OREGON
DESERT GUIDE

70 HIKES

OREGON
DESERT GUIDE

70 HIKES

Andy Kerr

Photography by
Sandy Lonsdale

THE
MOUNTAINEERS

Published by
The Mountaineers
1001 SW Klickitat Way, Suite 201
Seattle, WA 98134

First printing 2000, second printing 2003.

Published simultaneously in Great Britain by Cordee, 3a DeMontfort Street, Leicester, England, LE1 7HD

Manufactured in the United States of America

Project Editor: Dottie Martin
Editor: Mary Anne Stewart
Designer: Peggy Egerdahl
Book Layout: Jacqulyn Webber
Photographs: © Sandy Lonsdale, Wild Earth Imaging
Maps: Ecotrust

Cover photograph: *The Honeycombs in the proposed Owyhee Wilderness,* by Sandy Lonsdale
Frontispiece: *Wild rose in Succor Creek State Recreation Area,* by Sandy Lonsdale

Library of Congress Cataloging-in-Publication Data

Kerr, Andy, 1955-
Oregon desert guide : 70 hikes / Andy Kerr ; photography by Sandy Lonsdale.
     p. cm.
Includes bibliographical references and index.
ISBN 0-89886-602-2
1. Hiking—Oregon—Guidebooks. 2. Natural history—Oregon—Guidebooks.
3. Deserts—Oregon—Guidebooks. I. Title.
GV199.42.O7 K47 2000
508.795'9—dc21   99-050933

Dedication

To my Nancy
  wife, partner, friend, lover, rock, anchor
    —for all the reasons she knows and many more

In Memoriam

Denzel Ferguson
1929–1998

Zoologist, writer, teacher, activist, citizen, and husband of Nancy. Who, in the American South, stood up for black people, even as some bigots tried to kill him; and who later, back in the American West, stood up for nature, even as some ranchers tried to kill him.

They have cradled you in custom, they have primed you with their
    preaching,
They have soaked you in convention through and through;
They have put you in a showcase; you're a credit to their teaching—
But can't you hear the Wild?—it's calling you.
Let us probe the silent places, let us seek what luck betide us;
Let us journey to a lonely land I know.
There's a whisper on the night-wind, there's a star agleam to guide us,
    and the Wild is calling, calling . . . let us go.

Robert Service, "The Call of the Wild"

CONTENTS

BLUE MOUNTAINS ECOREGION

COLUMBIA BASIN ECOREGION

KLAMATH MOUNTAINS ECOREGION

LAVA PLAINS ECOREGION

OWYHEE UPLANDS ECOREGION

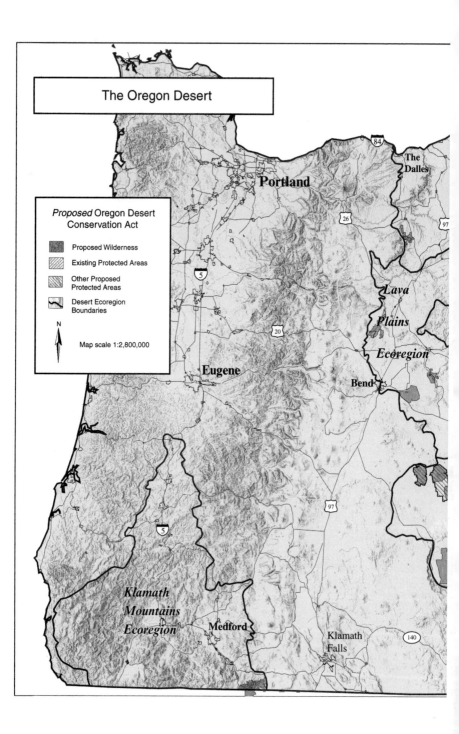

The Oregon Desert

Proposed Oregon Desert
Conservation Act

Proposed Wilderness

Existing Protected Areas

Other Proposed
Protected Areas

Desert Ecoregion
Boundaries

N

Map scale 1:2,800,000

Portland

The
Dalles

Lava

Plains

Ecoregion

Bend

Eugene

Klamath
Mountains
Ecoregion

Medford

Klamath
Falls

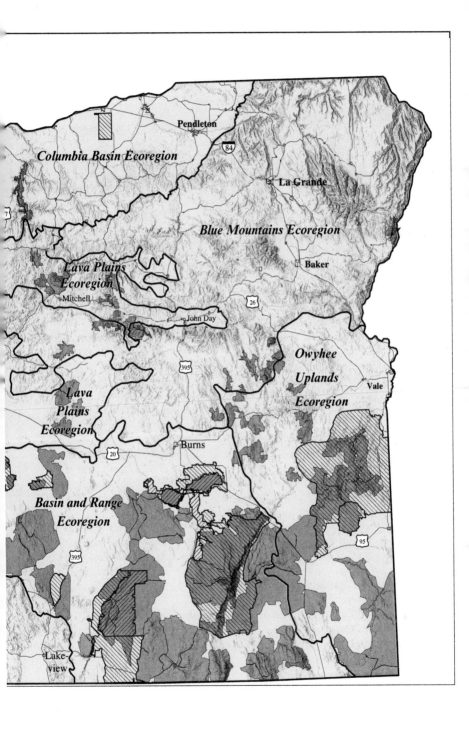

ACKNOWLEDGMENTS

Without the cooperation received, knowledge shared, files opened, time given, and the advice offered by so many people, you wouldn't be holding this book in your hand. I am in deep debt to all listed below and more (I've undoubtedly forgotten some—please forgive). I've decided to keep some people anonymous, lest their jobs or more be in jeopardy for being helpful.

All contributions, large and small, were appreciated. Rick Brown, Susanna DeFazio, Lizzie Grossman, Yael Hameiri, Tim Lillebo, Bill Marlett, and Nancy Peterson read nearly every word with red pen in hand.

Thanks also to Don Baccus, Ric Bailey, Borden Beck, Sheldon Bluestein, Gary and Carolyn Brown, Homer Campbell, Susan Campbell, Bob Cooley, Linda Craig, Sally Cross, Alice Elshoff, Cal Elshoff, Katie Fite, Bob Freimark, Paul Fritz, Dave Funk, Tony George, Kevin Gorman, Dave Green, Ashley Henry, Dennis Hill, Gary Kahn, Barney Kerr, Connie Levesque, Lance and Missy Litchey, C. D. Littlefield, Marc Liverman, Gilly Lyons, Maitreya, Craig Miller, Ann Mitchell, Tom Myers, Kathy Myron, Jim Myron, Reed Noss, Mary O'Brien, Bob Phillips, Elaine Rees, Kirk Shimeall, John Sherman, Paula Surmann, Jerry Sutherland, Mary Swanson, Pepper Trail, Irene Vlach, Dave Willis, Joe Walicki, Randy Webb, Russ Wilbanks, Harold Winegar, Wendell Wood, Jill Workman, George Wuerthner, and Berta Youtie.

For the geologically retarded, John Howell is a godsend. Joy Belsky provided the scientific rationale to support my visceral antipathy to livestock.

Public servants graciously provided information and/or review. Thanks to Larry Cooper, Tom Keegan, Don Whitaker, and especially Claire Puchy of the Oregon Department of Fish and Wildlife. From the Bureau of Land Management, I want to thank Lisa Clark, Scott Florence, Dave Harmon, Lucile Housley, Trish Lindaman, Fred McDonald, Heidi Mottl, Vern Stofleth, and Doug Troutman. Jenny Barnett, Mike Nunn, and Jenny Russell of the U.S. Fish and Wildlife Service were also quite helpful, as were Scott Moore (formerly of the Burns District BLM) and Paul Patton of Oregon State Parks. The willingness of these public servants to provide information or critique for this book should in no way be construed as an endorsement.

Many authors unknowingly contributed (see Recommended Reading), but I would especially like to acknowledge the Oregon Biodiversity Project. Their

Oregon's Living Landscape was invaluable to me in getting the natural history, hopefully, straight.

The staff of The Mountaineers Books were always professional and often fun to work with, especially Margaret Foster, Margaret Sullivan, Alison Koop, Dottie Martin, Peggy Egerdahl, and my fine copyeditor, Mary Anne Stewart.

Mike Mertens of Ecotrust did an excellent job in producing the maps.

I cannot conclude without especially acknowledging these especial people:

Lizzie Grossman, a recovering literary agent who went off the wagon long enough to shepherd me through the world of publishing.

Sandy Lonsdale for generously donating the photography.

Rick Brown, a fine naturalist who knows I'm ecologically retarded, but most patiently and helpfully answers my many questions anyway.

Susanna DeFazio for ideas, advice, and critique.

Dick Vander Schaff for his patient and informative explanations to my uncountable questions regarding flora and fauna.

Tim Lillebo, for advice on explorations in every ecoregion.

Finally, Nancy Peterson for putting up with me for being gone during looming deadlines and for subsidizing this endeavor in countless ways.

PREFACE

I wrote this book to bring public attention to thousands of square miles of the nation's public lands. The goal is to protect these treasures from development and to restore them to full ecological productivity.

My first purpose is to seduce you into loving the Oregon Desert, at least as much as I do. Maybe you've been there already, know its charms, and are adequately seduced. Maybe not. Follow both your heart and the directions in this book; then exercise both your legs and some common sense and get to know the Oregon Desert.

My second purpose is to inform you of the threats. The Oregon Desert is being despoiled and degraded, defiled and defaced, desecrated and denatured. Its wildness is being diminished both intentionally and unconsciously. The wildest part of Oregon is in danger of being lost because not enough people are standing up for it. The Oregon Desert's biggest problem is its benign neglect by most Americans, all of whom are co-owners of these public lands. A few elite exploiters, operating under the guise of jobs and tradition, are robbing Americans of their birthright: millions of acres of wild and natural public lands. The exploiters are often aided and abetted in their endeavors by the Bureau of Land Management, an agency of the U.S. Department of the Interior that often views itself more as handmaiden to the cattle and mining industries than as trustee of the public's lands.

The third purpose of this book is to inspire action. The above-mentioned threats to the desert, as well as others, can be addressed by the enactment into law of the Oregon Desert Conservation Act, which would permanently protect 6.2 million acres of your public lands. This legislation will only pass if enough Oregonians and other Americans speak up for these forgotten lands.

So let's get moving. Read on to find out more about the desert, its wonders and the threats to it, and how you can help conserve and restore it for this and future generations.

Some desert rats (desert aficionados) will be horrified by this book. They naively believe that the best way to preserve the desert is to keep it a secret. They seem to fear increased wildlands recreation more than increased wildlands exploitation. If the miners, ranchers, off-road drivers, developers, and energy corporations didn't already know about the desert, this argument might hold water. But exploiters do know. The Oregon Desert can be saved only by persuading enough citizens to first fall in love with and then to stand up for it. (See Appendix B.)

Let me now make an author's Big Fat Disclaimer:

By buying this book, you've presented evidence that you have good judgment and taste, but most important, that you are prudent. You're interested in visiting the Oregon Desert, and you want to know more about it and how to enjoy it safely. Most likely you'll have a great time and be nothing but the better for it.

However, it is possible that something bad will happen. If it does, don't try to blame the book or the author. Every reasonable (and some unreasonable) effort has been made to ensure the accuracy and safety of the suggestions in this book. If you follow them, you'll undoubtedly love the desert, and you'll probably love the book and the wonderfully witty and irresistibly charming author who wrote it. You're likely to come back safe, but you're not likely to come back the same.

Errors were undoubtedly made while producing the book, despite the best efforts and intentions of myself and all whom I consulted. Also, conditions will have changed after the book was written.

Be careful out there. Pay attention to the weather. Get the hell off a mountain top in a lightning storm. Watch those slippery rocks when crossing a stream. Be properly supplied with adequate gear and provisions. Have reliable transportation. Don't drive your rig down a road that makes you nervous. Watch where you step. Don't overexert yourself. Don't climb unless you know what you are doing. Don't play with rattlesnakes. Walk only as far as is safe. Don't be hesitant to change your plans. Have a first-aid kit and know first aid. Do what your mother told you. You're responsible for your life. Don't do stupid things. Pay attention.

Thanks! We need all available hands to help pass the Oregon Desert Conservation Act for this and future generations.

Andy Kerr
The Buckaroo Room
Frenchglen
Spring 1999

P.S. If the reading public demands a second edition, it shall be supplied. Please contact me through The Mountaineers Books with your criticisms, comments, and suggestions, and to point out errors in fact, logic, or opinion.

INTRODUCTION

We are not so poor that we have to spend our wilderness, or so rich
that we can afford to.

—Newton Drury

The Oregon Desert is far from being one huge sagebrush-covered flat. While significant portions do host vast stands of big sagebrush and little topographic relief, the Oregon Desert has seasonally snowcapped mountain ranges, forested hillsides, deep river canyons, and more. Take the time to see what the desert has to offer, including those sagebrush-covered flats.

It has also been called a "high desert" because it is much higher in elevation (colder in winter and not as hot in the summer) than the Sonoran, Mojave, and Chihuahuan Deserts.

The Oregon Desert includes part of the fourth kind of North American desert, the Great Basin, which is both a name for a type of desert and a region where the streams never reach the ocean. The Oregon Desert also encompasses arid lands that drain into the Pacific Ocean.

It is a sparsely populated land, though sprawling Bend-Redmond-Prineville is infringing upon it. Oregon's three largest counties in size—Harney, Lake, and Malheur—comprise the heart of the desert. Yet, while covering 29 percent of Oregon's land area, these counties contain only 1.4 percent of its citizens.

The Oregon Desert is the wildest part of the state—6.2 million acres of de facto wilderness remain. Wildlands are the reason that pronghorn and bighorn sheep still range free. They are the reason that sage grouse still gather in their fascinating and marvelous mating rituals.

Wilderness is the highest value for most of the Oregon Desert. Oregonians need to protect all the wilderness we have left and to restore much of what has been lost. Senator Clinton Anderson, a sponsor of the first wilderness bill in Congress, said:

> *Wilderness is an anchor to the windward. Knowing it is there we can also*
> *know we are still a nation, tending to our resources as we should—not a*
> *people in despair, scratching every last nook and cranny of our land for a*
> *board of lumber, a barrel of oil, a blade of grass, or a tank of water.*

Edward Abbey, the desert rat of all desert rats, in his classic *Desert Solitaire* noted:

> *A man could be a lover of wilderness without ever in his lifetime leaving the boundaries of asphalt, powerlines, and right-angled surfaces. We need wilderness whether or not we ever set foot in it. We need a refuge even though we may never need to go there. I may never in my life get to Alaska, for example, but I am grateful that it is there. We need the possibility of escape as surely as we need hope; without it the life of the cities would drive all men into crime or drugs or psychoanalysis.*

Our voracious rates of consumption and suicidal rates of reproduction are using up the Earth. But there is time to ensure that this large bioregion always functions ecologically. We still have time for the northern sage grouse to avoid the path of the northern spotted owl. The Oregon Desert provides the opportunity to leave room for nature. David Brower, the greatest living conservationist, noted:

> *We dare not let the last wilderness on earth go by our own hand, and hope that technology will somehow get us a new wilderness on some remote planet, or that somehow we can save little samples of genes in bottles or on ice, isolated and manageable, or reduce the great vistas to long-lasting videotape, destroying the originals to sustain the balance of trade and egos.*

Farsighted Oregonians have developed a political solution to the ecological and economic problems facing Oregon's forgotten corner. The Oregon Desert Conservation Act (ODCA) would set a new direction of working with, and no longer against, nature. It is bold and visionary legislation. Nothing like it has ever been enacted. But there are few places like the Oregon Desert.

The Oregon Desert Conservation Act recognizes that some people need help in making an economic and social transition away from exploitation, depletion, and unsustainability and toward conservation, restoration, and sustainability. ODCA is ecologically sound, economically rational, and socially just.

In *Walden*, Henry David Thoreau wrote: "If you have built castles in the air, your work need not be lost; that is where they should be. Now put foundations under them."

THE BASICS

For you, most likely, the Oregon Desert is a long way from home. When you are in the desert, it is often a long way between settlements and help if you need it. Knowing both where you are going and how to get along while you are there can make the difference between an enjoyable and memorable experience and a horrible and unforgettable one.

HOW TO USE THIS GUIDE

On the author's shelf is a hiking guide for a wilderness area. Three hundred pages intimately describe every trail in the 580-square-mile wilderness. Each trail description includes a graph of the elevation change along the route and describes the route in minute detail. This is not that kind of book.

The twenty-six proposed wilderness and ten special management areas described here encompass over 11,000 square miles (6.2 million acres). While undoubtedly an expert, the author obviously hasn't (yet) sauntered every stream or rambled every ridge.

Almost no actual hiking trails are in these Oregon Desert wilderness proposals. Nor are they much needed. The lack of trees greatly eases the tasks of ambulation and navigation (you can often see farther than you can walk).

This book is a hybrid of natural history, political future, and hiking guide. None of the areas in this book has (yet) been congressionally protected as wilderness. Most guidebooks concentrate exclusively on recreation, with perhaps a smattering of natural history. The lands in this book are in danger, so their potential fate is also discussed. If you haven't yet taken any steps to help save these places, now is the time. Exploiters wait for no one.

This book contains:

- *Information and natural history about the Oregon Desert and the threats to it.* Included are overviews of the physical and biological environments and the threats to them. Those wishing to delve deeper should turn to the Recommended Reading list at the end of the book.

- *An overview and explanation of the proposed Oregon Desert Conservation Act.* ODCA is proposed legislation that protects and restores what is ecologically and economically necessary for the Oregon Desert while at the same time addressing legitimate social needs brought on by such a transition.

➷ *Descriptions of the proposed wildernesses and other protective designations in the Oregon Desert Conservation Act.* These note the specific wilderness values for these last wild desert lands. They are individual briefs in support of protecting each area.

➷ *Ways the reader can help save the Oregon Desert.* ODCA won't be enacted by Congress unless there is a showing of massive and sustained political support. You can be part of it (see Appendixes C and D).

➷ *Specific suggestions for explorations.* A multitude of recreational opportunities can be found in each proposed wilderness and special management area. See the "Wilderness, Natural, and Recreational Values" table in the Natural History chapter for information on the most outstanding opportunities offered by proposed wilderness.

Information Blocks

In the information block at the beginning of each area description you'll find:

1. The name of the area and proposed protective classification
2. A summary "teaser" about the area
3. A county location and distance and direction from the nearest town
4. The area's size in square miles (and acres)
5. A description of terrain (not a particular exploration—see below)
6. Elevation range of the area (not a particular exploration—see below)
7. The managing agency (usually, but not always, a district of BLM)
8. The current agency wilderness status (not shown for proposed special management areas other than wilderness—national conservation areas, national monuments, and national wildlife refuges—please see wilderness proposals that overlap such areas)
9. The appropriate (usually BLM recreation) map
10. The narrative

After the narratives come the recommended explorations. The seventy-one explorations in this book are usually more than hikes on any well-defined route. The instructions are detailed enough to get you there and back, but the reader is encouraged not just to hike some route, but to explore a region. Another information block tells:

1. The exploration name
2. What to expect
3. The distance (either a round trip or loop total)
4. The elevation range for the exploration
5. Drinking water information
6. Best times to visit
7. The USGS 7.5' quad map(s) covering the exploration
8. The Oregon Official State Map starting point
9. The narrative

This book uses distinct terms to describe a hiking course:

Cross-country   No path, except perhaps game paths

Way	A two-track travel course caused by the passage of four-wheeled motorized vehicles
Path	A single tread made by the passage of humans, wild-life, or livestock
Route	A suggested course of cross-country travel
Trail	A course of pedestrian travel constructed and maintained by humans
Ex-road	It was a road, but now it is not, either by governmental or natural action

The suffix -*erly* is often added to compass direction points, not to be majorly annoying, but to clarify the general, not exact, direction. Travel by foot rarely fits into just four or eight directions.

Acreage numbers are approximate and subject to change because of refinement of measurement and/or revision of boundaries.

Below are some suggestions and matters to keep in mind as you visit the areas described.

Keep this book with you. Don't leave it at home or on the dashboard (if you do, please put it face up so others can see it).

Getting to the Embarkation Point

Unless otherwise stated, the hikes in this book can be reached in normal passenger vehicles. It is rarely pavement all the way, however, and backcountry driving is harder on vehicles than highway or city driving. Some of these improved roads are good for 55 miles an hour. Some of the unimproved roads will require a first-gear crawl.

Mileages mostly are taken from USGS 7.5' quad maps. References from mileposts are by odometer. (Warning: Odometers vary.) This book favors the use of direction and distance, rather than road signs. Signed intersections in the Oregon Desert are rare. Where signs were erected, more often than not, they have been knocked down, torn down, worn down, or gunned down.

After the Embarkation Point

This is not a "0.14-miles-down-the-trail-after-crossing-a-little-spring-you'll-see-this-big-cottonwood-next-to-a-giant-rock-that-looks-like-a-cougar-with-a-nice-log-to-sit-on-if-it-is-dry-and-sunny" kind of guidebook. This guide gives enough specifics to get there and back. Expect to explore along the way. In some cases, the route is so obvious as to preclude much need to describe. The descriptions are designed to be followed using just your own senses and the map (and compass). For example, a reference to "peak 6675" refers to an unnamed peak on the USGS 7.5' quad map at 6,675 feet elevation.

Government Jurisdictions

Most of the public land in the Oregon Desert is managed by the Bureau of Land Management. The BLM has four districts east of the Cascade crest:

District	Counties	Ecoregion
Burns	*generally* Harney *some* Grant	*generally* Basin and Range *some* Blue Mountains
Lakeview	*generally* Lake	Basin and Range
Prineville	Deschutes, Crook, *some* Grant, Morrow Gilliam, Wasco, Jefferson, Sherman, Wheeler	High Lava Plains *generally* Columbia Basin *some* Blue Mountains
Vale	*generally* Malheur Morrow, Baker *some* Grant	Owyhee Uplands *some* Blue Mountains *some* Columbia Basin

The Soda Mountain area is in the Medford District in Jackson County in the Klamath Mountain ecoregion.

National wildlife refuges (Hart Mountain and Malheur) are under the jurisdiction of the U.S. Fish and Wildlife Service.

The John Day Fossil Beds National Monument is under the jurisdiction of the National Park Service.

Portions of the Fremont, Ochoco (and Crooked River National Grassland), Malheur, and Wallowa-Whitman National Forests (all under the jurisdiction of the U.S. Forest Service) are in the Oregon Desert and are included in at least one wilderness proposal.

The Bureau of Land Management, the U.S. Fish and Wildlife Service, and the National Park Service are in the U.S. Department of the Interior; the U.S. Forest Service is in the U.S. Department of Agriculture (see Appendix A).

Ecological Classifications

One way scientists categorize landscapes is to classify them into ecoregions, based on characteristics of geology and vegetation. Oregon has ten (not counting the near Pacific Ocean) ecoregions. The Oregon Desert (roughly that part of Oregon that does not have or did not have major forests) covers all of the Basin and Range, Columbia Basin, Lava Plains, and Owyhee Uplands ecoregions, as well as a goodly portion of the Blue Mountains, a small bit of the East Cascades (not mentioned further here since said portion has no "desert" wilderness remaining), and a minor portion of the Klamath Mountains ecoregions.

The proposed wilderness and other special management areas described in this book are categorized by ecoregion.

The Oregon Biodiversity Project

A consortium led by Defenders of Wildlife and The Nature Conservancy, the Oregon Biodiversity Project published *Oregon's Living Landscape*, an excellent natural history overview of the state. The book recognized a series of conservation opportunity areas, which had both high biodiversity and good opportunities for conservation improvement. They are noted throughout this book.

A Word on Other Words
This guides focuses on wild places. There are many other natural and cultural attractions in the Oregon Desert that are not described in this book. See Recommended Reading.

THE RIGHT MAPS
There is no one great map to the Oregon Desert.

You will need small-scale (large-area) maps to figure out where you are going. Medium-scale maps are best to comprehend the general landscape and vicinity. Finally, large-scale (small-area) maps will show you where you actually are.

Each area description notes the maps you'll want.

Some maps are *planimetric,* showing legal descriptions (township and range), land ownership, political boundaries, and major streams. Other maps are topographic and show elevations and landforms, as well as most features found on planimetric maps.

If you don't know how to read maps, especially topographic maps, it is a useful skill to learn. (See Recommended Reading.)

First, the directions in this guide begin at a location specified on the (free) Oregon Official State Map. Accept no substitute. It is available at many tourist information, chamber of commerce, Driver and Motor Vehicle Services, and police offices. As a last resort, ask the Oregon Department of Transportation to send you a copy (135 Transportation Building, Salem, OR 97310; telephone 503-986-3200; fax 503-986-3446). On this map, 1 inch equals approximately 16 miles on the ground (a scale of 1:1,000,000—that is, 1 distance unit on the map equals 1,000,000 distance units on the ground).

Second, you must have the appropriate BLM recreation maps ($4 each), which depict the various state and federal agency holdings in different colors. On BLM maps, 1/2 inch equals 1 mile (a scale of 1:126,720). An index is available from the BLM Oregon State Office's Public Room (1515 SW 5th, P.O. Box 2965, Portland, OR 97208; telephone 503-952-6001). BLM recreation maps are available from other BLM offices, many map stores, and local tourist haunts.

Third, you should have an atlas of the state. There are two fierce competitors, both of which are invaluable for getting the lay of the landscape you're visiting. Both are Global Positioning System (GPS)–friendly with latitude/longitude ticks in the margins and give an excellent medium view of your exploration.

The *Oregon Atlas & Gazetteer* covers the state with seventy color topographic maps. For eastern Oregon, each map covers four times the area the maps for western Oregon do. On the eastern Oregon maps 1 inch equals 4.8 miles (a scale of 1:300,000). Each map covers 1 degree of longitude and 1 degree of latitude, with an elevation contour interval of 600 feet. The *OA&G* shows many, but not all, roads. BLM and state lands are distinguished by color, but national forest lands only have exterior boundaries depicted as the traditional green was already used to depict tree cover, which is annoying.

The *Oregon Road & Recreation Atlas* has two scales and kinds of maps. The eight recreation maps show major landowners in color (1:750,000, about 10 miles/inch). Their thirty-seven double-page landscape maps are scaled at about 4 miles/inch (1:250,000) and are beautifully colored (shades correspond to elevation). Though Benchmark brags that its maps "are diligently field-checked by certified map fanatics—you can be certain that if we show a cut-off, it will not turn out to be a power line maintenance track!" the author found several examples where the *OR&RA* indicates high-standard roads that are, in fact, low-standard tracks.

Any one map, especially covering the Oregon Desert, is prone to errors. The author has both (one cannot have too many maps) but uses the *Oregon Road & Recreation Atlas* more than the *Oregon Atlas & Gazetteer*.

A new challenger, but no competitive threat, is *Pittmon's Recreational Atlas of Oregon*, which is simply a bound version of their black-and-white county maps.

The United States Geological Survey (USGS) also puts out a folded series of maps at 1.5 miles/inch (1:100,000), which are pretty, but are otherwise of marginal utility. The same goes for the Metsker and Pittmon county map series, except they aren't even pretty.

With the right maps and this guide, you will generally know where you are going. But to know *exactly* where you are going, you'll need the mother of all maps: the U.S. Geological Survey Standard 7.5' Series Quadrangle Maps ("USGS quads"). These exquisite maps have a very large scale of 2.64 inches/mile (1:24,000) and show nearly every road, track, trail, water body, and cultural feature. By reading the contours you can "see" the landscape. (It takes 456 of these beauties if you want to fully cover every proposed wilderness, national conservation area, national monument, and national wildlife refuge in the Oregon Desert Conservation Act.) These maps are not cheap, going for $5 to $7 each. But to see yourself walk across the map as you walk across the land, the USGS 7.5' quad maps are the ones.

You can get the *USGS Oregon Index to Topographic and Other Map Coverage* and the companion *Catalog of Published Maps* from Map Distribution, USGS Map Sales, P.O. Box 25286, Federal Center, Building 810, Denver, CO 80225; telephone 800-USA-MAPS (800-872-6265); http://mapping.usgs.gov. Many map stores will have the former to give away, but they don't like to give out the latter because it lists competing map dealers and the government prices. Dealers understandably mark up the price of these maps far over the government's retail price. It may be cheaper to order directly from USGS, but consider convenience and speed.

New topographic digital databases are coming onto the market. With a fast computer (Windows only, I'm sad to say), a large color monitor, and a decent (and increasingly affordable) color printer, you can print your own custom maps.

Other special maps are sometimes handy to have if you're going to that particular area. They are noted in the area descriptions.

To obtain these and other maps, look under "Maps" in the Yellow Pages. Many stationery, book, and/or sporting goods stores in small towns carry maps.

In Portland, Captain's Nautical Supply (138 NW 10th; telephone 503-227-1648), Pittmon Map Company (732 SE Hawthorne Blvd.; telephone 503-232-1161), and Nature of the Northwest (800 NE Oregon; telephone 503-872-2750) have the best selections. The latter has the best prices. REI stores also carry topographic maps but are biased toward the forested wilderness areas, the coast, and alpinelike Steens Mountain. Perhaps this book will help them diversify their map selection.

Finally, while you won't need them for the explorations in this book, you'll very likely want a set of large-scale color quad maps depicting land ownership, proposed wilderness, and other special management area boundaries, major roads, and streams, and so forth, obtainable from the Oregon Natural Desert Association (see Appendix C).

GETTING AROUND AND BACK WELL

The Oregon Desert doesn't care about you. It is neither trying to kill nor not kill you. It just is. The better educated, prepared, and aware you are, the better time you'll have in the desert.

Driving

This book's explorations try to avoid routes to areas that require a high clearance and/or a four-wheel-drive vehicle. If these conditions are unavoidable, it is noted.

Driving can be especially challenging. Not only are the roads generally much worse than what you're used to, if something happens, help can be a long distance and time away. Cellular coverage is expanding, but don't count on it.

Take your time. Don't rush. If a road obstacle can't be overcome, go to plan B. Devise plan B before you need plan B. If you can't reach your chosen area, choose another. Have a plan C.

Snow can be an obstacle. Always carry traction devices. A little rain on the right soil type, even regularly maintained county roads, can make it slicker than nasal drip. Or wet dirt can ball up on your tires and bog you down. (Life is not complete until you've chained up to get out of the mud.)

Fill up with fuel anytime you can.

If you haven't already, it is time to have a talk with your car. Will it allow you (or you it) to go on rough roads? If it (or you) anguishes at every bump and grind, then perhaps it's time for a new car (or at least a new attitude).

The more clearance the better. A high-clearance two-wheel-drive vehicle can usually get farther than a low-clearance four-wheel-drive one. The latter may be fine in the mud or snow but bottom out in a rutted or rocky road.

These "roads" are tough on tires. Modern tires are generally excellent against punctures, but defenseless against sidewall-attacking rocks. Bitterbrush (yes, the plant) can puncture a tire (another reason not to drive off-road).

For field research, the author drove a 1995 four-cylinder Toyota Tacoma semi–high clearance four-wheel-drive pickup with the next size bigger tires to get the higher ply rating. Three skid plates gave their lives for the engine. It was kept in two-wheel drive as much as possible, reserving four-wheel drive to get *out* of, not further into, trouble.

Killer Cows

Even driving the paved roads, you face a very major road hazard. Under Oregon's open-range laws, a black cow at midnight has more right to the road than you do. If you hit a bovine, you (or your estate) bought it. Under the law, you have no beef.

When approaching livestock on or near the road, slow down. The younger the livestock, the more need to slow. The adults know about cars, and so do the yearlings. It is the little calves bolting straight for mom that are the most dangerous.

Wildlife on the Road

Deer and elk can also total you and/or your car. At night, wildlife can fixate on headlights, and you can often see the light reflected in their eyes. Interestingly, with cattle you cannot. Is it that they look away, or is it that their eyes don't reflect? Perhaps this is a reflection on the dullness of the species.

If one deer safely crosses in front of your car, most likely there are others. *Slow down.* Night driving can also result in collisions with owls and other large birds and small mammals. Rabbits in particular seem to have a game in which they run under your car as you run over—but not squish—them. The rest of the rules to the game are unclear to humans.

Ambulation

If you're not in shape, get so before you visit the Oregon Desert. Backcountry walking requires basic fitness.

What's your average walking speed? With day pack? With backpack? If you don't know, take time to find out before you hit the Oregon Desert. The mileage, elevation change, and terrain are noted for each exploration, but you must estimate the time and decide whether the route is easy, moderate, or strenuous for you. How many miles can you (and your party) walk in a day, both comfortably and uncomfortably? Remember, the air is thinner, as you may be hiking a mile or more higher in elevation than at home.

As you walk, pace yourself. Remember the tortoise and the hare.

Of course, you need good walking shoes. This guide doesn't insist on "sturdy boots." The right shoe varies for each individual. Some need the arch and ankle support of the sturdy boot. The heaviest "boot" the author ever uses is a bootlike cross-trainer. These can be waterproofed, but you should also carry dry socks. However, what works for someone else's feet may be podiatric hell for another's. Only you and your feet can know. If you are a new hiker, practice in all kinds of shoes and socks, after having read up on the subject (see Recommended Reading).

Though the author has quite nice legs, he never walks in shorts in the desert. Walking in ankle- to waist-high sagebrush and other scratchy vegetation calls for long pants. Trails are rare.

Just as in town, as you walk, pay attention. Loose rocks on talus slopes can be quite treacherous.

To Backpack! Or Not to Backpack?

That Is the Question! This book describes "explorations." Some are no more than day hikes, and some are no less than backpacks. In between you find some that can be either, depending on you. In the driest parts of the Oregon Desert, consider day hikes over backpacking. Having backpacked extensively (including the Oregon portion of the Pacific Crest Trail), the author is not averse to it. But the critical factor that pushes one toward *long* day hikes is water. In the water-free areas, you will have to carry your own. At certain times of the year in certain areas, you could carry a water filter and drink off the land, but this is unreliable except in the higher mountains or along rivers and major creeks.

When preparing to dry-camp, calculate the weight of your backpack with the necessary complement of water and overnight gear (sleeping bag, tent, stove, food, and so forth). (See "Hydration" later.) It may be that you can cover more country in a day hike with a much lighter pack. Consider food. Freeze-dried won't help you here, as you must carry the water to rehydrate it. It is just as efficient to carry a watermelon.

Comfort is another factor. By car camping, you can often hike more country, carry less gear, sleep on thicker pads, eat better food (nothing like a big slab of dripping tofu on the grill), drink colder beer, use comfortable lawnchairs, and so on.

Navigation
Because of the lack of trails (or trail signs), it is especially important to pay attention to where you are going in the desert.

The good news is that there are few trees in the way to confuse you. You can usually see a long way. If you can't, you can usually climb a knob or ridge until you can see a good distance. A far-off prominent and unmistakable landmark can serve as a beacon.

Always carry a map and compass, which should be called mapandcompass. One is of very little use without the other. And both of are little use if you don't know how to use them. See Recommended Reading for some books on navigation and map reading.

Before you begin the hike, study the maps, not only those in this book, but also the Oregon Official State Map (which doesn't depict BLM lands, but could if enough people complained to the governor), and the appropriate BLM recreation maps and USGS 7.5' quad maps. Get a good sense of where you are going.

Very occasionally, the author gets disoriented (real men don't get lost). It is nice to punch up one's exact coordinates using a Global Positioning System (GPS) receiver, but don't get addicted. One could spend too much time looking at the screen instead of paying attention to where one was.

If you do get lost, it is best to sit and wait for help. This assumes that you have followed the advice of safety experts and are not traveling alone and that you have told responsible people where you are going and when you expect to return. If you don't check in after the appointed time, they may alert authorities to begin a search.

For the record *(and not as advice),* the author admits that he often travels alone and that his spousal unit only has a general idea of where he is. He's comfortable and experienced traveling in the backcountry, and it is a risk he chooses to take. He also packs his GPS receiver and a cell phone to provide his exact longitude and latitude to Search and Rescue. (Cellular coverage is incomplete in the Oregon Desert, but if one can climb to a high enough point, one can usually get service.) It is possible that he will eat these words posthumously in his obituary. He has on occasion eaten them financially.

Hydration

Kidney stone survivors believe doctors when they say to drink more water. On a hot summer day hike, carry at least three liters of water, and tank up on a liter before starting the hike.

The experts agree: lack of water can either kill you directly or disorient you so you make mistakes and kill yourself.

In the desert, you should drink water even when you are not particularly thirsty, as thirst is a poor indicator of adequate hydration. While the body manifests dehydration in a variety of ways, the single best indicator is the color of your urine. The darker yellow, the more dehydrated you are. You should aim (so to speak) for as light a yellow as possible (past pastels).

If you are in a group and don't yet know each other well, in the name of group safety and preventing dehydration (and possibly worse), ask someone about the color of their urine—a great icebreaker in desert social situations.

Now that you've promised to drink lots of water, where does it come from? More often than not from carrying it. Be concerned about both water quantity and quality.

In the spring (and through the fall in the higher mountains), carry a water filter and drink off the land. While you can obtain water from small streams and seeps, this source can be unreliable—not the filter, but whether the water is there. Spring can come early or late and stay long or short.

The desert offers many springs. If you've found one, so likely have the livestock. Some springs are fenced off or are protected by terrain, so you can get some water sans cow feces. It is a sad state of affairs when you have to not only worry about the fecal coliform in the water, but can see the fecal matter in the water.

Another scourge to your gastrointestinal system is the nasty protozoan *Giardia lamblia.* If you get it, your bowels won't quit rebelling until medical treatment. Bringing water to a boil (more boiling wastes fuel) kills *Giardia,* as will iodine (but not chlorine) treatment. Chemical treatment of water is not recommended, as it leaves a bad taste in your mouth. However, additional pills can now be added to iodine-treated water to neutralize taste, odor, and color.

Even where the water appears clear, it is best to filter or treat it. Buy the best filter you can afford.

Plan ahead. Carry enough water to allow for an expected source being dry.

Thermoregulation

In the desert, you must be concerned about being too hot (hyperthermia) and too cold (hypothermia), often within a few hours of each other.

Say "desert" and "death," and most people first think of dying of dehydration from the heat. Most desert survival literature was written for the Sonoran

Desert around Tucson. While it doesn't get anywhere near that hot in the Oregon Desert, people can die of heat-related injuries. They have to be quite stupid and/or work hard to do so, however. Hyperthermia is being dangerously hot. It usually can be prevented easily by proper preparation and actions.

Be aware of heat-related health concerns. Master the accompanying box, and know the difference between mild hyperthermia (heat cramps and heat exhaustion) and very serious hyperthermia (heat stroke). Treatment is quite different.

Seek shade during the summer midday. Hike early or late. If water is plentiful, take a dip with clothes on. Be careful. Think ahead.

Except for Steens Mountain, try to avoid the Oregon Desert in August, the month for which forests were invented.

Symptoms and Treatment of Heat-Related Injuries and Heat Stroke

I. **MILD HEAT INJURIES**
  A. *Symptoms*
      1.   Heat cramps
           a.   Caused mainly by loss of salt from the body.
           b.   Symptoms: moderate to severe cramps in legs, arms, or abdomen.
      2.   Heat exhaustion
           a.   Caused by large loss of water from the body.
           b.   Symptoms: headache, excessive sweating, weakness, dizziness; skin is pale, moist, cold and clammy.
  B. *First aid for mild heat injuries*
      1.   Create shade for victim.
      2.   Have victim lie down.
      3.   Loosen victim's clothing and sprinkle victim with water.
      4.   Fan victim to cool.
      5.   Give victim water from a canteen.
      6.   Let victim drink small amounts of water every 3 minutes.
      7.   Call a medic immediately.

II. **HEAT STROKE** (a medical emergency): A severe heat injury caused by an extreme loss of water. The victim has lost the ability to cool his own body and may die if not cooled immediately.
  A. *Signs and symptoms*
      1.   Sweat stops forming, and the skin feels hot and dry.
      2.   Headaches and dizziness.
      3.   Fast pulse.
      4.   Nausea and vomiting.
      5.   Mental confusion leading to unconsciousness.
  B. *First aid for heat stroke*
      1.   Immediately send for medic.

2. Create shade and move victim under it.
3. If possible, get victim off ground (about 18 inches or 45 centimeters).
4. Loosen victim's clothing.
5. Immediately pour water on victim.
6. Fan victim to cool.
7. Massage victim's arms, legs, and body.
8. Cool victim off—but do not use ice (it may cause shock).
9. Evacuate victim to an aid station as soon as possible.
10. If victim regains consciousness, let him or her drink small amounts of water every 3 minutes.

Adapted from *The Basics of Desert Survival*, by Dave Ganci, ©1991, ICS Books, Merrillville, Ind. Used with permission.

Worry more about hypothermia than hyperthermia. Even if it's a scorching day, it always cools off at night. Even when days reach 100 degrees Fahrenheit, it can still frost at night. Carry long underwear and sock cap on every trip, anytime of the year. If you get too cold, you become disoriented and incoherent and can die.

Carry an outfit of polar fleece–like material (get the stuff made out of recycled pop bottles) as it is very warm (even when wet) and lightweight. Carry rain gear (coat and pants) all the time (it can thunderstorm in August). Even if it doesn't rain, rain gear can help keep you warm. One can die of hypothermia in above-freezing temperatures, especially if windy. The key to keeping warm is keeping dry.

If someone is hypothermic, get the person out of wet clothes into something dry, and administer warm fluids (but only if the victim is conscious!).

Please see Recommended Reading for books on backcountry medicine that cover hypothermia and hyperthermia.

Preparation

Always have the Ten Essentials with you. They are the ten things that most survival experts agree everyone should have with them and know how to use if the need arises:

1. Extra clothing
2. Sunglasses
3. First-aid kit
4. Extra food
5. Flashlight (and extra batteries and bulb)
6. Map *and* compass
7. Whistle
8. Matches (in a waterproof container)
9. Firestarters
10. Knife

If you are not sure why you may need these things, it is time to do some reading (see Recommended Reading).

Check the weather forecast before starting your exploration, but that's no substitute for reading the sky yourself. In any case, you should be prepared for any kind of weather, not just dry and hot, but wet and cold.

It is a good idea to have first-aid and cardiopulmonary resuscitation (CPR) certification. You can read up on mountain medicine, first aid, survival, campcraft, no-trace camping, and the like. Do it before you go.

You should also pack your eleventh essential(s), which is a matter of individual choice. It may be medicine, snakebite kit, gun, cell phone, camera, chocolate, and/or condoms.

Lightning

Summer thunderstorms can form quickly in the desert mountains. At first notice, get thee off the high ridges. Don't be in the open where you are the tallest object. Don't seek shelter under a single tall object, be it rock, tree, or shrub. Avoid both the highest and lowest ground. Don't touch metal, unless you are totally inside of it, like a car (absolutely the safest spot in a lightning storm). If a *dry* cave is nearby (what are the odds?), use it, but don't touch the walls or ceiling or stand at the mouth. Do seek shelter in a stand of trees or rocks if the trees (or the rocks) are all of similar size (a high one sticking up may draw the lightning). If in a group, spread out, but not out of sight.

Having said all this, the odds of being struck by lightning are really low.

Ticks

Tick bites are another matter. The blood-sucking little bastards are quite disgusting on general principles. They can be vectors for Rocky Mountain spotted fever (hasn't been a case in Oregon in two decades) and the new favorite: Lyme disease (if you see the characteristic bull's-eye pattern—red spot with white ring—get thee to a doctor).

Lyme disease is carried by very tiny little ticks; so small that you don't notice them (you notice Oregon Desert ticks!). Cases have been reported in Oregon along the lower Columbia River, but not in the Oregon Desert.

Ticks are a problem in the late spring and early summer.

Bathing will remove unattached ticks. Look for ticks *everywhere* on your body after hiking. (Lovers, of course, should inspect each other.) Prompt inspection means easy removal by scraping and plucking before the ticks have securely fastened themselves. If the tick is engorged with your blood and/or securely fastened, plucking it off with tweezers and scraping off any remaining mouth parts is best followed by soap-and-water cleaning and maybe an adhesive bandage. If the tick takes a bit of your skin as you take it off your skin, that means you got it all. Disinfect the tweezers.

Hot matches, petroleum jelly, hot wire, glue, fingernail polish, and so forth don't work. All you will have is a mess. Just yank the damn thing off and be done with it.

Rattlesnakes

You have nothing to fear but fear itself.

Besides not knowing where to go, the most common reason why people don't visit the Oregon Desert is the fear of rattlesnakes. Scientists have documented our deep genetic (and cultural) fear of serpents. Human babies, who have to learn to fear most things, instinctively fear snakes. But you're not a baby, and it's time to grow up.

The facts are that you have extremely little to fear, and it is rattlesnakes who should be afraid. Odds are that you won't even see one on a desert trip. Rattler survival strategies are camouflage, escape, and defense. In that order.

Most human encounters with rattlers go unnoticed, since the snake simply lies still and blends in.

If hiding fails, then the rattler seeks escape. You might see the snake "run" for it, but you'll likely miss that too.

Only if the rattler feels trapped will it move into the defense posture: head high, neck in a loop, and the rest of the body coiled. And only then will it "sound off" (rattle). The purpose of this bone-chilling sound (you'll know instinctively) is to warn off potential attackers. It *really* wants you to leave it alone.

In Oregon, the only dangerously poisonous reptile is the western rattlesnake (*Crotalus viridis*). We don't have any sidewinders, diamondbacks, or timber rattlers. The venom of the western rattlesnake isn't as toxic as many of the

Great Basin subspecies of the western rattlesnake

twenty-nine other species of rattlesnakes found in the Americas. It is made up of enzymes designed not only to kill the prey, but to aid in later digestion. The venom of Oregon rattlers is more hemotoxic than neurotoxic, affecting the blood and circulatory system rather than nerves.

There are two subspecies of the western rattlesnake: the northern Pacific (*C. v. oreganus*) and the Great Basin (*C. v. lutosus*). The latter is found throughout most of the Oregon Desert, the former being more probable in forested areas. According to the Oregon Department of Fish and Wildlife, the back of the Great Basin rattlesnake will have "relatively small, widely spaced oval blotches that are dark-edged." It will have a background color of light to golden tan. It will not have white rings on the tail. It is found in sagebrush country of northern Great Basin deserts.

The northern Pacific rattler displays "large, closely spaced, squarish blotches that are light-edged." The background color will be brown, gray, or olive green-ish. It will have alternating black and white rings on the tail. It inhabits "rocky open woodlands of oak, pine, or juniper."

Shy and retiring types, Oregon rattlers are "moderately" sized (fear makes them appear *much* bigger in person, and they are always reported to be *much*, *much* bigger in the retelling), on average 2 to 3 feet long. Occasionally they reach 4, and very rarely, 5 feet in length. They are generally not found above 6,000 to 7,000 feet elevation.

The Oregon Department of Fish and Wildlife recommends that in the spring and fall, one try to avoid "open, south-facing, dry rocky areas" because the snakes sometime congregate in communal denning sites (to keep warm).

In Oregon, the gopher snake mimics some of the posture, blotching, and sound of the rattler (it works for them, even though they have no rattles).

More people die in the United States each year from lightning strikes and bee stings than from rattlesnakes. Your chances of dying are many magnitudes greater driving to and from the desert than from being bitten. In the *extremely* unlikely event that you are bitten, your chances of survival are very good. Bites to the head and torso are more serious (and more rare) than those to the extremities. Modern transport to modern medical care means an extremely high chance of survival.

Americans receive forty-five thousand reptile (snakes and lizards) bites a year, eight thousand of which are envenomations (venom injected), but there are only five to twelve deaths per year. Sixty percent of the venomous bites are from rattle-snakes.

If the rattler does bite, it *often* first does a mock bite (mouth closed), *often* followed by a dry bite (no venom). A rattler can only strike from one-third to one-half the length of its body. The fangs approach at 6 to 10 feet per second.

If you are bitten (*and* venom is injected), you'll feel immediate pain at the bite site and experience massive bruising and internal hemorrhaging. There will be some permanent tissue damage.

If you are bitten, follow the guidelines below:

DO:
1. Remain calm.
2. Rest.

3. Get to a medical facility as soon as possible (if the bite is serious enough, you might receive antivenin, but the medics will definitely treat your symptoms).

DO *NOT*:
1. Panic.
2. Suck the venom out with your mouth (even if you're the one that's been bitten).
3. Ice the bite.
4. Elevate the bite above the heart.
5. Use tourniquet or pressure dressing.
6. Incise the bite site.

If you need to walk out (imperative if you are alone), severe manifestations of poisoning may not occur for several hours, so you can *calmly* walk out.

According to the Wilderness Medical Society, the only scientifically proven method for extracting venom from a bite site is with the Extractor® device by Sawyer Products. Tests in animals have shown that 30 percent of the venom can be removed, *if* done within 3 minutes of bite.

Rattlesnakes have much more to fear from humans than we from them. They are subject to relentless persecution through organized "round-ups," road kill (snakes are the only animals that evoke the "swerve to hit" response), and habitat destruction (development, farming, chemicals, and so forth). A poor snake doesn't have a chance against a determined attack by humans, be it with firearms, shovels, clubs, or vehicles.

Humans, not rattlesnakes, are the wanton killers.

The data are clear; you've little to fear. Your chances of being bit—such that they are—are much greater if you are male, in your twenties, and intoxicated. Why? Because a significant portion of this cohort thinks their penis size increases by harassing rattlesnakes. Silly boys. That's only (possibly) true if the harasser is naked.

In the herpetological world, bites are quaintly classified as "legitimate" (accidental) and "illegitimate" (harassing).

If you are lucky enough to encounter a rattlesnake, withdraw to a respectful distance and enjoy it respectfully.

Fences

Be careful when crossing a fence (most will be barbed wire). Take your pack off and put it on the other side first. Crawling under is usually best. If you find a sturdy rock jack or post, you can go over on it. You can step through if the wire is loose, especially if someone steps on the lower wire and tugs on the higher one.

Leave gates as you found them. Study how the gate is fastened, so you can put it back exactly as you found it, if for no other reason than it will likely be the easiest. (As you open a gate, watch for livestock lurking in the bushes, just waiting to make their run for freedom.)

USGS 7.5' quad maps only show fences that can be seen from the air.

Perilous Plants

Not much to worry about here.

A few areas offer small cacti, which have little spines you certainly don't want to sit on. The spines stick to shoes and are difficult to remove. It is the only cactuslike thing out there, so it is pretty obvious.

Stinging nettles are found in riparian areas. The young green leaves are edible (steam them first). Native peoples used them for fiber items, and gadwalls (ducks) nest in them.

Poison ivy and poison sumac can be found along low-elevation canyon bottoms of the John Day, Malheur, Owyhee, and so forth.

If you are not expert on your parsleys and parsnips, stick none in your mouth, lest you get the deadly water hemlock, arguably the most gruesome death possible.

Private Land

While the vast majority of the land proposed for protection in the Oregon Desert Conservation Act is public, significant amounts of private land do exist. While ODCA would seek to acquire several hundreds of thousands of acres of private land (essentially all uninhabited) from willing sellers, it is still private land and must be respected.

Much of the private land is not "posted," and landowners allow people to walk over and even camp, hunt, fish, and so forth, on their property. The normal rule of "ask first" doesn't work well in the more remote portions of the Oregon Desert, in that these are for the most part unoccupied inholdings within the vast public domain. There is no one around to ask.

The rules of doing no damage, leaving no mess, leaving gates as you found them, and so on, still apply.

If a property is posted, *don't* cross it. Go around or go back. Otherwise you have committed criminal trespass in the second degree, a Class C misdemeanor (ORS 164.245), and are now liable for up to $1,000 in civil damages.

You may come across:

- ❧ "No Trespassing" signs mounted on fenceposts adjacent to the road in a way to suggest that going farther on the road would be trespass.
- ❧ A little signboard, with no sign, but creating the lingering impression that the sign has been torn off (perhaps the corner is left).
- ❧ A fancy gate (not locked) with ranch brand/logo across the road (notice that it has no "No Trespassing" signs).

The author has experienced numerous instances such as these in which, in fact, the road in question was a public right-of-way. All were designed to intimidate public land users. While the land on both sides of the road may be privately owned, the road itself may be a public access to public land. If sure, proceed.

Sometimes you may come upon a "No Trespassing" sign facing the way you are leaving private property. Many private landowners don't fully post their property. If you are driving, even if the gate is locked, before turning around, inspect for another gate or spliced fence nearby through which to safely get back to public land or roads.

The 1999 Oregon legislature tightened the trespass law to allow "posting" with a blaze of 50 square inches of fluorescent orange paint, or less if it is the top of metal fenceposts. Such blazes or other postings must be no more than ¼ mile along a roadway and may not be on posts where a public road enters private land. If signs are used, they must be at least 8.5 x 11 inches and include the name, address, and telephone number, if any, of the owner or agent (House Bill 2801 as enrolled, 70th Oregon Legislative Assembly, 1999).

The BLM recreation maps show land ownership, but they aren't perfectly accurate. If not sure, don't proceed.

The author has also experienced several instances in which a very large bull was pastured in a small fenced area where someone had to exit the vehicle twice to deal with gates. It is another way the rancher tells you that you aren't welcome, even though it is a public road on or to public land.

Proposed Wilderness Boundaries

The boundaries of the proposed wilderness and special management areas have yet to be legislated by Congress. In many instances, it is quite legal (but not moral) to do things in these areas that wouldn't be allowed after enactment of the Oregon Desert Conservation Act—actions such as driving motor vehicles, mining, grazing livestock, and so on. Even in the wilderness study areas designated by the BLM, it may be legal to drive on the "ways" (vehicle paths that don't qualify as roads).

The boundaries were drawn to ensure the long-term ecological protection and restoration of the Oregon Desert. In those cases in which you could (physically and legally) drive farther, please don't. You may be walking along on a route described in this book and be overtaken by a motorcraft. Let it slide, and take solace in being ahead of your time. Remember to contact your elected officials when you return home.

Cultural Resources

Both as a matter of law and respect, leave all historic and prehistoric human artifacts, including those very tempting little arrowheads, where you found them.

It is a federal offense to remove antiquities and other cultural resources from federal lands.

More important, it is disrespectful of Native Americans and their cultures.

Campcraft and Backcountry Ethics

This book assumes that you know how to car camp and/or backpack (both, no-trace camping) or are going with someone who does. Most of the skills and equipment are the same for forest or desert. If you need help in this regard, see Recommended Reading for some suggestions.

This book also assumes you are of good moral character and that you respect private property, and so forth. If you need help in this regard, see a priest, lawyer, therapist, or guru.

Don't litter. Even beer cans, though they be worth a nickel in this state, are far too common in the Oregon Desert. Careful field work by the author revealed that in each and every case, the tossed beer containers were "yahoo fuel" (Bud,

Coors, and the like). In not one instance was a container that held an Oregon microbrew ever discovered out of place.

While there are few campgrounds, car-camping locations in the desert are plentiful. Often, but not always, water sources have good camp spots. As in the forest, don't camp right next to the water (200 feet away is ideal). If only livestock would do the same.

If building a campfire, make sure you need it and that it is small. Dead juniper and especially mahogany, aspen, and cottonwood should be used minimally. Dead sagebrush makes a nice-smelling smoke. If car camping, bring your own wood and use a fire pan (for example, a metal garbage can lid). Camp stoves are more convenient and efficient.

During the hot summer, avoid a fire altogether by not warming food at all. Go to bed at dark and get up at dawn. Under certain circumstances, sitting around staring into a campfire can be little different than sitting around and staring at a television.

The Best of Times and the Worst of Times

The Oregon Desert, being a cold desert, has definite seasons. During each season, elevation is the best indicator of temperature and rainfall.

Winter. Snow covers the mountains in winter and can periodically blanket the lower flatlands. Winter hiking is possible during certain times at lower elevations. One must be flexible. It can be extremely windy and cold.

Spring. The snow will keep you out of the mountains (unless you are cross-country skiing), but the lower elevations are very accessible. The earlier in the season, of course, the greater the chance of inclement weather. Depending on the rains, travel on backcountry roads can be a problem. In the late spring, what a difference a day makes in drying out a road. Again, be flexible.

Summer. Go to the mountains, where the water flows from the snowmelt and the air is cooler. The lower flatlands and canyonlands can be unbearable.

Autumn. A great time to be in either the mountains (when the quaking aspen are turning color) or the flatlands and canyonlands. The days are warm and the nights frosty. The later in the season, of course, the greater the chance of inclement weather.

Hunting and Hunting Seasons

Some may wish to keep in mind the various hunting seasons as they plan their trips. Opening day of each season (often a Saturday) is usually the busiest. In general, those wearing camouflage are stalking their prey with a bow and arrow; those trying to be seen by wearing flourescent orange are rifle hunting.

If you are out during hunting seasons, it wouldn't hurt to wear colors not usually found in nature (Day-Glo orange is visible even to those colorblind to red). Inexpensive vests can be found at sporting goods stores. Put an orange T-shirt on the dog.

The seasons can vary greatly from year to year and from game unit to game unit. Various Oregon Department of Fish and Wildlife (ODFW) synopses (available from local sporting goods stores) contain the most accurate information but are rather daunting to understand. Call ODFW at 503-872-5268 to inquire about your intended destination.

Wear orange and forget about it. Most hunters don't get far from a road anyway.

Hot Springs

The Oregon Desert is thermally blessed (or cursed, if we're talking potential geothermal power plants).

Hot springs are often overused, and ecological damage can occur. There is something about a hot spring that says if there is one other person there you don't know, it is overcrowded. Hot-springs elitists agonize about any written word describing how to get to a hot spring (though they don't mind telling their friends, who tell their friends, who tell . . .).

Hot springs have an etiquette. It is polite to ask people there first if they mind if you join them. It is not polite for them to refuse. Clothing is not required at hot springs on public land. If you have a problem with that, you may not want to visit. Counseling may also help.

If the hot water is adjustable, do so carefully. At the Alvord Hot Springs in particular, the tubs are far easier to heat up than to cool down. Turn the heat off when you leave.

Numerous hot springs in the Oregon Desert are little known or visited (the author doesn't tell his friends, either). To experience a better-known hot spring, see the appropriate area description.

Hot Spring	Area	Exploration
Willow Creek	Trout Creek Mountains Wilderness	Little Whitehorse Creek
Alvord	Steens Mountain National Conservation Area	(General description)
Hart Mountain	Bighorn Wilderness	DeGarmo Canyon and Warner Peak
Warm Springs Canyon	Owyhee Wilderness	Three Forks

One other of note is Snively Hot Spring, about 12 river miles downstream from Owyhee Dam on the way to Lake [sic] Owyhee State Park in the proposed Lower Owyhee National Conservation Area.

Commercial operations do exist at Summer Lake (on OR 31) and at Crystal Crane Hot Springs (25 miles southeast of Burns on OR 78).

Hot springs are for spiritual and emotional, not physical, cleansing. You don't want to know the bacteria counts, and some springs are best visited in the dark. You also don't want to know about those little mites that cyclically exist in many hot springs and may enter your body through any orifice.

Don't use any soap anywhere near the hot spring. If you can drive to the spring, park the car a fair distance away, and don't do cannonballs off your rig into the pool like some yahoos do at Willow Creek Hot Spring.

Deviation

Hike off on your own, either by doing entire hikes of your own invention, or by making a side trip on one of the described hikes. Drive off on your own, too. Know what you are doing and pay attention.

Other Than Walking

River running (see Recommended Reading) is an option for the Lower John Day and Owyhee Wildernesses. You can do a private trip or utilize one of the many commercial outfitters.

Oregon Guides and Packers (P.O. Box 340, Springfield, OR 97477-0340; telephone 800-747-9552; ogpa@ogpa.org) has a directory of most licensed and bonded outdoor guides. In the Oregon Desert, guiding is mostly limited to running the Deschutes, John Day, and Owyhee Rivers, but other options do exist, including some hunting and fishing trips.

Fecal Matters

Though properly near the end, this is important. This author, at least, rarely defecates the first few days out. When finally moved by the moment, it is into a shallow (4 to 6 inches) trench dug with a boot heel or a stick (why buy and carry a trowel for the purpose?), located if possible in an area of good sunlight (heats the soil and accelerates the decomposition process). Into the trench also goes the toilet paper and then the dirt kicked back into the trench. Some advocate burning said paper, but it does decompose, and more than one unintended wildfire has resulted from such. (A female friend highly recommends sagebrush in lieu of paper for No. 1—make sure no insects are along for the ride—but this author cannot testify to it.)

In heavily defecated areas or river corridors, coyotes (like domestic canines) will dig up and consume your deposited delectable delight, leaving the toilet paper visible. Portapotties are now required on river trips.

A resealable plastic bag (one inside the other if you don't trust technology) can be used to pack out toilet paper and those uniquely feminine items.

For more on the subject (and there actually is quite a bit more), see Recommended Reading.

Leave No Trace

The National Outdoor Leadership School (NOLS), in cooperation with the Forest Service, National Park Service, Bureau of Land Management, and the Fish and Wildlife Service, promotes "Leave No Trace" (LNT) outdoor recreation. Boiled down, LNT means:

1. Plan ahead and prepare.
2. Travel and camp on durable surfaces.
3. Dispose of waste properly.
4. Leave what you find.
5. Minimize campfire impacts.
6. Respect wildlife.
7. Be considerate of other visitors.

While leaving no trace is the goal, the result is minimum impact. For more information contact NOLS (telephone 800-332-4100; www.lnt.org). They have excellent and detailed recommendations on LNT skills and ethics, both for major ecosystem types and for different recreational activities.

Settlement Services
Material needs can be met in the larger communities, such as Baker City, Bend, Burns, Lakeview, Ontario (Mountain Time Zone), Prineville, and so forth. In the desert, small settlements are few and far between, especially if you're running on your spare or forgot to fill your tank.

If a hamlet isn't listed in the accompanying table, it is just a once-was place on the map, and no services are available other than perhaps a post office (always the last to go). If it ever was, it is not now.

Only essential goods and services are rated. All listings have public telephones. In multiestablishment communities, the ratings are an amalgam of businesses.

Not rated is the amount of antienvironment(alist) material on walls, which generally inversely correlates to the coffee, beer, ice cream, and restaurant ratings.

Bring your own fresh fruits and vegetables. You can sometimes negotiate with a restaurant to sell you lettuce, tomatoes, and other things that garnish a burger.

Goods and services are rated in the table as follows:

| Goods / Services (no stars equal none) | | | |
	*	**	***
Coffee	"Eastern Oregon" coffee	Good coffee	Espresso drinks
Auto Services	Gasoline*	Flats	Other repairs
Beer	All the same color	Token beers of color	Microbrews
Ice Cream	Basic	Hägen Dazs-esque	Homemade
Restaurants	Diner fare	Somewhat more	Excellent

* Often not diesel and sometimes not premium.

If you've spent one too many nights on the hard ground, or if the weather and/or your body odor is just too foul, *Where to Stay in Oregon* (distributed widely, or available from the Oregon Lodging Association, 12724 SE Stark, Portland, OR 97233; telephone 503-255-5135) lists hotels, motels, resorts, bed and breakfasts, and recreational vehicle (RV) parks everywhere, including many of those little out-of-the-way places.

Not listed is the nonprofit Malheur Field Station, which has dilapidated (considered quaint in foul weather) trailers and dorms. Meals also available. Great ambiance. Telephone 541-493-2629 for more information.

SETTLEMENT SERVICES*

Community	Coffee	Auto Services	Beer	Ice Cream	Restaurant
Adel	*	*	*	**	*
Adrian	*	*	*	*	*
Alfalfa	*	*	***	*	
Antelope	*	*	*	*	*
Arock	*	*	*	*	*
Brothers	*	*	*	*	*
Buchanan		*	*	*	
Burns Junction	*	*		*	*
Christmas Valley	*	***	**	*	**
Culver	*	*	**	*	*
Condon	***	***	**	**	**
Crane	*	**	*	*	*
Dayville	***	***	***	***	*
Denio, NV	*		*		*
Denio Junction, NV	*	*	***	*	**
Diamond	***	*	***	***	***
Drewsey	*		*	*	*
Fields	*	**	*	***	*
Fort Rock		*	*	*	
Fossil	*	***	**	**	*
Frenchglen	***	*	***	**	***
Frenchglen (outer)	*		*	*	
Halfway	**	***	**	**	**
Hampton	*	*	*	*	*
Harper	*		*	*	
Jordan Valley	*	***	*	*	**
Juntura	*		*	*	*
Kimberly	*	*	*	*	

Community	Coffee	Auto Services	Beer	Ice Cream	Restaurant
Malheur Field Station[†]					*
McDermitt, NV	*	***	**	*	*
Millican	*	**	**	*	*
Mitchell	*	***	**	**	**
Monument	*	*	**	*	*
Paisley	**	***	**	*	*
Paulina		*	*		
Pine Creek[††]	*	*	**	*	*
Pinehurst	**		**	*	
Plush	*	*	*	**	*
Post		*	*	**	
Riley	*	*	*	*	
Rome	*	***	*	*	*
Service Creek	*		**	*	*
Silver Lake	*	***	**	*	*
Spray	*	*	*	*	*
Terrebone	**	**	**	**	**
Summer Lake[†††]	***	*	***	**	*
Unity	*	*	**	**	*
Vale	**	*	**	*	*
Valley Valls	*	*	**	*	
Wagontire	*	*	*	*	*
Wasco	*		*	*	*

Note: *Italics* indicate Mountain Time Zone.
*See the Goods/Services key for services rating information.
[†]Reservations required.
[††]West of Oxbow Post Office (Copperfield on Oregon official state map).
[†††]Two commercial establishments 1 mile apart on OR 31.

NATURAL HISTORY

One can have a fine enough time hiking in the desert just taking in the views and the smells. Many people do just that. However, one's appreciation can be enhanced by some knowledge of nature and its processes. The following is intended to intrigue you to learn more (see also Recommended Reading).

See the "Wilderness, Natural, and Recreational Values" table at the end of the chapter for a listing of outstanding features of proposed wilderness.

GEOLOGY

Geology does not hide well in the desert. The vegetation is sparse enough (or nonexistent) that one can often see the bare rock in all its color, shape, size, form, and texture.

If you are quizzed about a random rock in the Oregon Desert and you have no idea as to its kind, guess basalt. You would be right more often than not. The second guess should be rhyolite. Both are volcanic.

Basalt is a fine-grained dark-colored igneous rock that often has a smooth texture. It is black when "fresh." If weathered or otherwise altered, it tends to greenish black or shades of rusty brown. On occasion, it is red as a brick.

Rhyolite is light-colored pastels of yellow, gray, and pink.

Essentially all of the Oregon Desert rock is volcanic. Some rock is quite old, while other deposits have been identified as having been molten just 100 years ago. Some of the most ancient rocks in the Oregon Desert, between 215 and 190 million years old, are in the Pueblo Mountains. They are the rare nonvolcanic formations.

Many forces and events have shaped the desert to date, the most significant being volcanism, uplifting and faulting, and erosion by wind and water.

Nearly everywhere you look at the desert, if you know what to look for, you see lava flows, cinder cones, volcanic plugs, the ghosts and corpses of old calderas, and other evidence of volcanism.

To see representative samples of the freshest volcanic activity, start at the Newberry National Volcanic Monument southeast of Bend in the Deschutes National Forest and then travel to the Fort Rock Lava Beds, Diamond Craters, and finally Jordan Craters (all proposed national monuments).

The Basin and Range ecoregion is a series of long and narrow, north-south-trending fault-block mountain ranges separated by sediment-filled basins. Steens Mountain is a classic example, sloping gently up from the Catlow Basin on the west in a 1-mile rise over a distance of 18 horizontal miles. From the summit, the mountain drops dramatically downward another mile over a horizontal distance of but 3 miles to the Alvord Desert. From the east side, one can easily see the numerous layers of volcanic deposits. Steens Mountain is high enough to have been glaciated during the four ice ages that have come and gone in the Oregon Desert. Classic U-shaped glacial valleys are still clearly visible.

Between the uplifts in the Oregon Desert are flat valleys that often have no outlet to the sea—hence the descriptor Basin and Range.

The Great Basin is the name given both to a huge area of land that has no outlet to the sea and to one of the four major types of American desert. It should have been called the Great Basins or Countless Basins, because it is actually a great number of basins with either a lake or a dry lake (due to evaporation) at their bottom. Alkali salts remain after evaporation in the dry season, leaving playas.

In earlier times, the climate was tropical and subtropical, and the land was covered with oceans. Mountain ranges have come and gone. In "recent" (geologically speaking) times, during the Pleistocene (2 million to 10,000 years ago), large pluvial lakes filled between the ranges. Christmas and Fort Rock Valleys were covered with water; Lake Abert and Summer Lake were one and called (later by us) Lake Chewaucan (CHEE-wah-CAN). Upper Klamath Lake hadn't yet found its way to the Pacific. The largest lake was in the Catlow Valley. It dried out enough to have the general appearance it has today. The ancient lake shore terraces can often be seen 70 to 300 feet above the valley floors.

Just as the desert isn't all sagebrush vegetation, it is not all basalt and rhyolite. Hot springs abound in many areas along fissures or breaks caused by uplifts. Boiling mudpots can be found. Glass Butte is a solid mountain of mostly black, but some reddish, obsidian.

The bright reds and oranges at the Honeycombs and Leslie Gulch (in the proposed Lower Owyhee National Conservation Area) resemble the canyonlands of Utah. For stark layers of reds, blues, greens, yellows, tans, oranges, grays, browns, and blacks, check out the John Day country.

More local geology is described in appropriate wilderness sections.

CLIMATE

Very little of the Oregon Desert is a true "desert," as defined by scientists. Any desert has a rate of evaporation at least seven times that of precipitation.

Some refer to the Oregon Desert as a cold desert, as it gets quite cold in the winter (it is still quite hot in the summer!).

The Cascade Mountains to the west wring most of the moisture out of eastward-moving Pacific air. Each mountain range along the way wrings out a bit more.

While the northern desert of Oregon doesn't get nearly as hot as deserts to the south, temperatures can be extreme in the Oregon Desert. George Wuerthner aptly describes the climate of the Oregon Desert:

> [O]verall the region is known for its aridity. . . . The driest recording station in Oregon is at Andrews, . . . where the average annual precipitation is a mere 7". Andrews rests in the "rain shadow" of Steens Mountain, . . . but even . . . Burns, located north of Malheur National Wildlife Refuge in an open valley, receives only 12" of precipitation a year. The climate can best be described as harsh, but healthful: hot, dry summers and cold, dry winters. The minimal precipitation comes primarily as snow and during infrequent summer thundershowers.
>
> But these averages vary more here than elsewhere in Oregon. For example, the record high for Andrews is 107 degrees, while the low is a frigid 33 below zero. And year-to-year variation is tremendous; Burns' average of 12" was topped by 17" in 1940 and cut in half in 1937 when only 6" fell.[1]

VEGETATION

It is not all sagebrush.

However, if you were set down randomly in the Oregon Desert prior to the European invasion, you'd most likely find yourself in sagebrush.

Desert sulfur buckwheat

That's true even today, even though vast areas have been converted to "unnatural exotic grasslands-rural pasture with remnant bottomland, agriculture, and urban-industrial," to use the classification in *Oregon's Living Landscape.*

It is also the case that, due to livestock grazing intrusion and fire exclusion, sagebrush—where it still exists—is in greater abundance now as compared to presettlement times, both in absolute numbers and relative to the bunchgrass.

Vegetation is primarily a function of soil type, elevation, and moisture.

Depending on where you are in the Oregon Desert, you'll see mountain big sagebrush, Wyoming big sagebrush, low sagebrush, black sagebrush, silver sagebrush, bitterbrush, salt desert scrub, saltsage, spiny hopsage (with shadscale and black greasewood varieties), and mountain mahogany communities.

If the site receives enough moisture from above and not too much fire, you'll see western juniper woodland communities. Forest—or at least woodland—communities of aspen can often be found at higher elevations, and sometimes relic stands of ponderosa pine or white fir or Douglas-fir.

If the ground is wet enough (and if the livestock have been restrained), you'll see willow riparian wetland and cottonwood riparian wetland communities.

If you go high enough, you'll be in alpine or tundra communities.

In extreme environments, such as on lava flows and sand dunes, you won't see any vegetation. The big lakes are open water, and the dry lakes are often bare playas.

Wetlands can also be found in the desert and include tule and cattail marshes (emergent wetlands) as well as sedge-dominated wet meadows.

Numerous species of plants are found only in the Oregon Desert. On Steens Mountain alone, at least thirty species of plants are of special interest (rare, endemic, threatened, endangered, and so forth). Newly discovered species are still being described to this day.

To repeat: it is not all sagebrush.

A Desert Without Cactus?

Most people never notice cactus in the Oregon Desert and understandably so. It is rather uncommon.

According to *Intermountain Flora,* by Arthur Cronquist, five species of cacti, in three different genera, can be found in Oregon. One usually first notices cacti when a spine pierces a foot, hand, or butt.

The hedgehog cactus *(Pediocactus simpsonii)* is round or barrel shaped and is found in certain sagebrush areas in hot canyons of eastern Oregon.

A newly discovered species of hedgehog cactus *(Pediocactus* sp. nov.) grows only in Harney and Wheeler Counties.

The brittle prickly pear cactus *(Opuntia fragilus)* has yellow flowers and can be found only in the dry hills near Mitchell and immediately eastward.

The red prickly pear cactus *(O. polyacantha)* has reddish to yellow flowers. It has a larger range than its brittle close relative and is found in widely scattered locations throughout the Oregon Desert.

The cushion coryphantha *(Coryphantha vivipara)* is found in several areas of southeast Oregon.

Hedgehog cactus (Pediocactus simpsonii) in Spring Basin unit of the proposed John Day Wilderness

Western Juniper: Loved and Loathed

Trees in the desert? Sure, along the streams (assuming no livestock). But evergreen trees? Yes—if the elevation, aspect, and soil are such that enough moisture is available, you'll likely find the western juniper *(Juniperus occidentalis)*.

A tree of seemingly unlimited shapes, juniper can grow as a lone specimen or in stands thick enough to be classified as woodland (denser than a savanna, sparser than a forest). Usually short, it can grow more than 60 feet high. The oldest junipers can approach 5 feet in diameter and exceed a millennium in age.

Juniper's distinctive fragrance comes from the needles (rub some on your hands as an all-day reminder). Juniper "berries" are actually a nonwoody cone and may be eaten (while edible, they aren't particularly tasty and are better left for the birds). They are remindful of gin, which is flavored by European juniper varieties. (Bendistillery [sic] makes a locally flavored gin. Tanqueray it is not, but it is fine with tonic water and a lime.)

Junipers have gender. Only the female trees have "berries."

Junipers live on less water than other trees and are often found between the slightly higher ponderosa pine forest and the slightly lower sagebrush steppe.

Though juniper is an extremely slow-growing wood, the timber industry is seeking ways to exploit the species. It is a pretty and enduring wood (juniper fenceposts have been known to outlast two post holes), but since it grows so slowly, any serious logging is nothing less than tree-mining. With the advent of new technologies to successfully exploit juniper wood, watch out.

To most ranchers, the juniper is the sylvan coyote. They view it as an invading weed, killer of springs and streams, reducer of biodiversity, eroder of soils, and degrader of forage quantity and quality for both wildlife and livestock. Some ranchers contend that the roots of a juniper tree extend halfway to the next juniper.

Because of these misconceptions and the fact that western juniper is presently expanding in its range, ranchers and their handmaidens in government favor aggressive "management." Burn it, spray it, log it, or otherwise kill it to make room for more forage for more livestock. While juniper is expanding in range, many of the oldest trees have been and are continuing to be lost to development. One Oregon specimen was found to be 1,700 years old.

Scientists aren't sure why juniper is spreading, but the tree-ring studies suggest that the species' range expands and contracts because of climate variations. Other factors are the exclusion of fire and the intrusion of livestock. In a natural desert, the bunchgrass was tall and fire was frequent. Periodic fire, carried by the bunchgrass, killed most of the tiny juniper seedlings. But now livestock eat up grass and humans put out fires, giving the juniper seedlings an unnatural break.

Grassland ecologist Dr. Joy Belsky, while on staff with the Oregon Natural Resources Council (she's now with the Oregon Natural Desert Association), examined common beliefs about juniper and compared them with the available science. Among her conclusions:

> In spite of the conviction that junipers are degrading western rangelands and wildlife habitat, there is little or no experimental evidence suggesting that this is so or that juniper control will (1) increase water yield to springs and streams, (2) increase water infiltration, (3) reduce erosion, or (4) improve fish and wildlife habitat. It is probably safe to predict that tree removal will increase the productivity of understory shrubs and herbaceous plants, including, in some case, the productivity of undesirable weedy annuals and shrubs. The trade-offs need to be recognized and analyzed.[2]

Modern sensibilities force ranchers and bureaucrats to now mask their arguments against juniper (and for livestock) behind claims that juniper removal is good for watershed and biodiversity protection. In fact, this type of juniper management is predicated on the belief that the ecosystem exists only to benefit livestock. If serious about healthy watersheds and biodiversity, public land managers would banish the bovine and bring back the blaze.

Unfortunately, the juniper cannot run like a coyote.

A Desert Without Crusts Is a Desert Without a Skin

Some things are easy to miss in the desert. Sometimes it is because you're not looking; other times it is because it is not there—or if there, just barely. Such can be the case with microbiotic crusts. Scientists first called them cryptogamic (literally "hidden reproductive organs") crusts, then cryptobiotic crusts. Let's just call them desert crusts.

Desert crusts are fibrous mats of interwoven lichens, fungi, and algae. A hundred tiny plant species may occur in the crust, along with thousands of species of bacteria and other organisms. Desert crusts usually look rather brown and dull, but they are nonetheless an essential part of healthy desert ecosystems (douse a patch with saliva and watch it turn bright green).

You may have noticed these crusts if you've looked under a big sage or in a crevice that a livestock's hoof, hiker's boot, or vehicle's tire couldn't get to. Less than 5 percent of the desert's original skin remains intact, mostly in large areas that haven't been destroyed by livestock hooves, vehicle tires, and hikers' boots. "The Island" in the proposed Deschutes Canyon Wilderness, the proposed Boardman Grasslands National Wildlife Refuge, and the Hanford Arid Lands Ecology Reserve in Washington are some of the more pristine examples of remaining desert crust. In natural conditions, desert crusts may cover 80 percent of the ground, with grasses and shrubs towering above on the rest. That this is still true in the Oregon Desert is evidence both that bison were never common here and that native ungulates more gently trod the land than the alien invaders of the same order. When desert crust is disturbed, recovery begins immediately, but it may take a century to fully recover.

Desert crust

Desert crusts:

🐾 *Enhance soil productivity.* Crusts include cyanobacteria, tiny one-celled organisms that fix nitrogen from the air and leak it into the soil as an essential ingredient in plant growth.

🐾 *Resist erosion.* An area of crustless desert can have ten times the erosion.

🐾 *Retain water.* Crusts are a natural sponge that retain water after brief desert rains.

🐾 *Resist exotic species.* Invasive species like cheatgrass can't get established in a well-crusted desert.

🐾 *Reduce the harmful effects of wildfires.* Bare ground favors cheatgrass, which grows rapidly in the spring and then quickly dries into fuel for fires. In Idaho, land managers are seeding recent cheatgrass burns with native bunchgrass and then excluding livestock. This allows the bunchgrass—and eventually the crust—to return. Fires in native bunchgrass- and crust-covered sites are both less frequent and less intense.

A good crust is not hard to find, if you know where to look. Fortuitous confusion by BLM range managers makes a fine stand of desert crust highway close. Between Hampton and Riley, US 20 is the practical dividing line between the Prineville and Burns Districts of the BLM. Two fences bound the respective cattle allotments, leaving a triangle where the Prineville fence went to the highway, but the Burns fence is somewhat back from the highway on the other side. The result is a lucky triangle that has been cow-free for decades. Continued evidence of lack of interdistrict cooperation is that each has erected highway boundary signs, which are 1/2 mile apart, even though they could have shared the same post. Look for the back of the Prineville District sign (when traveling west, milepost 82.1) or the back of the Burns District sign (when traveling east, milepost 83.4). You're in the lucky triangle bounded by highway (mileposts 80.9 to 83.4) on the north and fence on the south. Park safely at a road to the south at milepost 81.7 and take a little stroll. Stay off the delicate crusts, which can't distinguish a cow hoof from a shoe sole.

More information on vegetation is included in the specific area descriptions.

FISH AND WILDLIFE

Wildlife habitat is as diverse as the plant communities in the Oregon Desert. Even the sometimes monotonous-looking tall sagebrush-bunchgrass communities, as common and uncharismatic as they may first appear, are vital to 145 wildlife species for reproduction and feeding (and what's more important than sex and eating?).

Government scientists have inventoried at least 341 species of terrestrial (nonaquatic) species of wildlife, including 244 birds, 71 mammals, 18 reptiles, and 8 amphibians.[3]

Some charismatic megafauna have been extirpated from the Oregon Desert. Steens Mountain used to be home to wolf and grizzly bear (and could be again). Lynx and wolverine may or may not still be on the mountain.

Numerous wildlife species are in decline in the Oregon Desert. This trend can be reversed.

Below are descriptions of some selected charismatic megafauna. More local wildlife information can be found in the wilderness sections.

Northern Kit Fox

Forty percent of the total length of the northern kit fox (*Vulpes macrotis nevadensis*) is tail. The very large ears are a significant amount of the rest ("the better to hear you with, my dear"). It is a very small canid, weighing in at only 4 to 6 pounds.

The tail has a black tip, the back of the animal is gray, and the legs are yellowish.

Kit fox are found in deep southeast Oregon, southwest Idaho, and northern Nevada, in particular in portions of the proposed Steens Mountain, Sheepshead Mountains, Owyhee, Trout Creek Mountains, Alvord, Oregon Grasslands and Pueblo Mountains Wildernesses. The species favors flat habitats (old lakebeds) covered with salt desert scrub species, such as black greasewood.

Kit fox live year-round in rather elaborate mazes of dens, often with two to seven openings, and eat small rodents. Species tend to do best in the heart of their range, and the kit fox's range barely extends into Oregon. We therefore have to be extra careful to ensure that the species stays here. It is adversely affected by trapping programs targeted at coyotes.

The Wily Coyote

Few experiences in life compare with being sacked out in your bag, just after the sun gives way to the moon, and being surrounded by howling coyotes. Their a cappella yowls are songs, their barks sentences, if you take time to listen.

The coyote is no varmint. It is intelligent, social, cunning, opportunistic, adaptive, fun loving, and full of wonder. Native Americans grant coyote a special place in their lore, and for good reason. It is a species that can make humans wax poetic or evil.

There are at least nineteen subspecies of *Canis latrans* (Latin for "barking dog"). In Oregon, the two subspecies are *C. l. lestes,* which is larger and paler and occurs east of the Cascades, and *C. l. umpquenisis,* which is smaller and more richly colored and occurs west of the Cascades.

Coyote size varies with subspecies and habitat. The average weight is between 20 and 35 pounds. Their color varies as well. Usually silver or a grizzled gray, the color can change subtly in the summer to rufous.

Hundreds of millions of dollars have been spent—and tens of millions still each year—to "control" the species. Hatred of the coyote has brought out both the irrational and inhumane sides of the human species.

It is irrational, because the coyote is one species that we can't control, let alone kill off. As a species, coyotes mock human extermination efforts. For example, in heavily "controlled" areas, coyote populations respond by doubling the size of their litters. Efforts at coyote control have led to the unnatural selection of a "supercoyote"—those that survived the onslaught know best how to keep out of harm's way. Sometimes life is fair.

It is inhumane because of the lengths humans go in futile attempts to control coyotes. The species is shot from the air, trapped, snared, gassed, drowned,

Coyote and white pelicans on Malheur National Wildlife Refuge

poisoned, dynamited, strangled, and "denned" (the mother is tracked back to her den, and the puppies are killed). Many of these methods are harmful not only to coyotes, but to other wildlife species, domestic dogs, and humans as well ("collateral damage").

All of this is done in the name of protecting livestock that should not be on public lands at all, and which, when on private land, should be shepherded if left out at night.

Ironically, the more successful extermination of wolves, who prey on coyotes, is a major factor in the coyote explosion. As wolf numbers declined, coyote numbers increased.

It used to be common to see coyote bodies hung over fences by sharpshooting ranchers who wanted to send a message to other coyotes. Modern public relations concerns have dictated a change in the disposition of the bodies, not in the killing.

To behave this way toward a family-oriented species! Coyotes attempt to mate for life and have family units with brothers and sisters who help raise the young. Like many species, the babies are *very* cute.

In a time when most large predators are on the decline because of predation by the most powerful and meanest predator of them all—humans—coyotes have dramatically expanded both their range and numbers. Common in wilderness, they've also been spotted intermingling with Yellow Taxi Cabs in the Bronx and thinning the house-cat population of Los Angeles. A coyote was recently captured in the elevator of a downtown Seattle federal office building (one can only hope she was looking for the government trappers who "denned" her pups).

Coyotes rightfully fear humans. Humans should fear the coyote only for the irrational and inhumane ways it makes us behave.

Welcome Back the Wolf!

Since before Oregon became a territory, government has sought to eliminate the wolf in the name of protecting livestock. Such a policy, if it ever made sense, does not today.

The last documented wolf kill in Oregon was in 1946. It is time to welcome back the wolf.

In 1999, one unattached female from an experimental population in Idaho roamed into Oregon nearly as far as US 395 in Oregon's Blue Mountains before being captured and returned "home." Perhaps she (biologist called her "B-45," but a better name is Eve) was home and humans just didn't know it. Hopefully this two-year-old female is the vanguard of an invasion.

Wolves seem to be coming back on their own. There have also been recent and numerous reports of wolves in Oregon, most often in the Rogue River National Forest. The presence of young suggests that these wolves may be reproducing. Are they a relic of the Cascade timber wolf subspecies, believed to be extinct, or were they released by parties unknown, or have they moved in from elsewhere?

Wolves are approaching Oregon from Washington and Idaho. A wolf litter was born in Idaho, about 60 miles from the Oregon border. While the Columbia River is a large impediment, it may not be a barrier. As Eve proved, the Snake River poses little challenge to an expanding wolf population looking to fill suitable habitat.

Wolves need large areas of undeveloped land with low human population levels, such as there are in Minnesota, Wisconsin, and Michigan. The Oregon Desert, along with the Klamath, Cascade, and Blue Mountains, fits the bill.

While wolves were historically less common in the desert than in the forest, three subspecies of *Canis lupus* were thought to inhabit the Oregon Desert: *fuscus* in the western desert, *remotus* in the eastern desert, and possibly *youngi* in the southeast corner.

Deer, elk, pronghorn, and bighorn sheep all have been brought back from the brink. Unmanaged hunting and habitat degradation didn't help the game, nor the wild canines that preyed on them. Just as wild ungulates were brought back from the brink at the beginning of the twentieth century, large predators, such as wolves, should be brought back during the beginning of the twenty-first century.

The core of the wolf reintroduction zones would be wilderness (both formally protected and proposed for protection). Road closures would help the wolf as well as the taxpayers who can't afford to maintain the spaghetti road network. Major roads should be left open for adequate access.

The biggest conflict in bringing back the wolf is the livestock industry. A major cause of the extirpation of the wolf in Oregon has been trapping, mostly paid for by the taxpayers, in the name of reducing livestock predation.

On the public lands, it is inappropriate to slaughter native wildlife, thereby aiding domestic livestock to degrade watersheds—all in the name of a pitifully small amount of the nation's beef production (again at the expense of the taxpayers).

Even though wolves will mostly stay on public land (because that's where most of the suitable habitat and prey will be), some will enter private lands and occasionally kill livestock. In such cases, the government should compensate the rancher, using funds saved from not funding trapping and poisoning on public lands. (Defenders of Wildlife compensates ranchers for any livestock losses attributable to wolves.)

How to pay for the state agency's costs in bringing back the wolf? Sell "wolf stamps" and dedicate the proceeds to reintroduction. It worked fantastically for ducks.

When the wolves return, they will eat some game species, especially deer and elk. Oregonians who want the wolf back could buy deer and elk tags and assign their chance to kill big game to the wolves.

This is an excellent opportunity for the Oregon Department of Fish and Wildlife to prove that it manages all wildlife, not just the hunted.

Despite what you may have learned as a child, wolves pose very little risk to humans. The benefits of once again hearing the howl of the wolf in the wild by far outweigh any downside.

Some suggest that those who want to see wolves should go to Alaska, where they are very numerous and not in danger. By similar reasoning, those who want to see livestock could go back East, where they are very numerous and less damaging.

Desert Elk

Rocky Mountain elk (*Cervus elaphus nelsoni*) are being seen in the Oregon Desert of late. They seem to be either expanding (or reexpanding) their range. Historically, elk were a range and plains species, being found even in the mountains of the desert Southwest. In Oregon, excessive hunting caused near-extirpation around the turn of the twentieth century. From last refuges in the Cascades, Blue, and Wallowa Mountains and the Oregon Coast Range, elk have come back to huntable populations. Their move into the desert is surprising in that rising elk numbers are apparently not directly attributable to improved habitat.

Elk have been spotted in the Owyhee country, in the Stinkingwater Mountains, on Steens Mountain, in the Fort Rock Valley and Jordan Valley area, and traipsing across Hart Mountain. There are an estimated two thousand to three thousand elk in the Oregon Desert. A large population seems stable on the Hanford Nuclear Reservation in the Washington desert (though they are rumored to glow at night).

Elk in the desert are causing biologists to rethink the habitat requirements of the species. Perhaps they are more adaptable than originally thought. More research is necessary.

Bringing Back the Bighorn

> Originally, mountain [bighorn] sheep inhabited every canyon, cliff, and lava butte as well as many of the rough lava beds of Oregon east of the Cascade Mountains.
>
> —Vernon Orlando Bailey, 1936

The California subspecies of bighorn sheep (*Ovis canadensis caiforniana*) was extirpated from Oregon by 1915, the Rocky Mountain subspecies (*O. c. canadensis*) by 1945. The latter was found in northeast Oregon in the Grande Ronde, Burnt, and Imnaha Basins, while the former were nearly everywhere else east of the Cascade crest.

The Rocky Mountain subspecies usually has heavier horns and is a little larger, stockier, and darker in color than the California subspecies.

Unrestricted hunting, diseases carried by domestic sheep, and conflicts with other livestock contributed to the demise of wild sheep in Oregon.

California bighorn sheep

An aggressive reintroduction program by Oregon Department of Fish and Wildlife (ODFW) was first a failure and is now a conservation success story.

In 1939, twenty-three Rocky Mountain bighorn sheep were transplanted to Hart Mountain from Montana. The last survivor was seen in 1947. A major factor in the failure to reestablish may well have been that it was the wrong subspecies.

In 1954, twenty California bighorn sheep from Williams Lake, British Columbia, were brought to Hart Mountain. The population not only survived, but thrived, and is the major source of California bighorn transplants in Oregon.

Twenty more Rocky Mountain bighorn were transplanted in 1971 from Jasper Park, Alberta, to Hells Canyon but eventually disappeared. Another twenty were released that same year on the Lostine River. This population fortunately thrived and became the source of successful transplants elsewhere in northeast Oregon (including Hells Canyon) and other states.

Today Oregon has an estimated 2,500 California and 550 Rocky Mountain bighorn sheep.

ODFW has identified numerous other transplant sites, but many are deemed unsuitable because of the presence of conflicts with domestic sheep. These "hooved locusts," as John Muir described them, are vectors for *Pasteurella pneumonia* and other diseases. A big die-off of the Lostine herd in 1986–1987 was likely due to intermingling with the domestic sheep. Ironically, most of the domestic sheep conflict comes from public land grazing permits issued by the Forest Service for the Wallowa-Whitman National Forest.

Both successful and potential bighorn reintroduction sites are well distributed around the state and often include de facto wilderness. This is no accident.

While bighorn sheep are often classified as a wilderness species, not all of Oregon's bighorn sheep are found within designated wilderness areas. Designating bighorn sheep ranges as wilderness is beneficial to bighorn sheep because it will provide long-term habitat protection from industry and development. Therefore the Department strives to keep present and potential bighorn sheep habitat as remote and undeveloped as possible.[4]

Bighorn sheep may soon return to the Deschutes Canyon, Fort Rock Lava Beds, Sutton Mountain in the proposed John Day Wilderness, Succor Creek in the proposed Lower Owyhee National Conservation Area, and elsewhere.

Faster Than a Speeding Pronghorn—Not!

There are no native antelope species in North America. Pronghorn (*Antilocapra americana*) may remind us of antelope in Africa, but they are taxonomically distinct. Pronghorn currently range in every western U.S. state save Washington, three Canadian provinces, and three Mexican states.

Ranking very high on the charismatic-megafauna scale, pronghorn are unforgettable. With coats of tan and brown overlaid with liberal splashes of white (every one looks a little different), they can be seen across much of the Oregon Desert. Actually the size of a domestic sheep, pronghorn look much bigger because of their longer legs.

They are named for the distinct prong, or fork, in their headgear, which serves to prevent permanent harm in fighting among males (mostly over females).

Pronghorn commonly eat forbs in the spring and summer, but they often rely on sagebrush tips in the winter. They will most likely be found within 5 miles of water.

Like deer, the males are called bucks, the females does, and the little ones are called either kids or fawns. They prefer low sagebrush as it allows them to better see and run. As social animals they are quite vocal (their call can often sound like a sneeze). They also communicate by the use of the white splotches on their rear. All these behaviors provide for the common defense.

Historically, grizzly bears, cougars, and wolves were major predators of pronghorn, but today most of that work is done by coyotes, who along with golden eagles often prey upon kids.

Robert Frost be damned, fences do not make us good neighbors to this species. Pronghorn can't jump! They never needed to. While pronghorn don't jump, they do swim (see Jordan Craters National Monument).

Of most concern is competition with domestic livestock—particularly in drought years. Livestock eat forbs that would otherwise be available to pronghorn does. The result is the does go into the winter less healthy and have smaller fawns.

Biologists estimate that 30 to 60 million pronghorn existed at the time of the European invasion. Today, even though the population is only around 1 million (about 23,000 in Oregon), the pronghorn is an excellent conservation success story. In 1915, only 10,000 to 15,000 of the animals remained. Market hunting, wanton slaughter, sod busting, and other kinds of habitat destruction brought the species to the edge of extinction.

A federal excise tax on guns and ammunition provided money to state wild-life agencies to bring back the species. Pronghorn numbers increased 1,500 per-cent from 1924 to 1976 through the control of hunting, transplanting of herds on historical ranges, conservation, restoration of habitat, and other actions.

Most amazing is the pronghorn's speed. Other mammals may have faster bursts of swiftness, but they can't maintain it for miles. Accurate measurements are rare, but speeds of between 50 and 60 miles per hour have been noted. It is difficult to get the test specimen to precisely parallel the test vehicle for adequate measurement periods, however.

Pardon the anthropocentrism, but pronghorn run for fun. Numerous cases exist in the literature of pronghorn racing automobiles. Most memorable to this author were three bucks in Hawks Valley. The road was (relatively) straight and smooth, and the trio challenged the truck. The driver accelerated to pace them, all the while trying to stay on the road, avoid rocks, holes, and other animal life, and watch both the pronghorn and the speedometer (52 miles per hour!).

After a few miles, the leader burst ahead and across the road in front of the truck and slowed again to the pace of the vehicle. It is obvious that this rumi-nant racer knew full well of the pitfall ahead—a road washout. Brakes were immediately applied, and later so were new shock absorbers. It was worth it. A once-in-a-lifetime experience (and the new shocks have a lifetime guarantee).

Bring Back the Beaver

Yes, Oregon's official mammal is a rodent. Far from a riparian rat, however, the beaver (Castor canadensis) enriches its ecosystem in disproportion to its num-bers. It is what biologists call a keystone species—as the beaver modifies its environment to make a living for itself, it also creates habitat for numerous other species.

Perhaps 200 million beavers once inhabited North America. Beaver were ev-erywhere there was water. After centuries of severe overtrapping, the beaver has finally made a partial comeback.

Beaver live to dam moving water, and they don't care if it is irrigation ditches or highway culverts. They can be a nuisance to humanity's sense of order and territory, but on the whole, any annoyance or damage beavers do to human de-velopment is far outweighed by the great ecological benefit they provide. Ac-cording to Oregon's Living Landscape, beaver benefits include:

- Raised water tables and related sediment settling, which contributes to the creation of meadows behind beaver dams and to the enhancement of fisheries downstream
- Control of streambank and channel erosion by trapping silt eroding from adjacent lands
- Creation of large carbon-absorbing reservoirs that greatly boost the amount of nitrogen available to plants
- Regeneration of riparian vegetation, which increases food and shelter for numerous invertebrates, other mammals, waterfowl, and songbirds

As a keystone species, the beaver creates habitat for many other species of fish and wildlife. (Photo by William L. Finley, Oregon Department of Fish and Wildlife Collection)

- Enhancement of fish habitat behind dams by increasing water depth
- Reduction of stream velocity and overall improvement of water quality as riparian vegetation intercepts contamination from agricultural runoff
- Recharging of groundwater reservoirs and stabilization of stream flows throughout the summer and during droughts
- The protection of downstream croplands and urban areas from floods by the beaver's enhancement of upstream water storage (through the creation of meadows and wetlands)[5]

Domestic livestock essentially do just the opposite. Though beaver munch plenty of riparian vegetation, they don't eradicate it.

> *In southeastern Oregon, riparian-zone trees have been reduced or eliminated in many areas by browsing herbivores. However, comparison of growth of red willow (Salix lasiandra) in an area inaccessible to cattle, but occupied by beavers, with that in an area inaccessible to both cattle and beavers indicated that beavers were not responsible for the deterioration. Although beavers harvested 82 percent of available stems annually, they cut them at a season after growth was completed and reserves were translocated to roots. Subsequent growth of cut willows increased exponentially in relation to the proportion of the stems cut by beavers.*[6]

In 1997 in Oregon, five thousand pelts were taken, but not many from the Oregon Desert. Cow-bombed desert streams no longer support beaver.

The first major assault on North American streams was the trapping out of the beaver. The second was the introduction of domestic livestock. Riparian restoration in the Oregon Desert cannot fully occur until livestock are removed and beaver are returned. Once the livestock quit degrading the streams, and beaver begin rebuilding them, we'll see a dramatic improvement in the desert landscape.

Reading the journals of early European explorers and exploiters in southeast Oregon, such as that of Peter Skene Ogden of the Hudson's Bay Company, one is struck that though the writers complained about much, they rarely complained about a lack of water. Consider that they traveled with canvas, cast iron, and fur—not nylon, aluminum, and polypropylene. Such would not be possible today in a desert with streams more dry than not.

Sage Grouse: The Spotted Owl of the Desert

The sage grouse (*Centrocercus urophasianus*) is a species that can't tolerate destruction of its sagebrush steppe habitat any more than the spotted owl can tolerate destruction of its old-growth forest habitat.

About the size of a small turkey, sage grouse once occurred in fourteen western states and three provinces. It has been extirpated from several jurisdictions.

Scientists have recently reclassified the species. The old western and eastern subspecies that were both thought to occur in Oregon are no longer accepted. A newly classified species, the Gunnison (to be called *Centrocercus minimus*), is found in Colorado and Utah. All other sage grouse are now known as the northern sage grouse (*C. urophasianus*).

Wherever there was sagebrush, there were sage grouse. The bird relies on its namesake for cover, shelter, and food. As sagebrush habitats have been converted to fields of alfalfa, wheat, crested wheatgrass, or houses, the sage grouse has declined. Fifty percent of the sage grouse habitat had been destroyed by 1951, and the trend has continued. Sage grouse chicks, for the first month of life, rely on riparian areas, where they feed on insects. Cow-blasted riparian areas means fewer sage grouse.

From October to May, the sage grouse dines exclusively on sagebrush, as the evergreen leaves are nutritious through the winter. In the late spring and summer, the grouse switch to herbaceous plants and grasses. Young grouse especially will eat insects, in particular grasshoppers (locusts!) when abundant.

The mating ritual is fascinating to observe. In the early spring, the larger and more strikingly marked males congregate each dawn at leks (assembly areas for courtship), where they undertake elaborate rituals of display to entice the females to mate with them. All will gather again in the evening and often will pull an all-nighter when the moon is bright.

The leks are small openings (0.1 to10 acres) in the sagebrush that are used only for display and copulation, never for eating and nesting. The males strut among the females with tailfeathers fully erect and fanned, and head and neck held high. The yellow comb over each eye is expanded, the sagging chest sac partly filled with air, and the wings drooping slightly. The grouse take in, and rapidly exhale, a large volume of air and make a unique and unforgettable sound (one authority has described it as *swish-swish-coo-oo-poink*) while exposing yellowish skin patches on the chest. Males also do a "dance" in which they aggressively brush each other.

The males fail in the family values department, however: after mating they play no role in raising the chicks.

Even if the sagebrush habitat is not eliminated outright, the sage grouse still suffers from the degradation of the remaining habitat.

Sage grouse experts describe the species' optimum "loafing" habitat as stream bottoms, ravines, and draws—the same optimum loafing habitat of

Strutting male northern sage grouse

livestock. By eating or otherwise destroying streamside vegetation, livestock cause gully erosion that lowers water tables and dries out wet meadows and other valuable sage grouse feeding habitat.

Domestic livestock also harm sage grouse in at least two other critically important ways. While livestock grazing has increased the ratio of sagebrush to grass (in areas where sagebrush habitat hasn't been intentionally eliminated for other land uses), the limiting factor for the sage grouse is not the sagebrush, but the forbs and grasses that grow among the sagebrush. Livestock eat the forbs and other herbaceous material that the sage grouse require in spring and summer.

Livestock also turn the tall grass into short grass, so it doesn't provide adequate sage grouse nesting cover from predators such as coyotes and ravens. The more grass cover, the better the chances of the eggs avoiding predation. In fact, the standing dead grass from previous years provides critically important cover. Yes, it is true: sage grouse need old-growth grass.

Sage grouse populations are in long-term decline. Complicating the lives of biologists monitoring the species is that several factors, including some not clearly understood, result in populations that vary greatly from year to year. Sage grouse have very good years and very bad years. It's probably related to drought cycles. It is clear, however, that the good years aren't as good as they used to be and that the bad years are getting worse.

The sage grouse was also in decline in the 1930s. It rebounded, primarily because of effective restrictions on hunting and excessive predator control rather than any major habitat conservation or restoration. Hunting pressures have decreased; habitat elimination, fragmentation, and degradation have not.

Fortunately, the sage grouse is at least as mediagenic as the spotted owl.

Under the Endangered Species Act, a species can be listed as either threatened or endangered. An endangered species is one that is in imminent danger of extinction unless action is taken. A threatened species is one that can be foreseen as becoming endangered with extinction if nothing is done. The sage grouse certainly qualifies as threatened. It is not yet down to a few birds in the wild like the California condor, but it is heading in that direction.

By acting now, we can begin to reverse the loss of habitat and bring back this magnificent bird not only from the brink, but to healthy huntable levels.

Viewing Sage Grouse. You can view sage grouse strutting their stuff—and if you are lucky, actual sex (don't blink)—during April and May.

From OR 205 about 27 miles north of Frenchglen (about 11 miles south of the turnoff to the Malheur Field Station/Malheur National Wildlife Refuge head-quarters), go west on the road with a sign that says "Foster Flat 32 (miles)." It is just south of milepost 34. Go 8.4 miles on this road. The road will bend toward the southeast, and you'll be pointed directly at Steens Mountain. There will be two small juniper-covered buttes off to your left in the short-middle distance. The sage grouse are directly off the road to the left about 50 to 200 feet.

The best time to see them is between first light and sunrise. Eighty birds once were commonly observed. Now it's twenty to thirty.

It is taboo to get out of your vehicle! If you want to take a picture and you don't have the lens for it, tough feces. Go buy one and come back later.

> Daily human disturbances on sage grouse leks could cause reduction in mat-ing, and some reduction in total production. If flushed, grouse usually fly from the strutting ground and do not return again that day. Some leks are known to the public and are visited by photographers and other interested persons to watch the annual courtship rituals. Such activities need to be curtailed if they disrupt mating. Grouse are tolerant of automobiles and may be watched from fairly close range if the observers do not leave their vehicles. But the instant a person leaves a vehicle the grouse become alarmed and generally take flight, not to return again until the next day. Fortunately the mating season is fairly long (up to 2 months) so receptive hens will usually be mated.[7]

Fish

Fish in a desert!? Certainly.

It is difficult to estimate the number of fish species in the Oregon Desert, primarily because scientists are still naming and renaming them. Fish populations once thought to be the same species are turning out to be different subspecies, having evolved in isolation from each other. Suffice it to say that numerous species, subspecies, and varieties of trout, minnow, suckers, and other kinds of fish, both native and exotic, can be found in the desert.

During the Pleistocene epoch (2 million to 10,000 years ago), the basins be-tween the mountain ranges were often huge lakes. As the climate changed, the big lakes dried into smaller ones. Lake Warner, for example, lowered to become the Warner Lakes. Lake Abert and Summer Lake were once one lake. Malheur Lake was much bigger than today. The Fort Rock–Christmas Valley area today has no large lake save the mostly dry Silver Lake, but one can still see the shoreline etched on Fort Rock, just as can one see on Catlow Rim the shoreline of the lake that once filled the Catlow Valley.

As the lakes lowered, fish populations became isolated and eventually speciated. Scientists can distinguish a dace that lives only in a single water body. The only home to the Fosket speckled dace (*Rhinichthys osculus* ssp.) is Fosket Spring.

Irrigation withdrawals and/or the cow bombing of streams has diminished the habitat of numerous fish species native to the Oregon Desert.

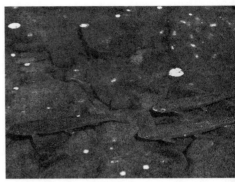

Redband trout are in decline.

Some are on the federal endangered species list, and others should be.

The 4-inch-long Borax Lake chub (*Gila boraxobius*) is found only in Borax Lake in the Alvord Basin. It has evolved to live in 97-degree Fahrenheit water.

The Warner sucker (*Castostomus warnerensis*)—lordy, do we need more charismatic names for these fish species—is found only in the Warner Basin.

Fish hang out not only in lakes, but also in the streams of the desert.

Trout, especially the Great Basin redband (*Oncorhynchus mykiss* ssp.), are also in trouble. The Great Basin redband is known to have six populations, which may actually be six distinct subspecies: Fort Rock Basin, Chewaucan Basin, Warner Basin, Catlow Basin, Goose Lake Basin, and the Harney Basin. The populations have been isolated for at least ten thousand years.

The Great Basin redband is a subset of a large inland redband group, which are cousins to steelhead and rainbow trout. The inland redband trout occur in arid areas between the Rocky Mountains and the Cascade and Sierra mountain ranges from British Columbia to Mexico. It is extinct in three-quarters of its original range. Over the millennia, the species has adapted to severe climate changes and water fluctuations by retreating to refugia when conditions are challenging and expanding when conditions are accommodating.

With a distinctive red stripe, redbands occur in semipermanent lakes, streams, and marshes. They have been found in streams with 75- to 80-degree Fahrenheit temperatures in summer, clearly lethal for their cooler kin. However, degraded desert streams often have temperatures in excess of 80 degrees—deadly even for the redband.

Redband trout are an excellent indicator of stream health, and few streams are healthy in the Oregon Desert. Grazing, logging, roading, mining, and irrigation withdrawal have degraded streams and therefore the redband populations. The introduction of exotic fish species and hatchery rainbow trout has exacerbated an already horrible situation.

Several other fish species of local note are described in various wilderness sections.

Wilderness, Natural, and Recreational Values

Wilderness Proposal	Lava Fields & Related Features	High Fault-Block Scarps	Unusual Erosional Forms	Uncommon Plant Communities or Diverse Plant Assemblages	Plants of Special Interest	Northern Bald Eagle	Existing or Potential Bighorn Sheep	Crucial Deer Winter Range	Sage Grouse Strutting Grounds	Excellent Raptor Concentrations	Rocky Mountain Elk in Desert	Cultural Resources	Paleontological Features	Most Exceptional Recreational Features*
BASIN AND RANGE ECOREGION														
Abert Rim		•					•			•		•		Ba, Hi, NS, P, Si
Alvord Desert			•	•	•			•						So, NS, Si, Bi
Bighorn		•				•	•		•	•			•	Ba, Bi, Hu, NS, P, Si
Buzzard's Creek									•					So
Diablo Mountain		•					•			•			•	Ba, Hi, Bi, NS
Fish Creek Rim		•		•	•		•	•		•		•		Hi, NS, Si
Fort Rock Lava Beds	•			•		•		•			•	•		Hi, NS, P, Si
Lonesome Lakes									•		•			So
Malheur Lake			•	•	•					•		•	•	
Oregon Grasslands		•	•	•	•		•	•	•	•	•			Ba, Hu, HR
Pronghorn				•	•								•	Hu, So
Pueblo Mountains		•		•	•		•			•	•			Ba, NS, Si, Hi, So, P
Sheepshead Mountains		•			•		•			•		•		So
Shifting Sand Dunes			•										•	Hi, HR, NS, P, Si
Steens Mountain	•	•	•	•	•		•	•	•	•	•			CCS, Ba, Hi, F, Bi, HR, Hu, NS, P, Si, So
Trout Creek Mountains				•	•		•	•		•				Ba, Hi, NS, P, So

	Most exceptional recreational features*
BLUE MOUNTAINS ECOREGION	
Homestead Addition	So, P
Sheep Mountain	Ba, Si
South Fork John Day	Ba, Hi, F, Hu
COLUMBIA BASIN ECOREGION (see John Day under Lava Plains)	
KLAMATH MOUNTAINS ECOREGION	
Soda Mountain	Ba, Hi, HR, CCS, NS, Bi, Hu, P, Si, So
LAVA PLAINS ECOREGION	
Badlands	Hi, NS, Si, Hu
Crooked	Hi, F
Deschutes Canyon	Hi, Bi, Bo
John Day	Ba, Bo, Hi, F, Bi, Hu, NS, P, Si
OWYHEE UPLANDS ECOREGION	
Malheur Canyons	So, Ba, Hi, F, Bi, NS, Si
Owyhee	Bo, So, Ba, Hi, F, Bi, Hu, NS, P, Si

*Key to most exceptional recreational features

Ba = Backpacking
CCS = Cross-country skiing
HR = Horseback riding
P = Photography

Bi = Birding
F = Fishing
Hu = Hunting
Si = Sightseeing

Bo = Boating
Hi = Hiking
NS = Nature study
So = Solitude

Expanded from Table 3-2 in *Special Wilderness Features in WSAs, Oregon Wilderness, Supplement to the Draft Environmental Impact Statement, Volume 1—Statewide* (Portland: Oregon State Office, USDI Bureau of Land Management), January 1987.

63

UNNATURAL HISTORY

One of the penalties of an ecological education is that one lives alone in a world of wounds. . . . An ecologist must either harden his shell and make believe that the consequences of science are none of his business, or he must be the doctor who sees the marks of death in a community that believes itself well and does not want to be told otherwise.
— Aldo Leopold, *A Sand County Almanac*

A desert, perhaps because to the uninformed it can be a perilous place, may appear at first glance to be a tough place that can withstand anything that humans try to do to it. In reality, this harsh desert is very delicate and quite fragile.

Humans have caused great damage to the Oregon Desert. It is down, but not out. It is natural enough to recover if we let it.

When most of us see a natural old-growth forest and a clearcut side by side, we instinctively know in our heart, if not our mind, that the forest is inherently good (alive, beautiful, verdant, diverse) and that the clearcut is inherently bad (dead, ugly, abused, simplified).

It is a bit different in the Oregon Desert. Often, to the untrained eye, an abused landscape can still appear beautiful. If the underlying geology is such, an eroded hillside can be aesthetically pleasing. A tree-free stream through a heavily grazed meadow can still look inviting if you don't know better.

Both because a desert is a much smaller, shorter ecosystem than a forest, and because ecological irritants such as domestic livestock have been pervasive for a century and a half, it is harder to see and understand the ecological damage. It is not impossible, however.

DOMESTIC LIVESTOCK: SCOURGE OF THE WEST

As sheep advance, flowers, vegetation, grass, soil, plenty, and poetry vanish.
— John Muir, founder of the Sierra Club, 1838–1914

The most pervasive and insidious threat to the Oregon Desert is domestic livestock grazing. Livestock have done more damage to the Earth than the chainsaw. Bovine bulldozers have impoverished the arid West at the expense of both water

Livestock have caused more damage to the Earth than bulldozers and chainsaws.

quality and quantity, native fish and wildlife, native vegetation, and soil. They are an abomination.

The sins of domestic livestock (a.k.a. meadow maggots) in the arid West are countless, but to enumerate a few:

1. *Domestic livestock consume forage at the expense of wildlife.* When you see domestic livestock on the public lands, you are not seeing bighorn sheep, pronghorn, elk, deer, or other forage-eating wildlife. In one study, scientists found that domestic livestock consumed 88.8 percent of the available forage (cattle 82.3 percent, feral horses 5.8 percent, sheep 0.7 percent), leaving 11.2 percent to wildlife species (mule deer 10.1 percent, pronghorn 0.9 percent, bighorn sheep 0.1 percent, elk 0.1 percent).[1]

2. *Domestic livestock endanger native fish and wildlife.* Scientists summarized the percentages of 1,880 species imperiled by habitat loss, alien species, pollution, overexploitation, and disease. In the United States, grazing has contributed to the demise of 22 percent of the species—compared to logging (12 percent) and mining (11 percent). In particular, livestock grazing is especially harmful to plant species, affecting 33 percent of endangered plant species.[2]

3. *Domestic livestock destroy streams by degrading both water quality and total water quantity.* Cattle devolved from species inhabiting wet meadows in northern Europe and Asia. They love water.

> *This is well illustrated in one study, which found that a riparian zone in eastern Oregon comprised only 1.9 percent of the allotment, but produced 21 percent of the available forage and 81 percent of the forage consumed by cattle.*[3]

Streams of the arid West are more defiled and tragic than wild and scenic. Dr. Joy Belsky (and associates), a world-renowned grasslands ecologist, exhaustively reviewed the scientific literature and found the following:

> A large number of studies document that cattle grazing degrades the environment. . . .   Locally, grazing affects
> - **Water quality:** livestock deposit pathogenic bacteria into streams and increase nutrient content, water turbidity, and water temperatures, all of which harm populations of cold water fish and other species.
> - **Stream channel morphology:** grazing results in stream downcutting and streambank loss, and reduces channel and streambank stability, number and quality of deep pools, and number of stream meanders.
> - **Hydrology (stream flow patterns):** grazing causes an increase in runoff, flood water velocity, number of flood events, and peak flow, while reducing (or stopping) summer flow and lowering the water table.
> - **Riparian soils:** grazing increases the area of bare ground, soil compaction, and erosion, while reducing water infiltration and soil fertility.
> - **Instream vegetation:** grazing causes an increase in algal populations but a decline in submerged higher plants.
> - **Streambank vegetation:** grazing reduces the cover, biomass, and productivity of herbaceous and woody vegetation, and impedes plant succession.
> - **Aquatic and riparian wildlife:** grazing leads to the reduction in diversity, abundance, and productivity of cold-water fish, amphibians, reptiles, and invertebrates and alters the composition and diversity of birds and mammals.
>
> Consequently, livestock degrade all aspects of local stream and riparian ecology.
> At the regional level . . . , grazing reduces the quality and quantity of water for domestic water supplies, reduces reservoir life and the hydroelectric capacity of reservoirs, increases maintenance costs of irrigation canals, and reduces commercial and recreational fishing opportunities. In addition, grazing fragments riparian corridors used by migratory wildlife, intensifies flood damage, and homogenizes the biotic landscape.[4]

4. *Domestic livestock are a hazard to human health.* The intestinal bacterium *E. coli* appears first in streams and then in us. The microscopic fecal parasite *Cryptosporidium* now contaminates nearly all surface waters that have been tested nationwide.[5] (No more euphemisms. Refuse to use the term *cow pies*. Pie is good and tasty and, unlike pumpkin pies or berry pies, cow pies aren't filled with cow.)

Eating beef contributes to heart disease. Cattle on open-range highways have more right-of-way than automobiles.

5. *Domestic livestock cost the taxpayers money.* Taxpayers are subsidizing live-stock grazing on the public land to the tune of $10.74 for every $1.00 received.[6] Because of these subsidies, it costs an elite set of ranchers only $1.35 per month to keep a cow and calf on public land. It costs more to feed a house cat. If it ever made sense to graze the public lands, it certainly does not now.

Don't expect most public land grazing permittees and many government bureaucrats to change their ways. Unfortunately, it is difficult to get someone to understand something when their livelihood, profits, or lifestyle depends on not understanding it.

THE TOP TWENTY THREATS TO ECOLOGICAL INTEGRITY

> *People have always chased around deserts looking for pots of gold. Such people have missed seeing the only real gold the desert offers—an occasional rainbow, hundreds of fantastic sunsets, interesting and secretive animals, pungent aromas of desert shrubs, droplets of dew on a hairy leaf, and a thousand other delights. As with every generation, we are duty bound to preserve all these for desert lovers yet born.*
> —Denzel and Nancy Ferguson, *Oregon's Great Basin Country*

Oh, my desert! How do humans threaten thee? Let me count the ways.

Below are the top twenty threats to the desert, arranged in descending order of proven or potential harm. Don't get fixated on the absolute order, though. The list changes daily because of relative threat, new information, and mood. The top and bottom ones don't change, but the ones in the middle move a lot.

1. Domestic Livestock
See "Domestic Livestock: Scourge of the West," earlier.

2. Human Population
It is not just the sprawling of Bend-Redmond-Prineville out into the Oregon Desert that is the problem; it is also the total number of Oregonians, Americans, and Earthlings. If human population is not stabilized at sustainable levels, then all bets are off. Any good cause is a lost cause unless population and consumption are addressed. To help save the desert, the rest of Oregon, and the planet, everyone should have fewer children and consume more efficiently.

3. Alien Species
The invasion of nonnative exotic plant species into native ecosystems is a serious problem. Exotic species often displace native species and are usually of little value to wildlife. Government land managers have significantly increased their talk about controlling exotic weeds, but unfortunately their walk has not increased commensurately.

BLM's color brochure entitled *Noxious Weeds: A Growing Concern* leaves one to believe that weeds are spread only by seed attached to tire treads and hiking socks or in pack-stock feces. Yes, one should not drive off-road anyway, but clean your tires if you do. Do pick your socks and burn or otherwise destroy seed before you go to the next area. Feed your pack stock on weed-free grain ninety-six hours before entering backcountry.

Government weed evangelists talk much about the impacts of exotic weeds but say almost nothing about *the* primary vector in their spread: livestock. Both through direct transport of seed in their guts and the trampling of ground crusts to bare dirt to make a seedbed for exotics, livestock are the biggest cause of weed spread. No serious progress in weed control will occur until livestock are controlled.

Land managers tend to reach for the herbicides first, which is easy if you ignore the effects of these highly dangerous poisons on other plant and wildlife species, not to mention humans.

Exotic plants are not the only problem. It has been easier for state fish and game management officials not to oppose the destruction of native fish and wildlife habitat, instead introducing new species into degraded ecosystems. Such has been the case with many exotic fish species now considered a problem to native species of fish. Wild species can lose out to exotics by direct competition or by hybridizing with exotics, thereby polluting the native gene pool.

One example is the chukar, an exotic game bird that was introduced by state game officers because they wanted a huntable species that thrived on another exotic species: cheatgrass. While the chukar has not been found to displace other wildlife directly, its presence masks the loss of native wildlife habitat that was caused by the invasion of cheatgrass, an introduced exotic plant. It is against the law to kill chukar out of season, but—at least from an ecological standpoint—it would be right.

Finally, let's not ignore another scourge of the wild desert: feral (please don't call them wild) horses and burros. While they may bring to mind a great western myth, while they may be cute when young and perhaps even majestic when older, they are nonetheless exotic intruders in the wild and an ecological nightmare. These horses were introduced from Europe and are not descendants of the horses native to the continent, which died out about 10,000 years ago, possibly extirpated by the first Americans. Herds can grow at 20 percent annually, and, with no predators except humans to control them, they take forage and space from indigenous wildlife. They destroy very sensitive habitats such as playa. The law should be changed to allow for their final round-up and adoption.

4. Off-Road Vehicles

If you've wondered why land management agencies are doing so much for off-road-vehicle (ORV) enthusiasts—much more than they are doing for hikers—just heed the advice of that great conservationist known as Deep Throat: "Follow the money." ORV owners pay a registration fee (and get a dedicated portion of the gas tax), and most of the money goes to develop staging areas, trails, and related facilities.

Meanwhile, hiking boots are not registered, and you get what you pay for.

The problem with ORVs is not just that they offend many people's aesthetic sensibilities. Although the loss of tranquillity is reason enough to restrict them, the noise harasses wildlife. Vegetation annihilation, soil compaction, and erosion are also products of off-road vehicles.

ORV enthusiasts often insist that they too are communing with nature, only they are doing so in a way that lets them get to areas they otherwise couldn't get to, and in a way that lets them see more. This is false economy. One cannot really enjoy and appreciate nature at 40 miles per hour.

Some also attack backpackers as rich elitist snobs. Some are elitist snobs to be sure, but the top-of-the-line collection of the finest backpacking gear is but a fraction of the cost of an average snowmobile or all-terrain vehicle.

Please remember that not all off-road enthusiasts are the problem. Ninety percent of all off-road-vehicle users give a bad name to the remaining 10 percent who follow the rules and try to minimize their impact.

5. Irrigation Impoundments and Withdrawals

No one should be allowed to dry up a stream. Minimum stream flows must be maintained. Enough water should be left in a stream so that it still supports fish, wildlife, recreation, and other purposes. Ninety percent of all water withdrawals are for cattle or for growing feed for cattle. Great damage has been done to the Snake, Owyhee, and Malheur Basins by the damming, ditching, diverting, diking, and destroying of native habitats.

6. Logging

Some desert areas have some very large and old, but very slow-growing, ponderosa pine trees. The timber industry, having gone through much of the big pine forests, seeks these as well. It is also turning to marginal timber species like western juniper. In the Rockies, the timber industry has discovered quaking aspen for chips for paper, but hopefully hauling costs to mills will dissuade logging of aspen in the Oregon Desert.

7. Roads

Roads, both their construction and use, have serious environmental impacts. Soil erosion harms streams. Roads are vectors for humans who, often unintentionally, harass wildlife and for the dispersion of exotic weeds. If large enough, roads can serve as migratory barriers to small species. Many so-called roads were created by casual use, rather than intent or design. A road closure and rehabilitation program could help wildlife, improve water quality, and save taxpayer money.

8. Altered Fire Regimes

Overzealous fire fighting, coupled with livestock grazing, has led to prevention of beneficial fires that clear out brush and juniper and favor grass (actually, such fires have just been delayed). Conversely, ecosystems in which native bunchgrasses have been replaced with the highly flammable cheatgrass are being overburned, creating a new unnatural equilibrium of low-diversity annual grasslands.

Consider the quaking aspen, a "keystone" species (many other species depend on it). Outside riparian areas, aspen stands contain the greatest numbers of wildlife and plant species in the desert. In many areas, the combination of livestock grazing and fire exclusion is a terminal combination. The lack of fire discourages aspen from sprouting, and the livestock browse off what does sprout.

9. Predator Killing

Each year, government "killers" slay about one hundred thousand coyotes, bobcats, mountain lions, and other kinds of the public's wildlife in the United States, all in the name of protecting livestock, much of which is on the public's land. The U.S. Department of Agriculture's Animal Damage Control Program has changed its name to Wildlife Services—a euphemism offensive enough to any thinking human, but more so to wildlife.

Besides rifles and traps, government killers use the M-44, a baited device that ejects a mixture of lethal sodium cyanide in the mouths of coyotes and other animals.

In Congress, efforts are increasing to cut the funding for this barbaric and unnecessary program. Congressman Peter DeFazio (D-OR) is a leader in that effort.

"Sure, coyotes eat sheep," said the late great Denzel Ferguson. "But the question is, do they get enough? Are their coats sleek? Do they have good conformation?"

10. Cyanide Heap Leach Mining

Less than a teaspoon of gold is yielded for every two dump trucks of earth that is dug up and piled and doused with cyanide to leach out gold (not to mention the eternal pits that remain). The resulting metal is in demand mostly for adornment and speculation.

Troublesome conservationists, costly (but inadequate) regulations, and depressed gold prices have kept transnational mining companies out of Oregon so far, but they aren't far away. These fools for gold think nothing of chemically stripping it from a land more precious than any mineral. The face of Nevada to the south is becoming pocked with this industrial-strength Earth acne.

11. Geothermal Power

Other miners seek to mine the heat of the Earth to produce unneeded electricity by building a large industrial facility at the base of Steens Mountain near Borax Lake (and perhaps running powerlines to power nearby gold mines). The factory, its smell, and plume would blight the desert and likely dry up the nearby hot springs, killing off the Borax Lake chub, the most unique fish in the Oregon Desert.

12. Groundwater Depletion

Electricity and deep-water pumps allow humans not only to dry up open watercourses but also to deplete underground aquifers. Along the old Oregon Trail, in the proposed Boardman Grasslands National Wildlife Refuge, was a spring that saved many a settler. Today the spring is dry, and the water table is at least 300 feet below the spring that flowed strong only 150 years ago.

13. Other Mining

Whether recreational panning for gold, quarrying of gravel for roads, taking lava rock for fireplaces, or excavating litter for kitties, mining takes its toll on the desert. Federal law, not materially changed since 1872, gives away the public's minerals and leaves the public with the mess.

Humans should fear the coyote only for the irrational and inhumane ways it makes us behave.

14. Fences

Any fence, no matter the number of strands of barbed wire or the spacing of the wire, is an impediment to wildlife. Fences to keep livestock out of riparian areas help riparian areas, but at the expense of upland habitat (since cattle numbers are rarely reduced) and species sensitive to fences, such as pronghorn. Fences are pasturizing the West.

15. Powerlines

The large swath cut through juniper woodlands by powerline corridors can impede wildlife migration. The smaller lines can be hazardous to raptors whose last act is a short circuit.

16. Militarization

With the end of the Cold War, Europeans became increasingly intolerant of close and low-level training flights. Much of this training has moved to the American West. Much of eastern Oregon is a military operations area and subject to low-level overflights by both jet bombers and fighters.

It is a memorable experience to be out in the middle of nowhere and then be buzzed by a jet fighter perhaps 50 feet above your head. If you have time to react, mooning is recommended. It is protected First Amendment speech, and it has been known to make a pilot waggle his wings.

17. Lights

As if conservationists didn't have enough already to worry about, we also need to advocate for the conservation of darkness. The feeling of vastness and humility that one receives in the middle of a flat desert as darkness falls and the stars shine on all horizons can be marred by inappropriate and unnecessary street and yard lights.

18. Development

Bend-Redmond-Prineville is sprawling out into the desert with first homes, second (sometimes third) homes, and the related commercial and industrial development. In Oregon, urban growth boundaries are actually urban growth bungies.

19. Recreation

All recreationists have impact, even those of us who mostly just walk the Oregon Desert. We should all strive to ensure that our impacts are the least possible (see "Leave No Trace" under "Getting Around and Back Well" in The Basics chapter). We also must guard against the industrial-strength recreation of huge resorts or off-road-vehicle havens, such as those in the Millican Valley.

20. Yahoos

Whether slaughtering road signs with guns or as grave robbers fancying themselves as amateur archaeologists, uncivilized yahoos do great harm to the desert.

POLITICAL FUTURE

The fate of the Oregon Desert is in the hands of politicians. A disturbing thought until we remember that all politicians want to be loved, and love voters who vote for them. A good majority of Oregon voters (if you don't vote, you don't count) love wilderness and want more of it preserved. If this love of wilderness is translated to votes for politicians who save wilderness, then Oregon's desert wilderness can be saved. If not, it will be lost.

INVITING NATURE BACK:
THE BIG VISION REQUIRES BIG WILDERNESS

We are in an unprecedented ecological crisis and are suffering an astounding loss of biological diversity. We are losing not only massive numbers of individual species, but also entire ecosystems and the services they provide.

We are consuming energy far faster than it is being produced and polluting our air, our waters, and ourselves in the process.

We are reproducing at astronomical rates, facing another doubling of the U.S. population in just a few decades.

We humans are living far beyond our means. We are so far beyond sustainable as to be downright scary. We are robbing from our grandchildren to pay our bills and the bills of our grandparents.

But we all know that. The challenge is not what to do. That's easy. We must (a) live within our means, (b) reduce our population to sustainable levels, and (c) conserve and restore the web of life. The challenge is doing it.

We have to use less. We northern industrial junkies are consuming at an unsustainable rate. We'd have to increase the world's industrial base twenty times for the rest of the world to catch up. Another way to look at it is that we need another three Earths.

Cutting our consumption by 75 percent is a very reasonable and achievable goal. Energy philosopher Amory Lovins has painted us the picture of how we can get by, just as sumptuously, on 25 percent of the energy and material we now consume. We can live, quite nicely, off of solar income. In terms of material consumption, by simply using half as much, twice as long, we can get by—just as well—on 25 percent of the resources we now consume. We have the technologies on the shelf today to do it.

Today we have 6 billion people on Earth, and 3 million in Oregon. Scientists have calculated that if we want to sustain the northern industrial lifestyle worldwide, albeit using less resources more efficiently, we can sustain 2 billion on earth (and 1 million in Oregon). Oregon had 1 million people just six decades ago. To achieve 2 billion on Earth (and 1 million in Oregon) in a hundred years, every family in the world (and in Oregon) must average 1.5 children. It is not that hard. That industrial giant Germany has already done it; Hong Kong, once again a part of China, is below the goal at 1.4, without any Chinese-style birth control. Finally, Italy, home of the Roman Catholic Church, is at 1.3. If every pregnancy were both wanted and planned, we'd be home free.

If we fail to limit population, we won't have any economic growth, no matter how much—or how little—we consume.

We can and will do these things because, (a) it is rational, (b) it is possible, and (c) the alternative is too horrible to contemplate.

Let us turn to the matter of restoring the web of life, first in general, then in the Oregon Desert.

Scientists call it biodiversity, shorthand for the term *biological diversity*.

> *Biodiversity is the variety of life and its processes. It includes the variety of living organisms, the genetic difference among them, the communities and ecosystems in which they occur, and the ecological and evolutionary processes that keep them functioning, yet ever changing and adapting.*[1]

Given that it is critical to stop the human-caused mass extinction of species now underway and accelerating, a new branch of science has formed to address how to do so. It is the science of conservation biology.

Conservation biology is developing guidelines that we must follow if we want to leave room for nature. Quite simply, habitat destruction must stop. And critical habitat that has been lost must be restored.

Integrating what scientists know about the habitat requirements of species, the dynamics of populations, the effects of pollutants, and so forth, conservation biologists have come to a not too surprising conclusion: the anchor of biodiversity is wilderness. Too much wilderness has been lost, and we must not only conserve every acre that remains but also restore much that has been lost— not just because we love wilderness emotionally and spiritually, but because it is ecologically imperative.

If the public wants the grizzly bear and the wolf to return, we need wilderness and lots of it. If we want salmon—not only as museum pieces, but in abundance—we need wilderness and lots of it (and fewer people).

Additionally, the spaces between wildernesses need to be managed better and as part of the greater ecological and economic system.

Dr. Reed Noss of Corvallis, a renowned ecologist and one of the founders of this new branch of science (he also loves the Oregon Desert), has set down four ecological goals that are necessary to conserve biodiversity:

1. *Represent, in a system of protected areas, all native ecosystem types and seral [successional] stages across their natural range of variation.*

2. *Maintain viable populations of all native species in natural patterns of abundance and distribution.*

3. *Maintain ecological and evolutionary processes, such as disturbance regimes, hydrological processes, nutrient cycles, and biotic interactions, including predation.*

4. *Design and manage the system to be responsive to short-term and long-term environmental change and to maintain the evolutionary potential of lineages.[2]*

Adequate representation includes *all* ecosystem types, from the common to the unique, from the lowest to the highest elevations, from the wettest to the driest climates, all soil and geologic types, and all vegetation types (including all age classes).

Because an ecosystem is more than a collection of species—it is an *interconnection* of species—we must be concerned about the health of each species. Many will get along without any special attention, but some will require our special attention. Wide-ranging carnivores, like wolves, bears, and wolverines, are excellent indicators of ecosystem health. Ensure for their continued existence, and you're taking care of many other species as well.

Noss has further generalized six guidelines for designating and protecting habitat for species:

1. *Species well distributed across their native range are less susceptible to extinction than species confined to small portions of their range.*

2. *Large blocks of habitat, containing large populations of a target species, are superior to small blocks of habitat containing small populations.*

3. *Blocks of habitat closer together are better than blocks far apart.*

4. *Habitat in contiguous blocks is better than fragmented habitat.*

5. *Interconnected blocks of habitat are better than isolated blocks; corridors or linkages function better when habitat within them resembles that preferred by target species.*

6. *Blocks of habitat that are roadless or otherwise inaccessible to humans are better than roaded and accessible habitat blocks.[3]*

Humans must leave enough of nature alone to allow ecological and evolutionary processes to function and change. Things change and nature adapts, but we must give it room.

Honing these and other principles of conservation biology and landscape ecology to apply them on the ground requires three essential kinds of land management: cores, corridors, and carnivores.

Cores are the heart of the conservation management system—the larger and more numerous, the better. They are the highest-quality habitat. This is best achieved by the designation of large wilderness areas and similar protective classifications.

To ensure the flow of individuals, populations, and species between the core areas, the system must also be connected by *corridors*, ideally by areas of high-quality habitat. This is best achieved by the designation of smaller wilderness areas, wild and scenic rivers, and other similar protective classifications to inter-connect larger wildlands or serve as stepping-stone habitats.

These cores and connectors must also be buffered with the most restrictions on human activities closest to the cores and corridors, with fewer restraints far-ther away.

The third essential is keystone species such as *carnivores*. As top predators, carnivores often regulate ecosystems and are essential components of ecosystem health. The large ones have generally been extirpated from most ecosystems.

> [M]any people are uncomfortable in proposing the reintroduction of large and politically troublesome carnivores. But this is no excuse. Timidity in conservation planning and implementation is a betrayal to the land. Even in relatively populated regions like most of the eastern United States, the land cannot fully recover from past and present insults and mismanage-ment unless its bears, cougars, and wolves return. The greatest impediment to rewilding is an unwillingness to imagine it.[4]

The cornerstone of any landscape conservation strategy is conserving what is still wild. Conservationists have inventoried the remaining Oregon Desert wild-lands and are recommending them for wilderness designation.

Since free-flowing streams and adjacent lands are excellent connector habi-tat, conservationists are inventorying them and will be making recommenda-tions for additions to the national wild and scenic river system.

No comprehensive and detailed ecological assessment has been done at the fine scale for the Oregon Desert. Such assessments done for other bioregions suggest that—if we want large predators and all other ecosystem functions to be working properly—at least one-half of the Oregon Desert needs to be either kept wild or rewilded.

Ecological realities versus political realities. Both are equally real, but since the former cannot be changed, the latter must be.

> A cynic might describe rewilding as an atavistic obsession with the resur-rection of Eden. A more sympathetic critic might label it romantic. We con-tend, however, that rewilding is simply scientific realism, assuming that our goal is to ensure the long-term integrity of the land community.[5]

Oregonians and all Earthlings are engaged in the greatest evolutionary test of all time. Humans, with our large brains and opposable thumbs, have conquered the world. Humans will determine whether any species or ecosystem will live or die. Humans (currently) have no serious predators, save ourselves. To date, as a species, we have successfully outmaneuvered all the major environmental checks and balances that keep all other species within their limits. Our popula-tion continues to grow in spite of diseases like AIDS. Because of environmental stresses (a.k.a. pollution), human sperm counts are down 50 percent in the last thirty years. What do we do about it? We don't address the underlying causes but simply learn to make babies in test tubes.

Humans are orders of magnitude more successful than any other species. We have—for the short term at least—transcended any limits. However, nature bats last. In the end, we humans must learn to live within our means on Earth or we won't be on Earth.

The evolutionary challenge is whether we, as a species, will evolve to have the wisdom to do something no other species has ever done or had to do— practice willful self-restraint. We must learn to live within our means, both economic and environmental.

Will we as a species learn that our long-term survival, as well as our short-term real comfort, depends upon a healthy, clean, and diverse planet?

We can. Establishing a model program in the Oregon Desert is a tangible step.

A SOLUTION: THE OREGON DESERT CONSERVATION ACT

As conservationists, ecologists, economists, and others began to turn their attention to the Oregon Desert, all soon realized that if the goal of conserving and restoring the web of life (biodiversity) in the desert bioregion for this and future generations was to be met, that it would take an act of Congress. The goals of the proposed Oregon Desert Conservation Act (ODCA) are to ensure that:

- The desert ecosystem would function across the landscape and over time.
- The primary provider of conservation would be public land, not private land.
- Government spending would be done in the most efficient manner possible.
- Local affected interests would be treated justly.

Combining their collective knowledge of the Oregon Desert with the principles of conservation biology, they set to work. First, de facto wilderness lands were inventoried. These lands qualify under the definition of wilderness as set forth in the Wilderness Act of 1964:

> A wilderness, in contrast with those areas where man and his own works dominate the landscape, is hereby recognized as an area where the earth and its community of life are untrammeled by man, where man himself is a visitor who does not remain. An area of wilderness is further defined to mean in this Act an area of undeveloped Federal land retaining its primeval character and influence, without permanent improvements or human habitation, which is protected and managed to preserve its natural conditions and which (1) generally appears to have been affected primarily by the forces of nature, with the imprint of man's work substantially unnoticeable; (2) has outstanding opportunities for solitude or a primitive and unconfined type of recreation; (3) has at least five thousand acres of land or is of sufficient size as to make practicable its preservation and use in an unimpaired condition; and (4) may also contain ecological, geological or other features of scientific, educational, scenic or historical values.

The 1964 law required the Forest Service, the National Park Service, and the Fish and Wildlife Service to review their holdings and make recommendations to Congress. The Bureau of Land Management was not required to review its lands until passage of the Federal Lands Policy and Management Act (FLPMA) of 1976. That law gave the agency until 1991 to complete the task.

Controversy immediately plagued the BLM's wilderness review process. The first task of the agency was designating wilderness study areas, areas of wilderness quality that would be managed "so as not to impair suitability" as wilderness "until Congress has determined otherwise."

To determine roadless areas, the agency first had to determine the roads. BLM took their definition of a road from the official report of the House of Representatives that accompanied FLPMA:

> *An access route which has been improved and maintained by using hand or power machinery or tools to ensure relatively regular and continuous use. A way maintained solely by the passage of vehicles does not constitute a road.*

An adequate definition, but the devil is in those details. In many cases, BLM misapplied the definition. However, it is in the gray area.

After determining the road network, BLM analyzed the areas between the "roads." If the area was five thousand acres or greater (criterion No. 3 in the Wilderness Act definition), BLM then determined whether the area was generally natural (criterion No. 1). If it wasn't, the area was dropped.

Much of the debate around wilderness designations has centered on the issue of roads. A designated wilderness area is an area without roads, and no mechanized uses are allowed. Humans and their machines have been nearly everywhere. We've all experienced motorcraft in the most surprising and/or inappropriate places. Those humans who love machines more than nature will argue that any discernible evidence of vehicle use constitutes a road (especially if they have the rig for it).

Proponents readily concede that several of the proposed wilderness areas in the Oregon Desert Conservation Act contain what all would agree are "roads," albeit of a low standard. As livestock grazing diminishes, for example, the only significant purpose of such roads no longer exists.

Rather than engage in interminable debates with bureaucrats over the shade of gray, conservationists asked, "Does the road have any legitimate purpose?" Fortunately, Congress is the final arbiter. On occasion, Congress has designated wilderness with a paved road in it (later removed). There was no longer any need (if there ever was) for the road.

USGS 7.5' quad maps distinguish five kinds of routes:

- ❧ *Paved:* further distinguished as "primary" or "secondary," depending on their construction
- ❧ *Improved:* engineered, constructed, surfaced (but not with pavement), and/or drained
- ❧ *Unimproved:* dirt, possibly having been passed over with a bulldozer blade

🐾 *Jeep trail:* a track established and maintained by use
🐾 *Trail:* pedestrian, or at least not four-wheeled motorcraft

BLM's wilderness inventory was done before most of the desert was mapped at the 7.5' scale, so the inventory did not have benefit of the USGS analysis. Conservationists generally draw the line between "improved" and "unimproved" as defining a "road."

If an area was roadless and generally natural, BLM then determined if it had outstanding opportunities for primitive recreation and/or solitude (criterion No. 2). In particular, this is where BLM disqualified millions of acres of Oregon de facto wilderness land from designated wilderness consideration. BLM interpreted this provision much more narrowly and arbitrarily than did the Forest Service, National Park Service, and Fish and Wildlife Service. These agencies assumed that an area that was generally natural and of sufficient size by definition had outstanding opportunities for solitude and/or primitive recreation.

Finally, BLM didn't let other supplemental wilderness values (criterion No. 4) influence its decision of whether to designate a wilderness study area.

BLM eventually designated 2,806,598 acres in Oregon as wilderness study areas. In 1991, they recommended less than half of these—1,278,073 acres—to Congress for wilderness designation. (Since then, as a result of land acquisition, BLM has identified two new wilderness study areas, totaling 38,920 acres. No recommendation has been made.)

In contrast, conservationists determined that over 6.1 million acres of wilderness-qualified lands are present in the Oregon Desert. These lands are the twenty-six proposed wilderness areas described in this book. To provide for better integrity and long-term management, in drawing the proposed boundaries, certain presently nonconforming lands and roads were included. Over time, they will naturally rehabilitate.

Wilderness designation, while the most essential and most important land conservation tool, isn't adequate to fully protect the Oregon Desert. Certain lands, while of a nonwilderness character, are nonetheless of critical ecological importance.

ODCA would establish or expand several new units of the national park system and the national wildlife refuge system. These units would be managed by the National Park Service and the Fish and Wildlife Service, respectively, because of their respective expertise in managing people and wildlife. The legislation would also establish the Steens Mountain and Lower Owyhee National Conservation Areas, both managed by the Bureau of Land Management. Where possible, the acreage inside all these special management areas also include designated wilderness and wild and scenic rivers.

The wilderness and other special management areas proposed in ODCA comprise the core of ecological protection. Both to provide connecting corridors between the large reserves and to protect and restore ecological values associated with them, ODCA would designate several hundred miles of additions to the national wild and scenic rivers system, to be managed under the Wild and Scenic Rivers Act of 1968. ODCA would specify expansion of the protective river corridor from an average of 1/2 mile in width to an average of 1 mile in width, following the precedent of the Elkhorn Creek Wild and Scenic River, designated in 1996 as part of legislation designed to protect the ancient forests of Opal Creek in Oregon's western Cascade Mountains.

ODCA would also require that—within three years—the Fish and Wildlife Service, with the cooperation of the Forest Service, the National Park Service, and the Bureau of Land Management, report to Congress on:

1. What additional measures and actions are necessary to conserve, protect, and restore the biological diversity of the Oregon Desert across the landscape and over time
2. Recommendations on the reintroduction of extirpated plant, fish, and wildlife species and the control or elimination of exotic plants and animals
3. Natural communities and ecosystems as they originally and currently exist
4. The state of Pacific salmon within the Oregon Desert and steps desirable and necessary to improve their numbers and health

The biggest and most vexing problem is what to do about livestock grazing in the wilderness and special management areas. Such must end if the web of life is to be maintained and restored. Yet it must be done fairly. ODCA would require that livestock permittees on federal land be fairly compensated when their grazing permits in the Oregon Desert are reduced or retired.

Presently under the Wilderness Act, any grazing that was occurring at the time of wilderness designation is permitted to continue. This was a political compromise with the livestock industry at the time of the act's passage in 1964. The livestock industry has broken its promise in the compromise by opposing every wilderness bill since then. While the Wilderness Act allows for a certain degree of regulation to ensure that grazing arrangements maintain "wilderness values," it is, in fact, impossible to simultaneously and fully conserve "wilderness values" and to allow any continued livestock grazing. If cattle continue to dominate and degrade the desert landscape, the overall quality of the ecosystems will not improve, the rare or endangered plants and animals will not be protected, and the quality of hiking and hunting will not be enriched.

ODCA would do several other important things:

- Designate the Desert Trail in Oregon as a scenic trail in the national trails system and provide for a 1-mile-wide protective corridor.
- Prohibit cyanide heap leach mining anywhere in the Oregon Desert.
- Prohibit military overflights under 10,000 feet above wilderness, wild and scenic rivers, and special management areas.
- Authorize acquisition of valid mineral claims at fair market value in wilderness, wild and scenic rivers, national wildlife refuges, national monuments, and national conservation areas.
- Authorize economic and other assistance to small communities and individuals in transition.

ODCA would hopefully result in the eventual acquisition of approximately 373,161 acres of primarily undeveloped lands with ecological values that are presently in private ownership. These lands could be acquired in a variety of ways, depending on the land designation and wishes of the owner.

Acquisition methods could include:

Donation. The owner of the property could donate it to the federal government and take a tax deduction.

Willing seller. The federal government would buy the land from the landowner at a mutually agreed upon price.

Exchange. The federal government and the owner of the parcel in question would exchange for an equally valued parcel elsewhere.

Eminent domain. As a last resort, the use of eminent domain would be allowed in units of the national park system and national wildlife refuge system and the two national conservation areas. Such use would be allowed under restrictions commonly imposed by Congress in land protection legislation. Condemnation is not allowed in the wilderness system in the West or in the wild and scenic rivers system, where 50 percent or more of the lands are already in federal ownership. Condemnation of state lands would not be allowed.

Life estate. In this option, the land would be acquired by the federal government, but the owners would be free to live out their lives on the property. (Extremely little of the private acreage proposed for acquisition for public purposes has anyone living on it.)

144,324 acres of state lands are also targeted for federal acquisition protection in ODCA.

Environmental Benefits of ODCA

- Maintenance and restoration of biological diversity of several endangered ecosystems
- Protection in a natural state of nearly 7.2 million acres for this and future generations
- Reduction in the rate of species extinction
- Elimination of off-road-vehicle damage in fragile areas
- Elimination of the threat posed by cyanide heap leach mining and other destructive mineral exploitation
- Prohibition of a geothermal power plant at the base of Steens Mountain and prevention of the possible extinction of federally listed endangered species
- Recovery and restoration of riparian areas to the great benefit of fish (including Pacific salmon stocks) and wildlife
- Restoration of watershed health (including water quality and quantity and other environmental values), resulting in increased stream flows, especially during dry months
- Significant improvement of bighorn sheep, pronghorn, Rocky Mountain elk, sage grouse, and other game numbers
- Increased scientific study and education opportunities
- Reduction of carbon dioxide contributions to global warming

Economic Benefits of ODCA

- ❧ Opportunities to diversify local economies by establishment of new businesses, such as tourist facilities (guides and outfitters, bed and breakfasts, restaurants, lodgings, and so forth)
- ❧ Reduction of government subsidies to a small group of livestock operators
- ❧ Increased streamflow for downstream uses
- ❧ More efficient production of red meat (emphasis of native over exotic species) as protein source

Recreation and Tourism Benefits of ODCA

- ❧ Outstanding wilderness recreation opportunities
- ❧ Superior hunting and fishing
- ❧ Highly scenic motorized (on-road) recreation
- ❧ Maintenance of a high-quality Desert Trail experience

What are the political chances for enactment of the Oregon Desert Conservation Act? In the beginning: zero. But that is no different from the history of any major piece of federal conservation legislation.

The proper question is: Can the political support be gained and the political opposition overcome to enact the Oregon Desert Conservation Act? The answer is: With proper leadership, adequate resources, and enough time, "Yes!"

A NEW MISSION AND NAME FOR THE BUREAU OF LAND MANAGEMENT

The Bureau of Land Management doesn't get much respect.

BLM wasn't nicknamed the Bureau of Large Mistakes, Bureau of Livestock and Mining, Bureau of Lumbering and Mining, or Bureau of Land Mismanagement without justification.

Born in 1947, out of a merger of the General Land Office and the Grazing Service, the BLM still shows its parentage. Knowingly or unknowingly, BLM officials have often served as a handmaiden to exploiter interests.

For most of its history, BLM has been the mere custodian of the federal public lands left over from the great giveaways to homesteaders, railroads, loggers, miners, and the like, and after the establishment of national forests, wildlife refuges, national parks, and military reservations. Since 1976, BLM has been charged with being the steward of the lands no one wanted, but it hasn't done the job that must be done.

BLM's stewardship failings can be attributed to a lack of money, vision, purpose, and leadership. Concerning the money, even though it has about four times as much land as the Forest Service, BLM has about one-quarter of the budget. While money isn't everything, it is something. The vision, purpose, and leadership are more difficult to achieve without it. BLM has been developing better leaders of late.

BLM's stewardship record is *slowly* improving, albeit in fits and starts and with some backsliding. For example, BLM has officially renounced its bias toward timber in western Oregon. The actions are still lagging behind the words, but that is not unusual in any government agency.

In 1976, Congress passed the Federal Lands Policy and Management Act, which ended the policy of giving away public lands. The federal public lands (other than those already reserved for parks, wildlife, forests, the military, and so forth) were to be retained and managed in the best interests of the American people. However, congressional direction for BLM lands allows for, or requires, greater levels of exploitation than are allowed for other federal lands.

While somewhat upgrading the status of the lands from giveaways to at least keepers, Congress didn't give BLM's lands the same status as other federal lands. The Forest Service has its national forest system, the Park Service its national park system, and the Fish and Wildlife Service its national wildlife refuge system.

All of these designations show up on road maps and atlases, but BLM lands do not. It is because the lands are not part of a formal protective system.

Until recently one could drive across the West and be viewing BLM lands more often than not, yet not know it. It is a good sign that BLM has started to put up some signs.

It is time for BLM to have its own land protection system: the national desert and grassland system. Congress should place most BLM lands into a system of national deserts and grasslands similar to its system of national forests. What! you say—there already is such a thing: the Forest Service manages several national grasslands (including Oregon's Crooked River National Grasslands) as part of the national forest system. True. These should be transferred to the successor to BLM.

Along with upgrading the status of the lands, it is also time for Congress to upgrade the status of the agency and give it a new vision, mission, and name. BLM has a second-rate name among the federal land-managing agencies. The others have employees in service to the nation, while BLM has bureaucrats.

Congress should write a new legislative charter for BLM lands so they have a comparable conservation mandate to other federal lands. It should also give BLM a new name: the U.S. Desert and Grassland Service (USDGS). Both morale and professional standards within the agency would improve and would result in better land stewardship.

The new USDGS should be structured like the Forest Service, with a National Desert and Grassland System branch dedicated to managing these unique public lands, and a scientific research branch dedicated to the understanding and recovery of desert and grassland ecosystems everywhere. It also needs a third branch, similar to the Forest Service's State and Private Forestry branch, to reach out to nonfederal desert and grassland owners and help them with the conservation and restoration of deserts and grasslands.

Those BLM lands that don't qualify as national deserts or grasslands should be transferred to other federal land management agencies. BLM's remaining Oregon coastal lands are best made part of the national wildlife refuge system. The same goes for BLM's vast holdings in Alaska. Congress should transfer BLM's forest lands in western Oregon to the Forest Service.

WHY SPECIAL DESIGNATIONS ARE NECESSARY

As conservationists developed the proposed Oregon Desert Conservation Act, they debated how much (if any) land and which lands to transfer from the jurisdiction of the Bureau of Land Management to the Fish and Wildlife Service and the National Park Service.

Notwithstanding our hopes—and *some* evidence—for a new and better BLM, our experience shows that the agency is nowhere near as conservation minded as the Fish and Wildlife Service and the National Park Service. Most important, the underlying statutory basis for the national wildlife refuge system and the national park system is much stronger for conservation than that for BLM lands.

While BLM's "Areas of Critical Environmental Concern" (ACECs) offer some recognition of important areas, such administrative "protection" is inadequate. Some ACECs have livestock grazing and are not permanently protected from mining.

There is also an issue of which way a land management agency "leans." The National Park Service and the Fish and Wildlife Service generally lean toward conservation. Of course, like any bureaucracy, they are always subject to political pressure and sometimes exercise bad judgment. But they lean toward conservation. As an agency, the Bureau of Land Management leans instead either toward development and exploitation or toward maintaining the status quo, which often amounts to the same thing.

An increasing number of conservation- and reform-minded BLM staff members are starting to have some effect on the "lean" of the agency. They are being allowed and encouraged by a *relatively* "green" Clinton administration, led by Interior Secretary Bruce Babbitt. How permanent the change in BLM "lean" is will be made clear upon the election of the next antigreen administration.

Supporters of BLM argue that Congress should not take away the agency's "crown jewels," leaving it with the public land dregs and no incentive to manage its lands better.

The fact that it is land—and public land at that—should be incentive enough to practice good land management. If it is not, the problem is with the quality of the BLM and its underlying congressional direction, not its land. Public lands belong to the public. Any agency is just a steward.

Congress long ago established the national park system, the national wildlife refuge system, and the national forest system for the nation's crown jewels. It has yet to establish any system for the nonforested arid lands presently in the custodial care of BLM. (See "A New Mission and Name for the Bureau of Land Management" earlier.)

Are the national park, national forest, and national wildlife refuge systems complete? Is nothing else worthy of addition? The answer is no.

The answer is also that BLM does not seem ready—either by agency culture or by statutory direction and authority—to fully protect and restore public lands. And they will not be until Congress amends the statutes under which BLM must operate to be clearly proconservation and antiexploitation. (Clinton, Babbitt, or the BLM have yet to ask Congress to change the agency's mandate.)

Having said this, the question is legitimately asked, then why not a Steens National Park (and/or National Preserve, the only difference being that hunting is allowed in a preserve)? Surely the parklike quality of Steens qualifies for the national park system. Yes, without a doubt.

Most conservationists, however, are not proposing Steens Mountain and the Lower Owyhee country to be part of the national park system, but instead are proposing congressionally designated BLM-administered national conservation areas. This was done because:

1. It avoids unnecessary controversy with conservationists who also hunt. Even if you don't like hunting, please keep in mind that wildlife are infinitely more threatened by the loss of habitat.
2. It avoids the political difficulties of transferring certain lands from BLM to the National Park Service. Any agency fights for its land, but BLM would fight extra hard to keep Steens Mountain. Additionally, the Park Service presently does not have an aggressive acquisition attitude and wouldn't be any political help in the effort.
3. BLM, with the stronger statutory mandate and increased funding that national conservation area (NCA) status brings, can do an adequate job of conserving and restoring land, if NCAs have mandatory livestock grazing phase-out requirements and are overlain with wilderness and wild and scenic river designations. Nonetheless, citizens will have to occasionally sue the BLM to enforce and/or obey these federal protective laws. Such is the case now and not just for BLM.

The political debate should focus on livestock, not bureaucracy.

Conservationists are seeking national monument status for four areas of the Oregon Desert. They are also seeking two new national wildlife refuges and expansion of another. All of these areas would consist primarily of public lands presently under the jurisdiction of BLM (or the navy).

Such areas are worthy of inclusion in the national park system and the national wildlife refuge system. They contain uniquely important geological, paleontological, and ecological features that are best conserved and restored under National Park Service and Fish and Wildlife Service management.

Finally, park system units—but also wildlife refuges—are more attractive to the local tourism and recreation economy than are BLM national conservation areas. As the economy of the Oregon Desert continues to diversify away from livestock grazing, such designations can play an important role in this diversification.

A NEW AND BETTER ECONOMIC FUTURE

Everyone is for change in general, but they're scared of it in particular.
—Bill Clinton

Most local sentiment in the West has always fought conservation, from Yellowstone National Park in 1872 through the Grand Staircase–Escalante National Monument in 1996. It is because people fear change.

During consideration of the Oregon Wilderness Act of 1984, the chambers of commerce in Union (La Grande) and Douglas (Roseburg) Counties voiced strong opposition to the legislation. Today, both market themselves as "wilderness" counties.

The choice facing Oregon Desert communities is not one of continuing with the status quo, but whether to embrace and make change work or to begrudge inevitable change at every step.

Accurate information is the foundation for good choices. It must be understood that:

1. The past is not sustainable in the future.
2. While socially significant, grazing is not economically significant.
3. The economy of the Oregon Desert has changed and will continue to change.
4. If locals choose to, they can move toward a better economic future.
5. Change is always a bitch.

Livestock grazing on the public lands is not ecologically sustainable (see "Domestic Livestock: Scourge of the West" earlier). Nor is it economically sustainable (see "Ending Public Land Grazing Fair and Square" later). Public land ranchers will continue to lose money and fail, irrespective of pressures from conservation organizations.

Statewide, the contribution of livestock grazing to the economy is insignificant. This is the case locally as well, especially for public land livestock grazing. If all the grazing on the 7.2 million acres addressed in the Oregon Desert Conservation Act were to end immediately, it would amount to perhaps one hundred full-time jobs lost to owners, operators, and ranch hands. (Grazing would continue on private lands, where most of the forage is.) This is a small number of jobs even in the sparsely settled Oregon Desert.

Unless it is your job. The consequences are little different whether you lose your job through an act of Congress or through inevitable market changes. Society has a moral obligation to help those in transition, even though the overall number is politically insignificant. It doesn't matter whether this change is due to the globalization of the economy, changing market preferences for goods and services, or government policies (interest rates, zoning, or grazing reductions).

The Oregon Desert Conservation Act would provide for (a) economic development aid for affected counties and (b) economic transition assistance to affected workers in the livestock industry.

Conservationists also support decoupling federal revenues to counties from resource extraction. Instead federal payments to counties should be based on a fair payment in lieu of the property taxes that would be paid if the federal land were private land.

Local government income that now comes from a portion of the revenues generated by exploitive and unsustainable activities on public lands should be switched to new and more stable sources. Most jurisdictions in the desert, for example, don't yet have a lodging room tax, and the few that do tax at a fraction of what most cities charge. A room tax is a politician's perfect tax: their voters don't pay for it.

Livestock grazing, while economically insignificant, is socially significant in the Oregon Desert. Far more people play cowboy (all hat and truck—no cows and calves), than are cowboys. They view themselves as part of cattle culture, though not economically dependent upon it.

The economy of the Oregon Desert has changed, however, and will continue to change. Espresso sales are up; barbed wire sales are down. The largest employer is still government, which will not likely change. Communities are transitioning from agriculture (including public land grazing) to modified service-based economies (and that doesn't mean everyone is flipping burgers or cleaning toilets). The largest economic activity is transfer payments (Social Security payments, retirement payments, nonlocal government salaries, and so forth), and it continues to grow. Few small towns of the desert are actually dying (unless you consider change death). Diversification brings uncertainty, while refusing to change brings certain death.

Though we live in a global economy, local citizens can choose their future. Will the local-economic-booster mentality lead communities to simply seek the next boom (with its inevitable bust)? Yes, if history is any guide.

Will communities change? Yes. Will they like it or, at least, be the better for it? It depends.

It is hard for most public land grazing permittees to change. A few have converted, and more will, to bed-and-breakfast operations. Some will convert to horse and llama operations hauling tourists into the backcountry (still get to wear the hat and drive the truck). Some will reconfigure their grazing operations solely to private lands. Some will not change.

Some people would rather die than change. For example, there is more money in raising domesticated bison than in cattle, yet few ranchers have made the switch. It is not what their daddy did. Resistance to change is not limited to ranchers. Most restaurants don't change their cuisine without also changing owners.

If you talk with many of the Oregon Desert "old guard" generation who fear change the most, you'll find that many have siblings who have long since moved to the city for economic advancement. The same is true of their aunts and uncles and great-aunts and uncles. Socially—if not genetically—selected, those left are often the least inclined to accept change, especially now, when change is visiting rural areas at a pace never before experienced.

In the range of the northern spotted owl, ten thousand timber jobs were lost when the government reduced timber cutting. Because of the controversy, $1.2 billion is being spent on economic transition. Unfortunately, most of this money is sucked up by bureaucracy or benefits mill owners more than mill workers.

Losing one's job to federal grazing reductions is no different and deserves no less attention. This time, let's spend the $120,000 per dislocated worker differently. One-third should go to range restoration projects (breaching cattle reservoirs, unchannelizing streams, fighting weeds, removing roads, and so on) that create temporary transition jobs; one-third should go to the affected county to spend as it—not the federal government—sees fit (mitigating transition effects or investing in the future); and one-third should go directly to the dislocated workers to spend as they see fit (coasting into retirement, paying off the place, going back to school, starting a new business, moving elsewhere, partying one's way through denial, and so on).

In the end, we must remember that this harsh land will never support very many people. History has shown us this time and again. We must also never forget that most of the Oregon Desert belongs to all Americans and shouldn't be exploited just to benefit a few locals or absentee corporations.

Those whom the land does support will exploit location more than resources. Burns is so unprone to earthquakes that it markets itself as the best place for data storage. Lakeview is specializing in tourism from hang-gliding. Done carefully, tourism and recreation hold more money and future for the Oregon Desert than does anything else.

The necessary shift in attitude is occurring, though not without stress. Increasingly, more are seeing the future in tourism or whatever, but certainly not in livestock and timber. An old guard, when it doesn't get its way as it used to, usually reacts by doing the same thing it always has, only louder and harder. This works for a while—as it intimidates those who would change—but in the end, such behavior is futile.

A friend was recently at the Safeway in Burns. By his outfit, he was marked as an outsider/westsider/tourist/birder/conservationist (amazingly, many locals don't distinguish any difference). Two cowboys (also marked by their outfits) approached, and one said: "Spend your money and go home." At least they recognize where the money is coming from. As American writer Bernard Devoto noted in the mid-twentieth century: "The average local response in the West to the federal government: give us more money and leave us alone."

Economists have documented the "designation effect" of increased tourism on designation of wilderness and other special management areas. To the degree that livestock are removed from the public land, the hunting, fishing, and hiking will greatly improve and attract more visitors (which will create more outfitting and other jobs). All will infuse money into the local economy.

Successful communities will be those that drive forward by looking through the windshield and not in the rearview mirror.

ENDING PUBLIC LAND GRAZING FAIR AND SQUARE[6]

Grazing on the public lands is not stable. Few, if any, bright spots are in the future of federal public land grazing permittees. Beef is losing market share to chicken, pork, seafood, tofu, cheese, and vegetables. Concerns about human health and food safety (heart disease, obesity, E. coli, mad cow disease, and so forth) are affecting the beef industry. Subsidies to farm and ranching industries are being phased out on private lands, which does not bode well for subsidies on public lands. Foreign competition is cutting into domestic beef sales. Domestic factory farming is changing the face of the cattle industry. The average age of the permittees is sixty years and rising.

Conservationists are increasing their attention on livestock grazing. Conflicts with recreationists are increasing. Enforcement of water quality standards is increasingly likely. More endangered species listings are inevitable. More litigation is probable. New planning and management processes by federal land management agencies will possibly reduce livestock grazing numbers and certainly place more restrictions on grazing. The latter scheme requires increased federal spending, which is increasingly problematic to secure. The fee on grazing is likely to rise. Bidding by conservationists on state grazing leases will increase pressure to reform the federal grazing fee.

The system for grazing on Forest Service and Bureau of Land Management lands in the West was established in 1934. Qualifying ranches ("base properties") were assigned an exclusive amount of AUMs (animal unit months: forage for a cow and calf for one month), theoretically based on the land's carrying capacity.

Public land livestock grazing is a privilege, not a right. If the government chooses to discontinue a "giving," that does not constitute a constitutional "taking." However, the real estate market—due to the certainty that the federal government will transfer grazing permits to the new base property owner—recognizes the value of a federal grazing permit so attached. So does the IRS. The result is that base properties have increased in market value to reflect the federal AUMs that are automatically transferred to new purchasers. In the rare instance when the government does reduce grazing, it is a loss of real money to the permittee. It is not only a loss of future subsidized grazing, it is also a reduction in the fair market value of the base property.

It is understandable that ranchers—not to mention the banks that hold the mortgages on the base properties—fight so hard to keep their AUMs up.

Public land grazing contributes only 2 percent of the feed to the nation's cattle industry, and only then with a large subsidy from the federal taxpayers. The 756,000 AUMs on federal lands (including forests) on the "east side" (Oregon and Washington east of the Cascade crest) provide a total of 243 livestock owner, operator, and ranch hand jobs, according to current government data.

Grazing permits have a capital value. According to Professor Robert Nelson, formerly with the U.S. Department of the Interior's Office of Policy Analysis for eighteen years, the West-wide capital value of a public land grazing AUM averages $75. (Notwithstanding reality, the air force recently compensated an Idaho BLM permittee $260 per AUM, in conjunction with an expanded bombing range, wanting—one can only assume—to remain competitive with $200 hammers and $400 toilet seats.)

The public land range fee for 1999 was calculated by an arcane and irrelevant statutory formula at $1.35 per AUM.

Even though the BLM admits spending more on grazing than it takes in, the agency considers only a small proportion of the costs. According to Nelson, the taxpayer expense in excess of revenue is conservatively $20 per AUM. While this includes direct and overhead costs, it does not include other subsidies, such as that for animal damage control.

In contrast, the gross income the federal treasury receives from an AUM is less than $1.35. From 50 to 62.5 percent (depending on the legal classification of the rangeland) of the $1.35 is dedicated to the Range Betterment [sic] Fund (the moneys are used for fences and water developments), and does not offset the federal taxpayer expenditure.

It would be easier—and more just—for the federal government to fairly compensate the permit holders as it reduces cattle numbers permanently. Since the government spends substantially more than it receives for grazing, buying and retiring AUMs has a fiscal payback of 3.75 years.

After recoupment, the continued savings could be used for national debt reduction and other beneficial activities such as stream restoration, erosion control, weed eradication, and so forth.

It would be less expensive—fiscally and politically—for the agency simply to buy out grazing permits and save extensive planning, monitoring, research, public involvement, appeal, litigation, and political costs. Given the vagaries of the cattle business, operators would benefit from compensation for retiring their permits. This is not possible under existing law, which mandates "use it or lose it."

How will public land ranchers feel about this? There is no reliable way to estimate. Factors include the financial viability of ranching operations, permittee age, and other personal situations of permittees, the existing and anticipated level of conflict regarding grazing on an allotment, the price of beef, and so on.

Several examples of retirement buy-out are encouraging. Anecdotal surveys suggest that about half of the ranchers who have taken advantage of buy-out offers have moved on to other things, and about half have purchased livestock operations not dependent on public land. The latter stayed in ranching but wanted to be the masters of their own domains.

What would be the benefits of such an option?

Species and ecosystems would recover at maximum rates and in the most cost-effective manner.

As permits are retired, taxpayer costs of subsidizing the forage are reduced proportionally.

Federal land management agencies could more easily meet the environmental protection standards if livestock grazing were reduced, resulting in better stewardship.

Controversy could be avoided or greatly diminished. There would be less litigation, less need for funds to be spent mitigating livestock grazing damage, and less call to overturn the environmental protection statutes.

While not vesting a legal right to graze (something permittees have never had), such a change in law would provide more options to livestock permittees. A permittee could choose to sell a federal permit but still live on and/or raise livestock on the base property.

The option to exercise the voluntary retirement option rests solely with the permittees. If they didn't want to retire, they would be free to continue to take their chances in a dynamic economic, regulatory, budgetary, and political environment.

The Oregon Desert Conservation Act would phase out livestock grazing permits in national monuments, national wildlife refuges, and national conservation areas ten years after the expiration of a current ten-year permit. Of course, permittees could choose to be bought out earlier.

While the retirement option is a radical departure from the traditional debates on public land livestock grazing, it is equally rational. It addresses directly the market value of federal grazing permits, which is the major subtext in the debate over public land livestock grazing.

Politically, the fairness and rationality of the proposed policy change can appeal to conservationists, taxpayers, politicians, permittees, fiscal conservatives, compassionate liberals, and others. Since it is a solution outside the box we are all in, it will require leadership in all camps and a willingness to try something different.

BASIN AND RANGE ECOREGION

Without a doubt, the Basin and Range ecoregion is the heart of the Oregon Desert. Extending into California and Nevada, it is named for the dominant topographic features that are caused by geologic action. Numerous generally north-south-trending mountain ranges have risen from the desert floor, leaving basins in between. Many are fault blocks with one very gentle and one very precipitous side. Elevations range from 4,100 to 9,700 feet.

According to the Oregon Biodiversity Project, the soils are thin and rocky, high in minerals and low in organics, making for a generally harsh environment. Temperatures reach extremes, both daily and seasonally.

Many, but not all, of the basins in the Basin and Range ecoregion have no outlet to the sea. The misnamed Great Basin is actually a collection of little basins that catch precipitation—including runoff from the mountains—into their bottoms, which can be permanent lakes, periodic lakes, seasonal playas, or marshes. When the evaporated water has left enough salts, you'll find alkali flats that harbor interesting plants or no plants at all.

As the huge Pleistocene lakes receded, trapped and isolated fish populations over time speciated into local endemics like the Borax Lake chub, Warner sucker, Lahontan cutthroat trout, Foskett Spring dace, and numerous races of redband trout and tui chub.

Two-thirds of the ecoregion is sagebrush steppe. The remainder is covered by areas of salt desert scrub, juniper woodland, mountain mahogany woodland, aspen groves, riparian habitats, and wetlands. On the summit of Steens Mountain, there is alpine habitat.

Where the soils are deep enough and the precipitation is adequate, one finds little stands of fir and pine trees, relics from an ancient time when the ecoregion was a much wetter place.

The Oregon Biodiversity Project has estimated that 7 percent of the ecoregion is adequately protected to conserve and restore biodiversity.

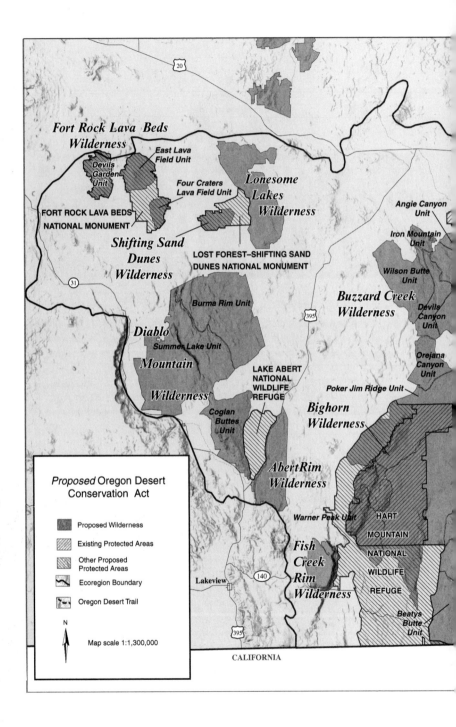

Fort Rock Lava Beds
Wilderness

East Lava
Field Unit

Devils
Garden
Unit

Four Craters
Lava Field Unit

Lonesome
Lakes
Wilderness

Angie Canyon
Unit

Iron Mountain
Unit

FORT ROCK LAVA BEDS
NATIONAL MONUMENT

Wilson Butte
Unit

Shifting Sand
Dunes
Wilderness

LOST FOREST–SHIFTING SAND
DUNES NATIONAL MONUMENT

Buzzard Creek
Wilderness

Devils
Canyon
Unit

Burma Rim Unit

Diablo
Summer Lake Unit

Orejana
Canyon
Unit

Mountain
Wilderness

LAKE ABERT
NATIONAL
WILDLIFE
REFUGE

Poker Jim Ridge Unit

Bighorn
Wilderness

Coglan
Buttes
Unit

Abert Rim
Wilderness

**Proposed Oregon Desert
Conservation Act**

Proposed Wilderness

Existing Protected Areas

Other Proposed
Protected Areas

Ecoregion Boundary

Oregon Desert Trail

Warner Peak Unit

HART

MOUNTAIN

Fish
Creek
Rim
Wilderness

NATIONAL

WILDLIFE

Lakeview

REFUGE

N

Beatys
Butte
Unit

Map scale 1:1,300,000

CALIFORNIA

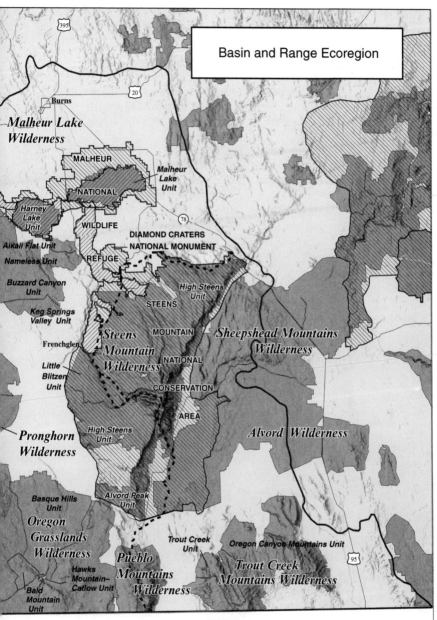

Basin and Range Ecoregion

Burns

Malheur Lake
Wilderness

MALHEUR

Malheur
Lake
Unit

NATIONAL

Harney
Lake
Unit

WILDLIFE

DIAMOND CRATERS

Alkali Flat Unit

NATIONAL MONUMENT

Nameless Unit

REFUGE

Buzzard Canyon
Unit

High Steens
Unit

STEENS

Keg Springs
Valley Unit

MOUNTAIN

Sheepshead Mountains
Wilderness

Frenchglen

Steens
Mountain
Wilderness

NATIONAL

Little
Blitzen
Unit

CONSERVATION

AREA

Pronghorn
Wilderness

High Steens
Unit

Alvord Wilderness

Basque Hills
Unit

Alvord Peak
Unit

Oregon
Grasslands
Wilderness

Trout Creek
Unit

Oregon Canyon Mountains Unit

Pueblo
Mountains
Wilderness

Trout Creek
Mountains Wilderness

Hawks
Mountain–
Catlow Unit

Bald
Mountain
Unit

NEVADA

ABERT RIM WILDERNESS (PROPOSED)

The largest continuous fault scarp in North America.

Location:	Lake County, 5 miles northeast of Valley Falls
Size:	105 square miles (67,478 acres)
Terrain:	Mostly flat and gently rolling hills, save for huge Abert Rim
Elevation Range:	4,289–7,040 feet
Managing Agency:	Lakeview District BLM
Agency Wilderness Status:	23,760-acre BLM wilderness study area; 23,760 acres recommended
Recreation Map:	Southwest Quarter, South Half Lakeview Resource Area, Lakeview District BLM

Abert Rim rises 2,000 feet above Lake Abert. The rim is vertical in most places and unscalable from the bottom at Lake Abert (see Lake Abert National Wildlife Refuge). At the base of the rim along US 395 is mostly sagebrush. Above the

Abert Rim in the proposed Wilderness of the same name

north rim is much of the same. Above the south rim are separate groves of mountain mahogany, ponderosa pine, and aspen interspersed with low sage.

The rim is highest at Abert Point on the adjacent Fremont National Forest, where Abert Rim meets the Warner Mountains.

Birds of prey include great horned owl, burrowing owl, short-eared owl, red-tailed hawk, northern harrier, rough-legged hawk, bald eagle, ferruginous hawk, peregrine falcon, golden eagle, turkey vulture, prairie falcon, and American kestrel. Golden eagles average two nests, and prairie falcons one nest, per mile of rim.

Evaporation of Lake Abert water significantly cools the adjacent Abert Rim, making it a haven for wildlife in the hot summer.

Sage grouse are found in the gently eastward-draining flats above the rim. Burrowing owls, downy and hairy woodpeckers, and a variety of songbirds are also known here.

The Oregon Biodiversity Project includes the area within its Honey Creek Conservation Opportunity Area. Much of the south part of the area drains into Honey Creek, one of the last best holdouts for the Warner sucker, a federally listed species.

Petroglyphs surround Colvin Lake.

1. Colvin Timbers

What to Expect:	Camping in an isolated pine forest and dangling your tootsies over the largest continuous fault scarp in North America
Distance:	20.4 miles round trip
Elevation Range:	6,320–6,620 feet
Drinking Water:	Some
Best Times:	Summer, fall
USGS 7.5' Maps:	Lake Abert South, Little Honey Creek
Oregon Map Starting Point:	Lakeview

Six miles north of Lakeview on US 395/OR 140, turn east where OR 140 leaves US 395. After 9 miles turn north on FS Road 3615. Go approximately 24 miles to the pavement end at the national forest boundary and park.

Hike northerly 5.8 miles (Little Honey Creek quad), first on an old way, then on a jeep trail to Colvin Timbers (Lake Abert South quad), a 600-acre grove of ponderosa pine (the most northerly in the Warner Mountains). Tank up at a BLM-developed spring about halfway between your vehicle and Colvin Timbers camp. From the shady forest, hike northwestward 2 miles over very rocky terrain to the rim at the head of Juniper Creek.

Excellent views of Lake Abert, Winter Rim, Summer Lake, Gearhart Mountain, and more are available. Walk north 2.4 miles along the rim, noting the vegetation change until it is just a few junipers at Poison Creek. It is tree-free to the north. Look for bighorn sheep on and below the rim.

Return as you came.

2. Poison Creek

What to Expect:	The hard way to the top of the largest continuous fault scarp in North America.
Distance:	2 miles round trip
Elevation Range:	4,300–5,940 feet
Drinking Water:	Yes
Best Times:	Summer, fall
USGS 7.5' Map:	Lake Abert South
Oregon Map Starting Point:	Valley Falls

Approximately 8 miles north on US 395 is the mouth of Poison Creek (the biggest break in Abert Rim). The land along the creek at the highway is private, so you have to park back from the mouth of the creek. Hike around the fence to the south to stay on public land.

This is an *extremely* rugged undeveloped "trail" to the rim. On your way to the rim you'll find good (not poison) water, good riparian vegetation, scattered white fir, mountain mahogany, quaking aspen, ponderosa pine, and western juniper. Watch for wildlife and watch out for ticks.

There are some nice petroglyphs at the Poison Creek pour-off at the top of the rim. Once on top, dangle your tootsies over the rim.

Return as you came.

ALVORD WILDERNESS (PROPOSED)

*Huge desert playas, unique flora and fauna
in the rain shadow of Steens Mountain.*

Location:	Harney and Malheur Counties, 10 miles east of Andrews
Size:	644 square miles (412,247 acres)
Terrain:	Gently rolling hills, sand dunes, playas, and vast flats
Elevation Range:	3,915–4,902 feet
Managing Agencies:	Burns and Vale Districts BLM
Agency Wilderness Status:	288,740-acre BLM wilderness study area; 69,165 acres recommended
Recreation Maps:	South Half Burns District BLM; South Half Jordan Resource Area, Vale District BLM

The area is characterized by gently rolling terrain surrounded by lava cliffs and plateaus. It also has three very large playas: the Alvord Desert, Alvord Lake, and Coyote Lake. During wet times, the water attracts migratory waterfowl.

Perhaps this area is most notable for its great herpetological diversity. Most of the herps found in the northeastern Great Basin are present, including the

Alvord Desert (middle) in the proposed Alvord Wilderness, from Steens Mountain

side-blotched lizard, sagebrush lizard, western fence lizard, desert horned lizard, Great Basin western rattlesnake, yellow-bellied racer, striped whipsnake, western whiptail lizard, leopard lizard, collared lizard, and Great Basin spadefoot toad. Northern kit fox may be here as well.

For discussions of the topography, vegetation, and wildlife here, please see the Steens Mountain National Conservation Area. The Oregon Biodiversity Project has included the area in its Crooked Creek–Alvord Basin Conservation Opportunity Area.

The proposal includes Mickey Hot Spring (see Steens Mountain National Conservation Area) and consists of three BLM wilderness study areas: Alvord Desert, East Alvord, and Winter Range.

The Desert Trail traverses the area (see Appendix D).

3. Alvord Desert

What to Expect:	Nude hiking by moonlight
Distance:	16 miles round trip
Elevation Range:	4,005–4,011 feet
Drinking Water:	Not likely
Best Times:	Summer, fall
USGS 7.5' Maps:	Alvord Hot Springs, Andrews, Miranda Flat SW, Tule Springs
Oregon Map Starting Point:	Andrews

Approximately 6.2 miles north of Andrews on the Andrews–Folly Farm County Road is an unimproved way down to the edge of the Alvord Desert (0.2. mile). Park. Water (not tested) is available at Frog Spring (marked, but not named on the Alvord Hot Springs quad).

The objective is Big Sand Gap and/or Big Sand Gap Spring (Tule Springs quad; you'll also be crossing the Miranda Flat SW quad). Big Sand Gap is a noticeable landmark 7.5 miles east-southeast from Frog Spring. As you get closer, distinctive vegetation should indicate Big Sand Gap Spring.

"What could go wrong?" you're thinking. "It is a flat walk and the destination is in sight." Plenty. This exploration should only be done in summer when the playa is dry. It will therefore be hot as hell during the day, so make this an overnight trip. Start this hike just as the sun sets over Steens Mountain. Take twice as much water as you might need as you may not find Big Sand Gap Spring.

You will make very good time on the playa, but your speed will decrease a bit as you hit the sandy soil and dunes on the east side. Walk gently as this is western snowy plover habitat.

Periodically turn around and determine appropriate landmarks to help your return. Frog Spring is not obvious from the other side of the playa.

At normal walking speeds in summer you should easily make the objectives before dark. If you don't, camp anyway.

Based on your walking speed eastward, determine your departure time for your westward return. Ideally you would be reaching Frog Spring as it just starts to get unbearable. As the sun rises in the sky, the desert heats up. The reflective white surface can move you past tan to burn in no time.

Timing your trip during a full moon not only adds to your nocturnal pleasure, you'll have some light to guide your westward return if you need to start before first light.

Unfortunately, the Alvord Desert is presently open to motorized use. Though pedestrians have the right-of-way, don't count on it. It is also prudent to assume that Alvord drivers are likely to be intoxicated.

A final request: no dumping on the playa, even if you bury it. Few microorganisms exist to aid decomposition. Manage your bowels or pack it out. Thank you.

Be prudent and you'll have a great time. Especially recommended is nude hiking.

4. Coyote Lake

What to Expect:	A surreal adventure into a land of stark contrasts
Distance:	8-mile loop
Elevation Range:	4,075–4,095 feet
Drinking Water:	No
Best Times:	Spring, summer, fall
USGS 7.5' Maps:	Coyote Lake East, Coyote Lake West
Oregon Map Starting Point:	Burns Junction (OR 78 at US 95)

Go south on OR 78 for 21 miles. Turn westerly on the Whitehorse county road. At approximately 10.6 miles is the turnoff southerly to Twelvemile Ranch (3 miles west after crossing the prominent Twelvemile Ridge). Continue 0.2 mile southwesterly to the intersection with a unimproved road to the northwest. Drive northerly 8.5 miles and park on public land.

Hike (Coyote Lake East quad) the way northerly 2.1 miles to Coyote Lake. Explore the vegetated islands in the playa.

(See the Alvord Desert exploration for special playa recommendations on timing, sun protection, moonlight hiking, and fecal matter disposition.)

To return, set cross-country course to vehicle.

BIGHORN WILDERNESS (PROPOSED)

The largest concentration of bighorn sheep in Oregon.

Location:	Lake County, 15 miles northeast of Plush
Size:	496 square miles (317,642 acres)
Terrain:	Precipitous fault scarps, deep canyons, rolling hills, and wetlands
Elevation Range:	4,460–8,900 feet
Managing Agencies:	Lakeview District BLM, Fish and Wildlife Service
Agency Wilderness Status:	20,390-acre FWS Poker Jim Ridge wilderness study area recommended; 14,800-acre BLM wilderness study area—9,800 acres recommended
Recreation Maps:	Southeast and Northeast Quarters, South and North Halves Lakeview Resource Area, Lakeview District BLM

The wilderness proposal consists of three units: Orejana Canyon, Poker Jim Ridge, and Warner Peak. It is also part of the Oregon Biodiversity Project's Hart Mountain Conservation Opportunity Area. (See also Hart Mountain National Wildlife Refuge Additions.)

Evidence of prehistoric human use around the lakes, along the rims, and across the flats can be observed.

Orejana Canyon Unit

The BLM's *Wilderness Report*, a document not renowned for eloquence, noted:

> *The incised canyon meandering through high elevation table lands, with the large boulders along the rim suggest not only naturalness, but a massive display of nature's grandness. The Island stands open and wild, free of human encroachment, symbolic of a once grander landscape now reduced in scale across the West to determined remnants.*[1]

Orejana Rim merges into Poker Jim Ridge, which merges into Hart Mountain farther to the south. All define the eastern edge of the Warner Valley. An ancient lakeshore can be seen along all three rims.

Geologically of interest are Orejana Canyon, Orejana Rim (especially the huge boulder piles at its base), and an exceptionally clear flow of obsidian.

Orejana Rim in the proposed Bighorn Wilderness

One hundred bighorn sheep from Hart Mountain move down into the Orejana area in winter, as do mule deer and pronghorn. Raptors include golden eagle, red-tailed hawk, and great horned owl. Large numbers of passerine birds and sage grouse can also be seen.

Poker Jim Ridge Unit

Two striking features stand out in this unit: the towering rim and the dramatic floor below. Poker Jim Ridge is as raw and rough a rim as you can find and is primarily on the Hart Mountain Refuge. It would get more attention if it were not next to the even more dramatic Hart Mountain to the south.

The second feature is a portion of the Warner Lakes (Flagstaff Lake on the south to Bluejoint Lake on the north). (See the Campbell Lake exploration in Hart Mountain National Wildlife Refuge Additions).

Warner Peak Unit

Hart Mountain is a classic Basin and Range fault-block mountain that rises several thousand feet above the Warner Lakes. From the precipitous rim, the mountain slopes upward to Warner Peak and then gently downward and always eastward for 20 miles (through the Pronghorn Wilderness) to the Catlow Valley.

This unit is primarily on the Hart Mountain National Wildlife Refuge and includes Warner Peak, the highest bump on Hart Mountain. Western juniper are scattered across many areas, sometimes being dense enough to be woodland. On Hart Mountain, vast and gorgeous stands of mountain mahogany and quaking aspen are common. In the steep canyons on the face of Hart Mountain, scattered old ponderosa pine can be found. Dry meadows are quite common as well.

Because of overhunting, livestock grazing, and diseases from domestic sheep, California bighorn sheep were extirpated from the state by 1915. They were reintroduced into the refuge from British Columbia in 1954. The very healthy population in this unit serves as the primary source for reintroductions elsewhere in Oregon.

5. Warner Peak and DeGarmo Canyon (Warner Peak Unit)

What to Expect:	Panoramic views; beautiful rugged canyons full of aspen, willow, and alder; old-growth white fir, western juniper, and ponderosa pine; dry and wet meadows
Distance:	11.6-mile loop
Elevation Range:	5,840–8,017 feet
Drinking Water:	Yes
Best Times:	Summer, fall
USGS 7.5' Maps:	Campbell Lake, Hart Lake, Warner Peak
Oregon Map Starting Point:	Plush

Drive north 1 mile and then northeasterly approximately 25 miles (following signs) to Hart Mountain National Wildlife Refuge headquarters. Drive southerly 1.1 miles to a fork. Go southwest (right) 2 miles to the Hot Springs Campground. Park.

Hike (Campbell Lake quad) 2 miles on the old jeep route, which initially parallels Rock Creek but then heads uphill to Barnhardy Meadow (Warner Peak quad). Continue on the old jeep route to the pass (elevation 6,899 feet) in 1.3 miles. Climb cross-country to Hart Mountain ridge. Throw down the pack and bag the Warner Peak summit (0.3 mile south). On a clear day, the views are fantastic. If you are day hiking to summit, return as you came.

From Hart Mountain ridge, backpackers continue cross-country into the headwaters of South Fork DeGarmo Canyon. Game trails exist along most of the way to the confluence with the North Fork DeGarmo Canyon (Hart Lake quad) in 2.7 miles. Continue up North Fork DeGarmo Canyon to the headwaters. Camp spots are numerous along both forks (or camp at Barnhardy the first night out). In 2.2 miles from the confluence of the forks, catch the jeep trail to the east. After 1.6 miles you are on the original jeep route, 1.2 miles from Hot Springs Campground. Return as you came. It is time for a relaxing bath.

Backpacking permits are required on the refuge.

6. Orejana Canyon (Orejana Canyon Unit)

What to Expect:	A steep canyon and a precipitous rim defending "a massive display of nature's grandness"
Distance:	8-mile loop
Elevation Range:	4,766–5,050 feet
Drinking Water:	During spring
Best Times:	Summer, fall
USGS 7.5' Maps:	Orejana Canyon, Steamboat Point
Oregon Map Starting Point:	Plush

Go north approximately 10 miles on Lake County 3-10 to an intersection. Turn northeast on Lake County 3-11. In 0.3 mile turn north onto a BLM road. Proceed northerly 22.8 miles to an intersection. A large rim is on your west. Proceed northerly (right, not northwesterly) 1.2 miles to an intersection. Turn east (right) and drive past Steamboat Point 5.2 miles to an intersection. Follow fence-line road east-southeast 2.9 miles to mouth of Orejana Canyon. Park.

From the mouth of Orejana Canyon (Steamboat Point quad), hike up the canyon (Orejana Canyon quad) either about 2 or 4 miles to a side canyon that grants access to the Island (not named on quad maps, but it is the large plateau bounded by Orejana Rim and Orejana Canyon) to the north. Hike across the Island to Orejana Rim on the west. Hike south along the rim back to your vehicle.

7. Poker Jim Ridge (Poker Jim Ridge Unit)

What to Expect:	Commanding views of the Warner Valley and maybe pronghorn and bighorn sheep
Distance:	12.2-mile loop
Elevation Range:	5,616–6,049 feet
Drinking Water:	Yes
Best Times:	Summer, fall
USGS 7.5' Map:	Campbell Lake
Oregon Map Starting Point:	Plush

Drive north 1 mile and then northeasterly approximately 25 miles (following signs) to Hart Mountain National Wildlife Refuge Headquarters. Park.

Walk 0.6 mile westerly on the main road to the turnoff to the appropriately named Petroglyph Lake. Hike to the lake in 1.5 miles. Proceed due north to the rim (1.1 miles). Set an easterly course for an unimproved way and continue on the way to Poker Jim Spring (Flook Lake quad) in 3.2 miles. Camp.

After detouring 0.3 mile to Poker Jim Lake to the east, set a course back to the refuge headquarters 5.5 miles southwesterly. You'll intersect Rock Creek, which will take you back to the headquarters.

Backpacking permits are required on the refuge.

BUZZARD CREEK WILDERNESS (PROPOSED)

Recreation by and for those at risk.

Location:	Harney County, 25 miles southwest of Burns
Size:	525 square miles (367,771 acres)
Terrain:	Lots of flat and gently rolling hills
Elevation Range:	4,112–5,464 feet
Managing Agency:	Burns District BLM
Agency Wilderness Status:	None
Recreation Maps:	Northwest and Northeast Quarters, North Half Burns District; South Half Burns District BLM

Southwest of Harney Lake, northeast of Hart Mountain, and west of the Blitzen Valley lies a whole lot of generally unremarkable country. It is flat and has gently rolling hills, where often a hill should be more properly called a rise. So gentle is the terrain, that rarely even a low rim gives relief to the relief. A few prominent landmarks like Iron Mountain can be distinguished from US 20, US 395, or OR 205. A few canyons do exist, like Buzzard Creek.

The proposal consists of eight units separated by low-standard roads: Alkali Flat, Angie Canyon, Buzzard Canyon, Devils Canyon, Iron Mountain, Keg Springs Valley, Nameless (not a named feature in it), and Wilson Butte.

Much of the area is a homogenous sagebrush panorama without even the lone juniper.

After studying the USGS 7.5' quad maps, an appellation comes to mind: "The land of the ten-foot contour maps."

Nothing appears to be the most, the deepest, the highest, the largest, the last, or the like in the area.

While there is little to attract most wilderness visitors, save for the vast littleness of it all (don't underrate it), the area does have important natural values. It is good sage grouse habitat. Mule deer and pronghorn can be found here. Where there is rimrock, there are raptors.

The area's numerous ephemeral lakes and streams are important stops on the mini-flyway between the Warner Valley (see Hart Mountain National Wildlife Refuge Additions) and the Silver Creek Valley on the Malheur National Wildlife Refuge, both of which are very major stops on the Pacific Flyway.

Most recreational use is by a few hunters in the fall. However, the area does get used by a large number of backpackers. Almost all of these backpackers are here against their will.

They are not being punished, though they may well think so. They are being helped.

Catherine Freer Wilderness Therapy Expeditions of Albany, Oregon, leads therapeutic backpacking treks into the wilderness. Its clients, from all over the nation, are minors with major drug (including alcohol), emotional, or behavioral problems. Frustrated and desperate parents—often with insurance companies picking up a large part of the tab—send their problem children into the wilderness, not for recreation, but hopefully for re-creation.

For 18 days, three leaders trained in both outdoor and mental health skills lead seven clients into the wilds and away from the distractions of people. The clients don't know where they are going. After a long drive from the Portland airport, they are marched up Iron Mountain, where they can see forever but cannot see a sign of human habitation or roads. To you this might be a very pleasant experience; to them the message is unmistakable: "I am safer staying with this group." The leaders try to avoid other humans at all costs to lessen the risk of clients attempting to run away. This is why they seek the boring Buzzard Creeks over the scenic Steens Mountain: fewer distracting people.

The clients don't know about the maps and cell phones carried or of the water and food cached. Most drinking water is strained through the bandanna on one's neck and boiled.

The experience includes a three-day solo. Hopefully by the end, the clients have begun to learn to trust others, and to learn something of the benefits of teamwork and the costs of personal irresponsibility (if you don't put up your tent properly and it rains, you get wet and miserable). Hopefully they gain self-confidence and self-esteem, so afterwards they are better prepared to face the challenges of the urban wilderness.

The institute explains "wilderness therapy" this way:

> *In the wilderness, young people leave behind the distractions and luxuries of their daily lives. Nothing comes easy or by itself.*
>
> *Consequences are meted out by nature in her simple, direct way, not by some authority figure of questionable motives and fairness. It is our belief that until young people experience the negative consequences of their choices, they won't perceive their behavior as a problem. Nature holds young people accountable for the choices they make and helps them rediscover the values that are important to leading successful lives: family, responsibility, honesty, trust, and respect.*
>
> *Wilderness living provides a naturally healing environment. It provides the physical activity and healthy conditions that are especially important to adolescents, and it is the best available means to promote self-explora-tion and self-esteem. This occurs in a setting where one naturally explores the meaning of solitude, daily work, play, and relationships, as well as life's larger spiritual questions.*

Seventy percent of its participants have had "marked improvement" from the experience, says the institute.[2] Not a bad use of land, don't you think?

Iron Mountain (back) in the proposed Buzzard Creek Wilderness

8. Iron Mountain Summit (Iron Mountain Unit)

What to Expect:	Vast exhilarating views
Distance:	1.2-miles loop/round trip
Elevation Range:	4,200–5,380 feet
Drinking Water:	No
Best Times:	Spring, fall
USGS 7.5' Map:	Iron Mountain Flat
Oregon Map Starting Point:	Riley

Drive east on US 20/395 11 miles and turn south on the Double O County Road. In about 20 miles the road comes to an unmarked T. Go west, immediately entering the Malheur National Wildlife Refuge. After 4.5 miles continue west through a gate onto BLM land. At 0.8 mile west of the gate, take the left (southwesterly) fork up and over the ridge. After 0.7 mile take southwesterly fork. After 2.7 miles take the northwesterly (north) fork. Go about 1 mile and park on public land (through the fence). This route may not be passable at times of high water.

It is 0.6 mile to summit, though nearly 1,200 feet in elevation gain. Take your time. The views are worth it.

If you see others in this area, in all likelihood it is best they not interact with you. Tactfully and tactically withdraw.

DIABLO MOUNTAIN WILDERNESS (PROPOSED)

The wild shore of a relic Pleistocene lake, steep escarpments, unique volcanic flows, and a species "hotspot."

Location:	Lake County, 10 miles southeast of Summer Lake
Size:	657 square miles (420,530 acres)
Terrain:	A large lake, very large flats, rolling hills, and steep escarpments
Elevation Range:	4,148–6,147 feet
Managing Agency:	Lakeview District BLM
Agency Wilderness Status:	113,120-acre BLM wilderness study area; 90,050 acres recommended
Recreation Map:	Northwest and Northeast Quarters, North Half Lakeview Resource Area, Lakeview District BLM

From OR 31—and even sometimes up close—much of the land in the area is outwardly barren. Seeing isn't always knowing. In this vast expanse of desert

Diablo Mountain across Summer Lake in the proposed Diablo Mountain Wilderness

range—with its great variation in character, topography, and hydrology—are unique lava flows, sedimentary fossil deposits, the high mountain escarpments of Diablo Mountain, the prominent Coglan Buttes and Burma Rim, and some of the least altered landscapes in Oregon. (The South of Ana River USGS 7.5' quad is the only quad map that the author has seen for Oregon that doesn't have *any* roads, not even jeep trails, and only one place name.)

As barren as it may appear at first look, the area has abundant life. The Oregon Biodiversity Project notes that the area is

> one of the largest intact blocks of salt desert scrub habitat in the Oregon portion of the Basin and Range and one of the largest roadless areas in the state. Summer Lake and the adjacent freshwater wetlands attract a high diversity of migrating and breeding birds, making it a key habitat along the Pacific Flyway. It has also been identified by the Interior Columbia River Basin Ecosystem Management Project as a "hotspot" of species rarity and endemism.[3]

Raptors utilize the cliffs adjacent to water habitats. Summer Lake is an important refuge for the declining western snowy plover (see Lake Abert National Wildlife Refuge) and for other shorebirds such as avocet and killdeer.

The area also includes historic homesteads, mollusk fossils, and archaeological sites.

Charismatic megafauna include bighorn sheep, pronghorn, and mule deer.

The proposal consists of three units: Summer Lake, Burma Rim, and Coglan Buttes. Both explorations are in the Summer Lake unit, which is no reflection on the others save for their remoteness and the difficulty in getting to them.

9. Diablo Peak (Summer Lake Unit)

What to Expect:	A lovely but strenuous climb from salt scrub flats through sage-covered foothills to unlimited views on the summit
Distance:	10.4 miles round trip
Elevation Range:	4,260–6,147 feet
Drinking Water:	No
Best Times:	Summer, fall
USGS 7.5' Maps:	Ana River, Diablo Peak
Oregon Map Starting Point:	Summer Lake

Take the county road east between the rest area and the church approximately 5.9 miles to a fork. Stay on the main road to the southeast (right). In 1.9 miles are green double gates to a ranch entrance. Park here or drive 200 yards north on an unimproved BLM way and park.

Hike (Ana River quad) easterly across the flat 1.6 miles, skirting the fence to avoid private land on the south. Climb up a low ridge (Diablo Peak quad) and bear southeasterly to intersect with a very faint jeep trail that goes up Cat Camp Draw (you really don't need it). At the head of the draw (2.2 miles from flat), climb steeply and northeasterly 1.4 miles to the Diablo Peak summit. Return as you came.

10. Sand Dunes Traverse (Summer Lake Unit)

What to Expect:	Easy walking across alkali flats and sand dunes into the deep wild and unparalleled solitude
Distance:	14.5 miles one way
Elevation Range:	4,260–4,450 feet
Drinking Water:	Yes, but . . .
Best Times:	Spring, fall
USGS 7.5' Maps:	Ana River, Diablo Peak, Loco Lake
Oregon Map Starting Point:	Paisley

This exploration ends at the same place as the Diablo Peak exploration (above) starts. One vehicle must be spotted there.

The embarkation point is at Fivemile Point north of Paisley. From the Chewaucan River Bridge, go 0.6 mile north on OR 31 to a dirt road, just past the high-standard county road that heads easterly. After you leave the pavement, three dirt paths present themselves. Take the middle one due north 3.6 miles to Fivemile Point and park.

No water is available for the first 10 miles, so pack plenty and hydrate well before you start. Almost all travel is on unimproved ways.

Begin hiking (Loco Lake quad) northerly on an unimproved way to Tenmile Ridge (about 5 miles). Passing just west of Tenmile Ridge, continue northerly 3.6 miles to Fourmile Point (Diablo Peak quad). As for place name logic, don't go there. Continue northerly 1.6 miles to a developed spring (it is on the Ana River quad). If you are tired (it has been rather flat hiking), camp here. Another spring is 0.5 mile northerly up the way. Several more springs are at Lost Cabin in another 0.8 mile northerly. The cabin is at an oasis, and many of the springs are on private property, so be extra respectful. From Lost Cabin head northerly 1 mile to a private land boundary. Continue northerly along the west side of the private property at Thousand Springs Ranch (fenced) to the road you came in on and to your vehicle in about 2 miles.

DIAMOND CRATERS
NATIONAL MONUMENT (PROPOSED)

"A museum of basaltic volcanism."

Location:	Harney County, 55 miles southeast of Burns
Size:	26 square miles (16,656 acres)
Terrain:	Rugged lava flows
Elevation Range:	4,150–4,700 feet
Managing Agencies:	Burns District BLM (present); National Park Service (proposed)
Recreation Maps:	Northeast Quarter, North Half Burns District BLM

From a distance it doesn't draw you. More sagebrush covering some lava flows and craters—something far from uncommon in the Oregon Desert. At first glance it "resembles a thin, rocky pancake with a few bumps," says Dr. Ellen Benedict of Pacific University. However, if you know what you are looking at, it is quite another matter. Another distinguished professor of geology calls Diamond Craters the "best and most diverse basaltic volcanic features in the United States and all within a comparatively small and accessible area."

The educational and research values are immense. In Diamond Craters, all those volcanic terms that some teacher tried to pound into your head during geology class begin to make some sense. You can see it. It is all here.

As molten lava repeatedly spilled from deep in the Earth over the past 25,000 years, nature has been at work in what is now called Diamond Craters. Basalt does fantastically different things, depending on such variables as mineral content, the presence or absence of water, how it reacted upon coming up against other natural forces, how much and what kinds of pressure, how fast it cooled, and so forth.

With a little interpretation you can see the difference between lava flows, pressure ridges, pahoehoe lava (smooth, billowy, or ropy surface), aa lava (rough, jagged, spinose, clinkery surface), tensional fractures, lava toes, ash fall lava tubes, trenches, collapse craters, natural bridges, shield volcanoes, spatter cones, ramparts, kipukas (areas of undisturbed vegetation surrounded by lava fields), plug domes, driblet spires, benches, tephra, grabens, cored bombs, scoria, breadcrust bombs, maars, calderas, walls, rings, and cones.

Significant portions of Diamond Craters are vegetated. It is an ecotone between western juniper/big sagebrush, sagebrush steppe, and desert scrub zones. Two hundred and forty species of vascular plants have been identified. A small stand of aspen on the south end is unusual because of the low elevation.

One hundred and eighty-nine species of birds and 52 species of mammals are thought to utilize Diamond Craters. It may also have a unique form of subterranean mite (bumper stickers to follow: "Save the Diamond Craters Mite!").

The craters even have some water. Most notable is Malheur Maar, a spring-fed lake with over 50 feet of sediment that has piled up over the last 7,000 years. According to Benedict, Malheur Maar is "one of the most significant desert lakes between Mexico and Canada, especially for the study of past climates."

WHAT TO DO

The best way to see Diamond Craters is by car, with short excursions by foot. An excellent informative and entertaining brochure ("Please don't break open or collect the bombs") describing a self-guided auto tour is available from Burns District BLM. The tour is about 30 miles in length from OR 205 and starts at the turnoff to Diamond on OR 205 between mileposts 40 and 41 (measured from OR 78 near Burns).

The Desert Trail traverses the area (see Appendix D).

Diamond Craters with Steens Mountain (back)

FISH CREEK RIM WILDERNESS (PROPOSED)

Great views of the Warner Valley, Warner Mountains, and Hart Mountain with a good chance to see bighorn sheep.

Location:	Lake County, 2 miles north of Adel
Size:	61 square miles (39,263 acres)
Terrain:	Gentle rolling hills and flats and one precipitous high rim
Elevation Range:	4,500–6,932 feet
Managing Agency:	Lakeview District BLM
Agency Wilderness Status:	16,690-acre BLM wilderness study area; 11,920 acres recommended
Recreation Map:	Southeast Quarter, South Half Lakeview Resource Area, Lakeview District BLM

The area is dominated by a very rugged east-facing scarp that rises steeply above the Warner Valley. To the west are broad sage flats with bitterbrush, other shrubs, and scattered pockets of juniper. Below the rim are some interesting benches in a completely natural condition with thickets of mountain mahogany and stands of juniper, ponderosa pine, and white fir. The area includes some of the largest and best-quality mountain mahogany stands within Oregon's Basin and Range. The white fir and ponderosa pine are disjunct from those of the Warner Mountains 13 miles to the west and include some truly old-growth specimens.

The sheer cliffs towering over the lakes below are habitat suitable for the reintroduction of the peregrine falcon. They also have high concentrations of other raptors.

Wildlife habitat and viewing are both excellent. Sage grouse, bighorn sheep, pronghorn, and mule deer are the most charismatic wildlife of the area. At least one prehistoric bighorn sheephunting complex, including rock blinds, is known. Rock art along the rim can also be seen. A pronghorn kidding ground (for giving birth, not joking around) is also in the area.

The area is included in the Oregon Biodiversity Project's Hart Mountain Conservation Opportunity Area.

Fish Creek Rim, Hart Lake, and Hart Mountain (left to right)

11. Fish Creek Rim

What to Expect: Great views, lots of raptors, and likely bighorn sheep
Distance: 8.3-mile loop
Elevation Range: 6,480–6,932 feet
Drinking Water: No
Best Times: Late spring, summer, fall
USGS 7.5' Maps: Adel, Priday Reservoir
Oregon Map Starting Point: Lakeview

Drive 6 miles north of Lakeview on US 395/OR 140. Continue east on OR 140 approximately 13 miles to Lake County 3-13. Drive northerly toward Plush approximately 11 miles (about 1.5 miles past a high-tension powerline). Turn southeasterly onto an okay road and drive approximately 7.6 miles to the Cleland Spring turnoff. Park.

Hike (Priday Reservoir quad) southerly on an old way 1.5 miles to a four-way intersection. Continue southwesterly 1.6 miles to a way that heads east. Nice camp here (Adel quad) with a 5-foot diameter white fir and a similarly sized ponderosa pine. These specimens are easy to find as they are noticeably taller than surrounding western juniper.

Follow this way 0.4 mile east to a southerly heading jeep trail. Follow the jeep trail southeasterly 1 mile beyond end to rim. Hike the rim north 0.6 mile to highest point (elevation 6,932 feet). Watch carefully for bighorn sheep both on the flat and below the rim. Continue hiking the rim 3.2 miles back your vehicle.

FORT ROCK LAVA BEDS NATIONAL MONUMENT (PROPOSED)

Thick forests to open sage with a wide variety of volcanic features in between.

Location: Lake County, 10 miles north of Christmas Valley
Size: 150 square miles (96,256 acres)
Terrain: Recent lava flows with a variety of volcanic features
Elevation Range: 4,315–5,612 feet
Managing Agencies: Lakeview District BLM (present); National Park Service (proposed)
Recreation Map: Northwest Quarter, North Half Lakeview Resource Area, Lakeview District BLM

The Fort Rock Lava Beds are a wonder of numerous volcanic events both in time and kind. Basalt flows, lava tubes, spatter cones, kipukas (areas of undisturbed

Three of the Four Craters in the proposed Fort Rock Lava Beds National Monument and Wilderness

vegetation surrounded by lava fields), and more are easy for the geologic novice to comprehend. But it is more than just lava. Much is vegetated. The lava flows are in an ecotone, a transition zone between the higher-elevation ponderosa pine forest and the lower-elevation open sage country. (See Fort Rock Lava Beds Wilderness.)

The proposed monument encompasses the proposed Fort Rock Lava Beds Wilderness and also includes additional lands with geological, ecological, cultural, historical, and recreational values. Several other features would be protected, including an ice cave, additional lava flows, and formations, as well as vast stands of western juniper forest.

WHAT TO DO

Starting at Christmas Valley, generally follow the BLM's backcountry byway noted on the BLM recreation map. The first required stop is Crack in the Ground (see the Crack in the Ground exploration in Fort Rock Lava Beds Wilderness). Continue northeasterly along the western edge of the Four Craters Lava Field to the summit of Green Mountain, which has a fire lookout and great views. A campground is located a few hundred yards away. Continue northerly to the southern edge of the East Lava Field and then westerly to the southeast edge of the Devils Garden unit of the Fort Rock Lava Beds Wilderness.

At this point, you can continue on the backcountry byway to Fort Rock (worth a side trip itself—the park, not the hamlet) or drive northerly along the east side of the Devils Garden unit to take in The Blowouts. The feature is not shown on the BLM recreation map, but it is just east of the "Derrick Cave" shown on the map. To confuse matters further, the one and only real Derrick Cave is in reality 1 mile to the north of where it is shown on the BLM recreation map. See the Little Garden exploration in Fort Rock Lava Beds Wilderness for more detailed directions. The Blowouts are huge and distinct spatter cones. Derrick Cave is a 30-foot-high, 50-foot-wide, 1/4-mile-long lava tube that has collapsed in two places. Exploring the cave requires both a bright light and the right attitude.

Continue northerly and then westerly into the Deschutes National Forest. The road soon reaches FS Road 23, which runs into FS Road 22, which goes to LaPine.

FORT ROCK LAVA BEDS WILDERNESS (PROPOSED)

The collision of lava, forest, and sage.

Location:	Lake County, 10 miles north of Christmas Valley
Size:	111 square miles (71,117 acres)
Terrain:	Rugged basalt lava flows with a variety of volcanic features
Elevation Range:	4,315–5,612 feet
Managing Agencies:	Lakeview District BLM, Deschutes National Forest
Agency Wilderness Status:	70,620-acre BLM wilderness study area; 58,270 acres recommended
Recreation Map:	Northwest Quarter, Lakeview Resource Area, Lakeview District BLM

The area is covered by vast expanses of extremely rugged, broken, and sharp basalt lava. Spatter cones, lava tubes, domes, cinder cones, vents, fissures, flows, and other results of volcanic action are evident.

While the lava flows dominate the area, other features also stand out. In this area, the lava flows are in a pine forest/sagebrush ecotone, which provides for a diverse range of habitats.

Mammals include porcupine, yellow-bellied marmot, badger, and big-eared bat. Cougar, bobcat, and black bear, all species with restricted ranges in the desert, are found here. Pronghorn are common. The area is crucial winter range for thousands of mule deer.

Bird species include bald eagle, golden eagle, red-tailed hawk, turkey vulture, great horned owl, raven, western meadowlark, white-crowned sparrow, lark sparrow, and sage grouse. Mountain bluebirds are quite common and are especially noticeable in the fall when they form flocks.

Numerous reptile species have been reported.

Kipukas (areas of undisturbed vegetation surrounded by lava fields) offer pristine grasslands. Because of the harshness of the terrain, many stands of relatively undisturbed native bunchgrass exist.

Of particular interest is desert sweet (*Chamaebatiaria millifolium*), an unusual shrub in the rose family that is abundant in the lava flows. It has a very sweet fragrance.

The proposed wilderness consists of three units: Devils Garden, East Lava Field, and Four Craters Lava Field. All are within the proposed national monument. (See Fort Rock Lava Beds National Monument.)

Devils Garden Unit

The unit is an area of rugged lava flows, dense vegetation, cinder cones, and highly broken terrain. The Devils Garden itself is a series of kipukas. The Blowouts are exceptional spatter cones. Derrick Cave is a well-developed lava tube cave. Little Garden is a pine-covered kipuka. The unit offers "truly exceptional opportunities for solitude," says BLM.

East Lava Field Unit

Containing both the aa (rough, jagged, spinose, clinkery surface) and the pahoehoe (smooth, billowy, or ropy surface) lava, the unit is the most rugged to

Ponderosa pine in the Devils Garden unit of the proposed Fort Rock Lava Beds Wilderness

hike. Tumuli (fractured basaltic domes), squeeze-ups (molten lava forced through fissures), spires, and ropy lavas can be found here.

Scattered aspen, juniper, and mountain mahogany stands exist, along with some shrub cover. In many areas, the lichens are quite colorful.

Four Craters Lava Field Unit

The Four Craters are cinder cones on a distinct linear alignment and the most obvious feature of the unit.

The most interesting feature in the unit is Crack in the Ground. With its cool temperatures, grasses, and ferns, it is in dramatic contrast to the desert landscape just above. The crack is a 2.5-mile-long rift along a fault formed along with the creation of Four Craters Lava Field several thousand years ago.

12. Crack in the Ground (Four Craters Lava Field Unit)

What to Expect:	A hike in and above a crack in the ground that in places is 70 feet deep
Distance:	2-mile loop
Elevation Range:	4,400–4,496 feet
Drinking Water:	No
Best Times:	Spring, summer, fall, winter
USGS 7.5' Map:	Crack-in-the-Ground
Oregon Map Starting Point:	Christmas Valley

Drive 1 mile east and turn north on BLM Road 6109-D. Drive northerly 6.9 miles to Crack in the Ground trailhead. Park.

A short hike takes you to a wide spot of the crack. Walk in the crack south as far as you can go or can stand, then climb out and return along the crack's edge. The deepest part of the crack is north of where you began your crack walk and is best viewed by hiking along either rim.

13. Little Garden (Devils Garden Unit)

What to Expect:	"The epitome of solitude"
Distance:	5 miles round trip
Elevation Range:	4,860–5,050 feet
Drinking Water:	No
Best Times:	Spring, summer, fall
USGS 7.5' Maps:	Fox Butte, Sixteen Butte
Oregon Map Starting Point:	Fort Rock

Drive east 8.25 miles, turn north for 1 mile, turn east for 1 mile, and then northerly for 2.1 miles to an intersection. Proceed northerly toward Fort Rock Fire Guard Station and Derrick Cave. Drive northerly 9.3 miles past The Blowouts and Derrick Cave (both worth detours—see Fort Rock Lava Beds National Monument) to an intersection 0.8 mile north of the unimproved way to Derrick Cave. Proceed westerly 0.8 mile to the four-wheel-drive trail to the south. Park.

"The aesthetics of the 'Little Garden' represent the epitome of solitude," according to BLM.

Hike (Fox Butte quad) southerly 1.3 miles to the Little Garden (Sixteen Butte quad). The demarcation of the Little Garden is striking as the lava abruptly changes to sandy soil and higher ground.

Campsites are plentiful. This exploration can be done as a long day hike or as an overnight backpack. Head west to reach the summit of the epitome of solitude at 5,050 feet.

HART MOUNTAIN NATIONAL WILDLIFE REFUGE ADDITIONS (PROPOSED)

A "hotspot" of species endemism and complete protection of the entire range of the Hart Mountain pronghorn herd.

Location: Lake and Harney Counties, centered 12 miles northeast of Adel
Size: 553 square miles (353,768 acres); existing refuge: 375 square miles (240,000 acres)
Terrain: Lakes and wetlands, high and low rims, rolling hills, and stream canyons
Elevation Range: 3,200–8,017 feet
Managing Agencies: Lakeview District BLM (present); Fish and Wildlife Service (proposed)
Recreation Map: Northeast and Southeast Quarters, North and South Halves Lakeview Resource Area, Lakeview District BLM

The expansion of the Hart Mountain Refuge would include two very distinct landscapes: the lakes, dunes, and playa ecosystem of the northern Warner Valley and the sagebrush steppe between Hart Mountain and the Sheldon National Wildlife Refuge in Nevada.

"[The Hart Mountain Conservation Opportunity Area] is an extraordinary landscape with high ecological integrity," notes the Oregon Biodiversity Project.[4] (Much of the proposed refuge addition is also described under the Bighorn Wilderness and Pronghorn Wilderness.) The proposed addition is one contiguous unit, but of two distinct characterizations.

Between the Refuges

One of the largest herds of pronghorn in Oregon summers on Hart Mountain and often winters in the Sheldon National Wildlife Refuge in Nevada. The herd sometimes chooses to winter in the Catlow Valley or at Oregon End Table, depending on the severity of the winter.

This proposed addition is to ensure that the entire "biological unit" of the pronghorn herd will be protected. It also includes numerous sage grouse leks.

The proposed addition (which also includes additional wildlands in Nevada) includes habitat for forty-six species at risk in either Oregon or Nevada: thirteen birds, four fish, eight mammals, one amphibian, one invertebrate, and nineteen plants. It would also include increasingly rare examples of three natural plant communities: basin big sagebrush/needle and thread grass, silver sagebrush/ wildrye, and winterfat/Sandberg's bluegrass flat.

Northern Warner Valley

"The Warner Valley includes a major wetland complex and extensive salt desert scrub," notes the Oregon Biodiversity Project. "The valley's lakes, springs, and streams provide habitat for a number of rare fish, and its wetlands are among the region's most significant for migratory birds. It is also considered a 'hotspot' of species rarity and endemism on a regional scale."[5]

The Warner Valley is comparable to the Malheur National Wildlife Refuge in its importance to migratory birds. The spring migrations of egrets, white pelicans, geese, ducks, and many other kinds of birds are quite impressive.

Inclusion of the northern Warner Valley into the national wildlife refuge system would also aid the recovery of the endangered Warner sucker.

Three people are most responsible for the conservation of Hart Mountain: President Franklin D. Roosevelt, who established the refuge; Ira Gabrielson of the U.S. Biological Survey (now Fish and Wildlife Service), who convinced him to do it (and later to issue an improved executive order putting wildlife ahead of livestock); and Barry Reiswig, the former refuge manager, who finally stood up to local (conflicts of) interests and said that livestock on the refuge was harmful to wildlife and therefore contrary to the executive order that established it.

"The current mandated 15-year exclusion of livestock from the Hart Mountain refuge presents a unique opportunity to explore strategies to restore native plant and animal communities at landscape levels," says the Oregon Biodiversity Project.[6]

Habitat recovery is quite evident. Rock and Guano Creeks, the main all-year watercourses, are sporting improving riparian cover. In the uplands, baby aspen are back.

Sage grouse are not yet rebounding with the absence of livestock. Scientists suspect drought to be the major continuous and unchangeable factor in varying sage grouse numbers. As we enter a wetter cycle, sage grouse numbers may increase. Another way to look at it: if the livestock hadn't been removed, sage grouse numbers on the refuge would have declined dramatically as they have in most other places where livestock continue to graze.

Reiswig's successor has apparently decided to make his legacy the slaughter of coyotes on the refuge in the name of increasing pronghorn fawn survival. Such wildlife management—though possibly well intentioned for pronghorn—disregards wildlife science, which says it is unnecessary and counterproductive for the health of the pronghorn herd (see Natural History chapter).

Crump Lake in the Warner Valley (front); the land between the refuges, both in the proposed additions to Hart Mountain National Wildlife Refuge (middle); Steens Mountain and Beatys Butte (back)

Though Roosevelt called it a national antelope refuge, the language of the executive order speaks to other "nonpredatory" wildlife (it was 1936). Subsequent congressional direction mandates a whole-ecosystem approach to refuge management.

WHAT TO DO

Hart Mountain has always been a magnificent place to visit, but even more so since 1993, when livestock grazing ended (until at least 2008, when it will resume, only over the conservation movement's collective dead body).

Starting with a full tank of gas, take a couple of days and drive from Adel to Frenchglen. Drive north toward Plush and along the proposed Fish Creek Rim Wilderness. From Plush continue northeasterly to the refuge headquarters (see the Campbell Lake exploration).

After you fantasize about living in the stone house for three seasons (forget winter), visit the little museum and interpretive center (write disparaging comments about coyote killing in the visitor's book) and grab a copy of the refuge brochure. Hot Springs Campground to the south is a great, and the only, spot to car camp.

South of Hot Springs Campground is a true wonder: the Blue Sky Hotel, a relic ponderosa pine forest on upper Guano Creek. The closest pine forest is about 25 miles away in the North Warner Mountains. Insanely, the U.S. Army established a winter camp here in 1866–1867 (at 6,250 feet elevation) and cut down most of the original old-growth trees trying to keep warm. They moved the camp the next spring to a lower elevation. A few original big yellow-bellies still exist, and the replacement stand is coming along nicely. Blue Sky is an alternative way to the summit of Warner Peak (follow ways and jeep trails, or hike cross-country).

Backpacking permits are required on the refuge.

14. Buck Pasture (Warner Peak Unit, Bighorn Wilderness)

What to Expect:	A stream and a wet meadow that hasn't been grazed since 1940 on a wildlife refuge that hasn't been grazed since 1993 in a landscape that has been grazed since the mid-nineteenth century
Distance:	3.2-mile loop
Elevation Range:	5,616–5,800 feet
Drinking Water:	Yes
Best Times:	Spring, summer, fall
USGS 7.5' Map:	Campbell Lake
Oregon Map Starting Point:	Plush

Drive north 1 mile and then northeasterly approximately 25 miles (following signs) to Hart Mountain National Wildlife Refuge headquarters.

Park at Refuge headquarters. From the westernmost bridge on the Plush-Frenchglen Road, hike westerly 0.4 mile to a sign saying "Willow Creek." Walk 0.8 mile south to an intersection with another way (bear west at a Y about half way). At the intersection, hike westerly for 0.4 mile to an official sign saying "Road Closed." Walk westerly a few hundred yards to a plank bridge across Willow Creek. Notice some rock weirs (big rocks wrapped in wire) that were placed in the creek to slow the stream, catch sediment, and such. A better solution, economically and ecologically, was to simply remove the livestock. Nature will heal itself.

Walk upstream on the east bank for about 100 yards. Notice the young grass growing in the very wide and shallow stream channel. Livestock were removed from the refuge in 1993. Before that, this stream had severe cutbanks and little vegetation. Continue your inspection upstream to a dramatic change in the creek character. At the former fence line, the creek channel deepens and narrows dramatically in the wet meadow. Buck Pasture has not been grazed for several decades. The exclosure fence was removed in 1994. Someday you won't be able to distinguish the recovering creek downstream from the recovered creek upstream. The Fish and Wildlife Service should re-erect four large corner posts to provide historical reference to where the fence was.

Return the way you came. When you can see the refuge headquarters, set out cross-country and walk down Rock Creek back to your vehicle.

15. Campbell Lake (Poker Jim Ridge Unit, Bighorn Wilderness)

What to Expect:	Large shallow lakes, countless potholes, marshes, desert scrub, sand dunes, short-grass meadows, countless waterfowl, and memorable views
Distance:	10.6 miles round trip
Elevation Range:	4,462–4,558 feet
Drinking Water:	Most always
Best Times:	Spring, summer, fall, winter
USGS 7.5' Maps:	Bluejoint Lake West, Campbell Lake
Oregon Map Starting Point:	Plush

Drive north 1 mile and then northeasterly approximately 20 miles to the Hart Mountain National Wildlife Refuge sign. Just as the road leaves the flat of the Warner Valley and begins to climb the rim, park at the junction of an unimproved way continuing northeasterly along the flat.

Hike (Campbell Lake quad) 2 miles along southeast shore of Campbell Lake to a jeep trail along the northeast shore of the lake. This way may be followed northwesterly 3.3 miles to the north shore of Stone Corral Lake (Bluejoint Lake West quad).

It is safest to return the way you came. The adventurous can set their own course back, but be aware that topographic quad maps are only somewhat useful here, in that the water levels shown on the map are but a snapshot in time. At any given time, water levels are likely higher or lower. Within a few years' time, these lakes have been both bone dry and overflowing to merge into one huge lake (during which time this exploration can only be done by canoe).

This exploration is on Lakeview District BLM land recommended for inclusion in the Hart Mountain National Wildlife Refuge.

(If the water levels are high, bring a canoe and put in on the south side of Flagstaff Lake and go exploring. Afternoon high winds can often be treacherous. If the water isn't too high, campsites are numerous. One best navigates by occasionally climbing "high" points and using Poker Jim Ridge as a beacon to the east.)

LAKE ABERT NATIONAL WILDLIFE REFUGE (PROPOSED)

Oregon's Mono Lake.

Location:	Lake County, 3 miles north-northeast of Valley Falls
Size:	64 square miles (41,154 acres)
Terrain:	Flat and quite wet
Elevation Range:	4,255–4,341 feet
Managing Agencies:	Lakeview District BLM (present); Fish and Wildlife Service (proposed)
Recreation Map:	Southwest Quarter, South Half Lakeview Resource Area, Lakeview District BLM

Brine shrimp (and, oh yeah, alkali flies) are the foundation of Lake Abert's (not Abert Lake!) fantastic biological productivity. Yes, the brine shrimp (and flies) have to eat something, but we don't need to discuss that here.

The brine shrimp handle water much saltier than the ocean as well as with an alkalinity up to a pH of 10. They tough out temperatures below 0 degrees Fahrenheit. When the lake dries out, the shrimp in their cystic form can survive with 2 percent of their normal moisture and can be carried by the wind to other water.

These millions upon millions of brine shrimp (and those alkali flies) make Lake Abert an attractive resting and forage stop for migratory waterfowl and shorebirds.

A significant portion of the Pacific Flyway populations of western snowy plover, eared grebe, Wilson's and red-necked phalaropes, and American avocet use Lake Abert.

Phalaropes twirl in the water to bring the brine shrimp to the surface. Up to fifty thousand of the birds have been estimated on the east shore at one time. It is quite a scene when numbers peak in mid-August.

The lake also provides seasonal habitat for 1.5 to 2 percent of the North American population of northern shovelers. It is also a rest stop for Canada geese, ducks, and cranes. The total waterfowl/waterbird use exceeds 3.25 million bird-use days annually.

Lake Abert is a feeding ground for raptors that use the adjacent Abert Rim for nesting.

Fourteen species of special status (various levels of worry and/or protection) are associated with the lake ecosystem: peregrine falcon, bald eagle, western snowy plover, white-faced ibis, loggerhead shrike, pygmy rabbit, Oregon Lakes tui chub, black tern, California bighorn sheep, long-billed curlew, ferruginous hawk, greater sandhill crane, white-tailed antelope squirrel, and white-tailed jackrabbit.

The lake has the third or fourth largest (depending on water conditions) breeding population of western snowy plover anywhere. Lake Abert's breeding population averages four to five times that of the species' entire coastal breeding population. The coastal population is a federally protected threatened species. It shares wintering grounds with the inland populations such as those at Lake Abert, so interchange is probable. The Lake Abert population isn't vulnerable to coastal winter gales or oil spills. However, it is vulnerable to off-road vehicles.

"Lake Abert is an aquatic ecosystem that is exceptionally productive and is comparatively close in functioning to its pristine state," says BLM. At 55 square miles, Lake Abert is what's left of the huge Pleistocene Lake Chewaucan (CHEE-wah-CAN). As the climate warmed and the lake shrank, the resulting water became more concentrated with briny mineral salts. And as the lake has no outlet, the salts continue to concentrate. The lake playa occasionally dries, and the saline dust blows away, making the lake temporarily less salty.

Lake Abert is the largest saline lake in the Pacific Northwest and among the five largest in the Great Basin. Its closest ecological relative is California's Mono Lake.

The amount of water inflow also affects lake productivity. The main source is the Chewaucan River, which enters the lake's south end over a 12-foot ledge—hence that end of the lake is the least alkaline. Some other streams and springs add fresh water at other places around the lake, serving onshore wildlife species from the sagebrush edge. Besides the lake habitat, the shoreline supports wetland, riparian, sagebrush/bunchgrass, and desert scrub communities.

The desert allocarya (*Plagiobothrys salsus*) is a wildflower that grew at an enclosed spring (to keep livestock out) on the west side of the lake until 1983, when cattle breached the fence and eliminated the entire remnant stand. It continues to live in one location in the Warner Valley and few locations in Nevada. Hopefully, it will be reestablished at the site.

The lake's salinity is too high to support any fish. XL Spring on the northeast edge of the lake is a refuge for the Oregon Lakes tui chub (*Gila bicilor oregonensis*).

The interface of lake and rim (now bisected by US 395) is an extremely rich cultural and archaeological district on the National Register of Historic Sites and Places.

Threats to the lake's ecosystem integrity include a potential for mining. There is moderate potential for gold, silver, mercury, and uranium. The potential for sodium and other evaporative minerals is high. Some geothermal power potential also exists. BLM cannot permanently withdraw the lands from the mining laws; only an act of Congress can do that.

An ambitious and stupid effort to develop a pumped-storage hydroelectric project has failed for now.

A small brine shrimp harvesting operation (mainly for pet fish food) exists on the lake. As it would be inconsistent with the purposes of a national wildlife refuge, the owner should be compensated at fair market value to end the operation.

Recent schemes to industrially harvest vast quantities of brine shrimp eggs are quiescent for now, but such harvesting is still a very serious threat to the lake.

Some key private lands should also be acquired to ensure the integrity of the lake's ecosystem.

The proposed Lake Abert National Wildlife Refuge

WHAT TO DO

The best way to enjoy the proposed refuge is a leisurely drive along US 395. The north and south shores are the most productive for birds. Most of the north shore is privately owned. From the few highway parking areas, small watercraft can be lugged for lakeside launching. Birding is excellent from April through October. One's attention will also be focused in the other direction to the incredible Abert Rim. The stretch from Valley Falls to Alkali Station compares with the Old McKenzie Pass as a highway wilderness experience.

LONESOME LAKES WILDERNESS (PROPOSED)

The wild does not reach out and grab you,
but is nonetheless there for the taking.

Location:	Lake County, 15 miles south of Hampton
Size:	168 square miles (107,468 acres)
Terrain:	Gently rolling hills and rims
Elevation Range:	4,562–5,238 feet
Managing Agency:	Lakeview District BLM
Agency Wilderness Status:	None
Recreation Map:	Northwest and Northeast Quarters, North Half Lakeview Resource Area, Lakeview District BLM

The area is typical of much of the Oregon Desert: a mix of sagebrush steppe and western juniper cover. The latter forms at the higher elevations in full cover, or in lower-elevation narrow bands where just enough moisture gathers.

123

The countless ephemeral lakes are used by Canada geese and many species of waterfowl. Remarkably, only a small fraction of these lakes have had a cattle pond bulldozed in their lowest spot.

Mule deer are present in good numbers. Pronghorn can be found here as well. Prairie falcon have been spotted.

Rocky Mountain elk are increasing in the area, a recent and not yet fully explained phenomenon. According to *Oregon Geographic Names,* Elk Butte received its name from local settlers in the 1890s who tracked a "lone" and "stray" elk to what they called Elk Butte.

BLM did not designate the area as a wilderness study area, marking it down for lack of solitude. Few people visit here, and none complain of crowding.

In the end, what is or is not "wilderness" is a subjective determination made by each person. Lonesome Lakes has no towering cliffs, no raging rivers, no snow-capped peaks, and no painted hills. Yet, it is wild and inviting. Go see for yourself.

Old-growth western juniper

16. Benjamin Lake and Benjamin Cave

What to Expect:	A pleasant stroll by lakeside, through sagebrush and juniper, and exploring a lava tube cave
Distance:	7-mile loop
Elevation Range:	4,850–5,103 feet
Drinking Water:	No
Best Times:	Spring, fall
USGS 7.5' Map:	Benjamin Lake
Oregon Map Starting Point:	Brothers

Drive 10 miles east on US 20. Turn south onto a county road (0.8 mile east of milepost 49). Go 12 miles south to an intersection (0.7 mile beyond the Lake-Deschutes county line at Frederick Butte) with a well-maintained dirt road. Proceed southeasterly 4.9 miles to an intersection where the road curves more to the south by Little Benjamin Lake to the west. Continue southeasterly, then easterly on a lower-grade dirt road 4.5 miles to the northwest side of Benjamin Lake. Park just short of a way to the south on public land. Skirt the private land and hike south along the lake edge, then turn westerly toward East Butte. Benjamin Cave is on the northwest slope of a slight saddle on the southwest side of East Butte. It is a noticeable hole where the top of a lava tube collapsed. Hike northerly, then easterly around the junipers' edge and back to your vehicle.

17. Elk Butte

What to Expect:	A pleasant climb through some gnarly juniper and nice grass to the summit
Distance:	5-mile loop
Elevation Range:	4,590–5,238 feet
Drinking Water:	No
Best Times:	Spring, fall
USGS 7.5' Map:	Elk Butte
Oregon Map Starting Point:	Riley

Drive southerly 37 miles on US 395 (9 miles south of Wagontire) and turn northwesterly (right) on Wagontire Road (Lake County 5-14). In about 10 miles the county road does a little wiggle and then a turn to the west-southwest. About 3 miles from said curve, turn due north (right) onto a dirt road. Head north 2.8 miles to the gate to the old cow camp. Take the fork to the right and veer eastward, then northward around the camp buildings, and very soon westward through a gate back onto public land. Park.

This exploration can be done either as a day hike or as an overnight backpack.

Hike north on the unimproved way. At the fork go west and upward, eventually bagging the twin summits of Elk Butte. Nice campsites can be found both in the draws and on top. Hike the edge of the juniper northward to the flatter country. You might want to hike farther north into the large flat with several ephemeral lakes, catching the four-wheel-drive track back to your vehicle.

LOST FOREST–SHIFTING SAND DUNES NATIONAL MONUMENT (PROPOSED)

Ancient pines and junipers, antediluvian fossils, and venerable dunes.

Location: Lake County, 30 miles northeast of Christmas Valley
Size: 577 square miles (36,624 acres)
Terrain: Open sand or gentle flats and rolling hills
Elevation Range: 4,290–4,792 feet
Managing Agencies: Lakeview District BLM (present); National Park Service (proposed)
Recreation Map: Northeast and Northwest Quarters, North Half Lakeview Resource Area, Lakeview District BLM

Three very different features are the centerpieces of the proposed national monument: Lost Forest, Shifting Sand Dunes, and Fossil Lake.

Lost Forest

Lost Forest is a unique ponderosa pine forest located at least 30 miles from any other forest outliers. The trees have genetically evolved to produce seeds that germinate more rapidly than other ponderosa pines. These pines survive on a mere 9 to 9.5 inches of precipitation annually. Other ponderosa pines need a minimum of 15 inches. The unique deep sandy soil conditions—dependent on the nearby Shifting Sand Dunes—allow the ponderosas to receive the water they need. Some are over six hundred years old. Some of the largest and oldest western junipers in Oregon are also found here.

Shifting Sand Dunes

The formation is the largest inland moving sand dune system in Oregon and possibly the Pacific Northwest. The moisture retained in the dune system and the resulting complex soil conditions contribute to the preservation of the nearby Lost Forest.

The dunes are nothing less than spectacular. Constantly sculpted by wind and rain, the dunes are ever changing. (See Shifting Sand Dunes Wilderness.)

Old-growth ponderosa pine in the proposed Lost Forest–Shifting Sand Dunes National Monument

Fossil Lake

The Fossil Lake area has numerous cultural and paleontological sites that have been recognized as extremely important for the study of Pleistocene-age mammals. It is the "type site" (where a species is first discovered) for a number of fossil species. The area is unique in the archaeological record of the northern Great Basin and is one of the more important paleontological areas in North America.

Fossils were first discovered here (by European Americans) in 1877. Paleontologists have identified twenty-three mammal, seventy-four bird, six fish, and six mollusk species from the fossils that lived 2 million to 10,000 years ago. Snail shells obtained 14 feet below the top of the lakebeds have a radiocarbon age of 29,000 years. Ancient horses (not the feral ones we have now), camels, ground sloths, flamingos, mammoths, pelicans, swans, elephants, salmon, and snails have been classified. Many of the species described are now extinct.

The area was the bottom of the ancient Pleistocene Fort Rock Lake (see the wave line on Fort Rock) and was approximately 200 feet deep. When the climate became more arid, the lake dried up. Fossil Lake is what remains.

WHAT TO DO

Following the directions to Fossil Lake below, continue due east 9.5 miles past the powerline to "The Crossroads" in the heart of Lost Forest. Park and walk in the direction that beckons most. The area's highest point is 1.2 miles southwest.

The Crossroads is located in a western juniper–ponderosa pine/sagebrush community. To the east a short walk is a tree-free sagebrush community. A short hike northwest is a ponderosa pine/sagebrush community. Northeast 1.5 miles is a ponderosa pine/bitterbrush community. Northeast 0.5 mile farther are dunes and shifting sand. East 1.8 miles and just south of road is a western juniper/Idaho fescue community without any ponderosa pine as it is too far from the Shifting Sand Dunes. East 0.2 mile of that is a small playa.

Sand Rock, 1 mile west of The Crossroads, is a fun little climb with nice views. If you plan to camp in the area and have a fire, bring your own firewood.

18. Fossil Lake

What to Expect:	A paleontological mecca
Distance:	1 mile round trip
Elevation Range:	4,292–4,302 feet
Drinking Water:	No
Best Times:	Winter, spring, fall
USGS 7.5' Map:	Fossil Lake
Oregon Map Starting Point:	Christmas Valley

Drive 2 miles due east and turn north on Lake County 5-14C and follow the signs to Lost Forest and/or Sand Dunes. In about 16 miles you'll be headed due east and cross under a high-tension powerline. East of the powerline 0.3 mile turn south on a dirt road. Go 1.5 miles and park at the fence and interpretive sign. Fossil Lake is a very flat 0.4 mile due southwest.

Return as you came.

MALHEUR LAKE WILDERNESS (PROPOSED)

Sporadically Oregon's largest lake.

Location:	Harney County, 25 miles south of Burns
Size:	144 square miles (92,303 acres)
Terrain:	Sand dunes and low hills and flats surrounding the lakes
Elevation Range:	4,093–4,145 feet
Managing Agency:	Fish and Wildlife Service
Recreation Map:	Northeast and Northwest Quarters, North Half Burns District BLM

The proposed wilderness includes two units: the "normal" Malheur Lake (see Malheur National Wildlife Refuge Additions) and Harney Lake.

Malheur Lake is a shallow alkaline marsh with dense growth of submerged and emergent aquatic plants. Sandy peninsulas and islands are common and are covered with greasewood and big sagebrush.

Scientists describe Harney Lake as a "large, shallow, intermittent, internally drained alkaline lake, remnant of a large Pleistocene lake, with alkali desert and sagebrush steppe vegetation, cold and hot springs, marshlands, sand dunes and abundant avifauna."

Harney Lake is sometimes dry with white alkali salt flats. Other times it becomes part of Malheur Lake. Historically, the "normal" Malheur Lake had periods of attempted farming and ranching (it got wet). Harney Lake was too harsh all the time to even try.

In particular, the sand dunes around Harney Lake are important western snowy plover habitat (see Lake Abert National Wildlife Refuge). The lake and immediate surroundings are a research natural area.

Waterfowl, shorebirds, and other avian species abound. White pelicans, Caspian terns, and gulls nest on the islands in Malheur Lake when water is present to keep away predators. Over 320 species of birds have been recorded since the refuge was established.

An ongoing management challenge is the exotic carp that were introduced into the lake system. The aliens churn up the lake bottom and reduce the productivity of the system for native species.

No exploration is given, as both Harney and Malheur Lakes are closed to the public save for a short duck hunting event on the north side of Malheur Lake. It wouldn't be any fun to be there then, unless you are hunting ducks.

Records of aboriginal settlement and use in the area date back nine thousand years. The closures are to protect wildlife and habitat and also to prevent the loss of archaeological resources. It is a federal offense to disturb or collect such resources. The feds frequently fly over looking for looters.

MALHEUR NATIONAL WILDLIFE REFUGE ADDITIONS (PROPOSED)

Expansion would help wildlife, ranchers, local government, and federal taxpayers.

Location:	Harney County, 20 miles southeast of Burns
Size:	159 square miles (101,079 acres); current refuge: 291 square miles (186,500 acres)
Terrain:	Very flat or nearly so, save a lone butte
Elevation Range:	approximately 4,100–4374 feet
Managing Agencies:	Private, Burns District BLM, State of Oregon (present); Fish and Wildlife Service (proposed)
Recreation Map:	Northwest and Northeast Quarters, North Half Burns District BLM

Malheur Lake, because it is so shallow and since precipitation varies dramatically from year to year, varies in size from a historic recorded (since 1903) minimum of 0 acres to a recorded maximum of 170,000 acres. Between 1825 and 1850, Malheur Lake likely dried up completely, as it did in 1934.

When it is high, Malheur Lake not only expands to include adjacent normally "dry" (actually much of it is wet) lands, it also completely swallows up both Mud Lake and Harney Lake. Harney Lake usually takes its fill from the Silver Creek and springs, while Malheur Lake suckles from the Donner und Blitzen and Silvies Rivers. Mud Lake is the connecting channel between the two. When the water rises, it all gets called Malheur Lake and is the largest lake in Oregon.

The problem is that about twenty-five ranches are *in* the lake. This is not a problem for the cows (and cowboys) when the lake is low. When the lake fills (it doesn't flood), it's a major problem not only for the landowners, but for the taxpayers as well. In the early 1980s, the lake rose dramatically. OR 205 had to be raised about 10 feet, and the higher lake level effectively finished off the Union Pacific railroad spur (it was on its way to abandonment anyway). Many miles of county road were inundated. The federal taxpayers got stuck providing both emergency flood and emergency drought (it didn't rain much the following summer) relief in the same year for the same ranchers.

Economically, the ranchland is worth $25 to $50 per acre. Because it is ranchland, it gets a big tax break, which is absorbed by other county taxpayers. Landowners (make that lake owners) pay an average of 10 cents per acre per year. (Four duck hunters spend more in Harney County on a weekend than the average property taxes paid by a lakebottom ranch.) In 1983, most of the landowners wanted the federal government to buy them out, and the Fish and Wildlife Service supported the idea. As in those towns on the Mississippi River, it makes more sense to spend the periodic federal flood and drought relief payments on moving people to higher ground and/or other pursuits.

Unfortunately, the county government opposes any net increase in federal land within Harney County, and some local interests are proposing that a drain be built connecting the Malheur Lake system to the South Fork Malheur River or a multi-pond pumped-storage irrigation scheme, or pumping the water into Diamond Craters (none with their own money by the way).

Conservationists propose that the boundaries of the Malheur National Wildlife Refuge be expanded to include the historic high lake level. Future federal disaster relief funds should be allocated to refuge land acquisition, instead of the periodic rebuilding of roads, barns, houses, and fences. On private property within the lake, owners should be covered by *one* more round of disaster relief. They could take the normal payoff, or be bought out at fair market value. If ranchers choose to stay, they would be "self-insured" from then on. Federal disaster funds should be used only for true disasters, especially those that cannot be foreseen. Anyone can foresee that ranching and living in a lake leads to trouble.

Of the proposed expansion, 15,908 acres is BLM land and 1,932 acres is state land.

Ecologically, the land is quite valuable. Over 320 species of birds and 58 mammal species have been observed on the adjacent refuge. Significant amounts of wetlands could be restored to productive fish and wildlife habitat. As the lake rises and falls, the wildlife would move with it as they did during presettlement times.

Fiscally, the considerable burden on the county funds would also be relieved.

Under current law, Harney County would receive more revenue from the federal revenue sharing program for refuge lands not being on the tax rolls than now collected from property taxes. A change in law is desirable, however. Presently the "payment in lieu of taxes" to counties to compensate them for the national wildlife refuge system lands within their borders comes from a special pot of money that is filled only from revenues from exploitive activities on refuge lands (oil, gas, grazing, logging, and so forth). Congress passed a new law in 1997 that is phasing out activities harmful to the purposes for which the refuge was established. Hopefully, this blood money will completely dry up; instead, Congress should continually appropriate an amount from the general treasury to fairly compensate the counties for refuge lands.

The rest of the existing refuge mostly includes the Blitzen River valley. Unfortunately, the river is channelized through much of its length on the refuge. According to the Oregon Biodiversity Project, "Restoration of a more naturally functioning river and floodplain would enhance the area's biodiversity values."[7] It would also likely be much cheaper as the refuge routinely spends large sums channelizing and repairing an extensive ditch system that suffers severe damage during most spring runoffs.

WHAT TO DO

No exploration is described, since most of the proposed expansion is private land and/or pasture. The existing Malheur Refuge has areas open to visitors in the Blitzen River valley. Seasonal and area closures are common, so check with refuge headquarters. A visit to headquarters is like a trip back to the 1930s.

Malheur Lake varies greatly in size, leading some to try things that just shouldn't be done in lakes.

OREGON GRASSLANDS WILDERNESS (PROPOSED)

Gentle rolling wide open spaces covered with bunchgrass and with other wonders, big and small.

Location:	Lake and Harney counties, 30 miles east of Adel
Size:	870 square miles (556,879 acres)
Terrain:	Lots of buttes, rolling hills, and gentle valleys, with many big flats interspersed with some major mountain peaks
Elevation Range:	4,390–7,918 feet
Managing Agencies:	Lakeview and Burns Districts BLM
Agency Wilderness Status:	393,605-acre BLM wilderness study area; 89,608 acres recommended (adjacent wilderness in Nevada)
Recreation Map:	South Half Burns District BLM

These grasslands are a long way from anywhere.

For the most part it is classic Basin and Range geology. Both Guano Rim (up to 900 feet high and 12 miles long) and Catlow Rim (up to 1,300 feet high and 15 miles long) are uplifted north-south fault blocks. Both are very pronounced on their west sides and gently give way to valleys to the east. Ancient features such as gravel bars, wave-cut terraces, wave-built terraces, and spits are obvious evidence that a lake existed in Catlow Valley during the Pleistocene epoch.

In between the rims are many ranges of rugged and rolling hills, broad and flat valleys, and relatively deep canyons. Low and high rimrock break up the landscape.

Numerous ephemeral lakebeds are scattered throughout the area, some covered with short vegetation, while others are alkali playas. Very few perennial streams exist.

While much of the geology and landforms of the area are typical, several areas are not.

Lone Mountain north of Hawks Valley stands out. Even from a distance, one is struck by the rock pinnacles of volcanic origin. One can find partially exposed columnar basalt, areas of colorful volcanic soils, and high tablelands incised by rocky draws.

There are very unusual eroded pinnacles in the small draw between the Buck Buttes. One can also find badlands in the area.

Two areas on the northeast side of Long Draw in the Hawk Mountain–Catlow Rim unit contain unique rock formations and include three balanced rocks in one of the more remote draws.

Fish Fin Rim in the northeast corner of the Basque Hills unit is just another rim, but Big Fish Fin is definitely worth seeing. It is easily seen from the road and reached in a 10-minute walk.

While sagebrush—both the common big and low varieties as well as some uncommon ones—dominates the first glance, the relatively undisturbed native bunchgrass in between the sage is a big part of what makes the Oregon Grasslands special. Because of the lack of surface water and/or livestock water developments, much of the area has been either grazed very lightly or not at all.

Vegetative communities found in the Oregon Grasslands include big sagebrush/ Idaho fescue; low sagebrush/Idaho fescue; low sagebrush/Sandberg's bluegrass; silver sagebrush; black sagebrush; bare playa and playa margin; winterfat; mountain mahogany; bitterbrush-sagebrush/snowberry; Indian ricegrass/needlegrass; big sagebrush/creeping wild ryegrass; big sagebrush/Thurber's needlegrass; aspen groves; willow/grass; and mid- to high-level vernal (spring) ponds.

On the northern edge in the Catlow Valley, salt desert scrub species can be found. Shadscale, greasewood, spiny hopsage, Nuttall's salt brush, and Great Basin wildrye are present.

The variety of soil types in certain small areas results in an array of plants not found in such proximity elsewhere in Oregon.

A recently discovered plant species, Crosby's buckwheat (*Erigonum crosbyae*), is testimony that all is not known about the vegetation of the Oregon Desert.

Tree species include scattered stands of mountain mahogany and western juniper. There are also some quaking aspen groves.

There are large numbers of sage grouse throughout the proposed wilderness. The Beatys Butte unit has the largest concentration, where 85 percent of the area is year-round habitat. Surveys in the 1980s found sixteen sage grouse strutting grounds, four containing more than thirty birds each. Eighty percent of sage hens nest within 2 miles of a strutting grounds.

Pronghorn are resident throughout the year. The western portion of the area lies within the migration route of the large pronghorn herd that summers on the Hart Mountain National Wildlife Refuge and often winters on the Sheldon National Wildlife Refuge in Nevada. The area includes crucial pronghorn winter range and spring kidding grounds. Another large herd migrates from Big Springs Table on the Sheldon Refuge to Oregon End Table.

Small mammals include badger, coyote, bobcat, mountain cottontail, porcupine, weasel, marmot, black-tailed jackrabbit, least chipmunk, antelope ground squirrel, kangaroo mouse, Great Basin pocket mouse, canyon mouse, bushy-tailed woodrat, small-footed myotis, and long-eared myotis. It is the northern edge of the range of the northern kit fox. The largest predator inhabiting the area is the cougar.

A rare population of white-tailed jackrabbits may inhabit the Bald Mountain unit. The more common jackrabbit is the black-tailed. White-tailed jackrabbits are more restricted to open grassland and don't do well in shrubby areas. Historically there were pygmy rabbits in the area. There have been no recent sightings.

Much of the area is bighorn sheep habitat, and reintroductions are planned.

Of particular interest is the large concentration of raptors. Excellent nesting and feeding habitat can be found throughout the area. One large concentration, not surprisingly, is at Hawk Mountain. Catlow Rim and other large rims also have dense populations. Species include Swainson's hawk, ferruginous hawk, golden eagle, red-tailed hawk, rough-legged hawk, and prairie falcon. Peregrine falcon may be reintroduced at Hawk Mountain. Migratory waterfowl use some of the surface water (streams and ephemeral lakes) in the spring.

Archaeological and historic sites are scattered throughout the area, including large lithic manufacturing and petroglyph sites.

A portion of the proposed wilderness is included in the Oregon Biodiversity Project's Hart Mountain Conservation Opportunity Area.

Of special note is Hawks Valley. In the 1960s, the Great Society extended even to the Oregon Grasslands. BLM planted a 3,800-acre seeding of crested wheatgrass to "improve" the range. To service it was an elaborate network of water tanks and pipelines. An airstrip was graded in Hawks Valley to make it easier to show off. All this was done to avoid reducing livestock to address overgrazing.

The sagebrush that was scraped off and/or sprayed once again dominates Hawks Valley. Old broken and twisted plastic pipe strewn across the landscape is easier to spot than the airstrip. Livestock are still a problem.

The proposal consists of four units—Bald Mountain, Basque Hills, Beatys Butte, and Hawk Mountain–Catlow Rim—and includes five BLM wilderness study areas: Basque Hills, Hawk Mountain, Rincon, Sage Hen Hills, and Spaulding. The total wilderness is much larger because the area abuts additional wildlands in the Nevada's Sheldon National Wildlife Refuge. The Fish and Wildlife

The Potholes in the Beatys Butte unit of the proposed Oregon Grasslands Wilderness

Service has recommended that Congress designate 277,200 acres as wilderness in eleven units on the Sheldon Refuge. Nevada conservationists are recommending 381,022 acres in ten units of refuge and BLM lands.

19. Beatys Butte Summit (Beatys Butte Unit)

What to Expect:	A relatively easy climb to one of most prominent points in southeast Oregon, with commanding views in all directions
Distance:	6.4 miles round trip
Elevation Range:	5,300–7,918 feet
Drinking Water:	No
Best Times:	Late spring, summer, fall
USGS 7.5' Map:	Beatys Butte
Oregon Map Starting Point:	Adel

Approximately 25 miles east of Adel (0.4 mile east of milepost 53) is a stop sign, just before OR 140 turns south and steeply upward. Go north on the Beatys Butte Road approximately 29 miles to the turnoff to Willow Spring. A house trailer marks the spot. Backtrack 0.3 mile and park on public land. Beatys Butte stands before you 3.2 miles to the south-southeast. The north side of Beatys Butte is a checkerboard ownership of public and private land (so please be extra respectful). The latter is not posted as of this writing.

Return as you came.

20. Lone Mountain (Hawk Mountain–Catlow Rim Unit)

What to Expect:	A maze of volcanic rocks and pinnacles and a pretty juniper canyon
Distance:	3.9-mile loop
Elevation Range:	5,590–6,675 feet
Drinking Water:	Yes
Best Times:	Late spring, summer, fall
USGS 7.5' Map:	Hawk Mountain
Oregon Map Starting Point:	Adel

Drive approximately 37 miles east of OR 140 to milepost 65 (just short of the Sheldon Refuge/Nevada border). Drive first northerly and then northeasterly 8 miles to a major intersection. Continue northeasterly (right) 5.8 miles to another major intersection. Continue east (straight) 0.5 mile to an intersection. Continue easterly 3.6 miles to a major intersection. Continue easterly (straight) 3.5 miles to Moss Waterhole on the south (right) side of the road. Immediately north of Moss Waterhole is the way to Scotts Cache Spring. Park.

Hike 0.8 mile to Scotts Cache Spring (private land). Hike beyond the fence at the spring and into the canyon. In 0.1 mile, you enter a small natural amphitheater. Keep climbing by staying in the main "channel" of the drainage. In the amphitheater, it is the channel to the west.

Keep your course northward. While it may look like you're heading to your end in a box canyon (you've been watching too many Hollywood westerns), there is always a route. As you rise to the gentle bench after another 0.8 mile, you'll see the summit (objective of the hike). Continue your gentle climb northward, gradually turning your course toward the ever-present peak 6675. It is about 0.7 mile. Some scrambling may be necessary. The more of the surface of your body that comes into contact with the surface of the rock, the safer you are. Friction is our friend.

From peak 6675 drop into the canyon above Juniper Spring and hike to Juniper Spring (0.5 mile). Hike the way 1 mile back toward the Hawks Valley Road and your vehicle.

21. The Potholes (Beatys Butte Unit)

What to Expect:	Petroglyphs, standing water in summer, and waterfowl
Distance:	15.6-mile loop/round trip
Elevation Range:	5,613–5,880 feet
Drinking Water:	Yes
Best Times:	Late spring, fall
USGS 7.5' Maps:	Chimney Rock, Rocky Canyon, Sage Hen Flat
Oregon Map Starting Point:	Adel

Drive east approximately 25 miles on OR 140 (0.4 mile east of milepost 53) to a stop sign, just before the highway turns south and steeply upward. Go northerly on the Beatys Butte Road 10.8 miles until you see a very primitive unimproved way off to the southeast (you're going north). (If you don't see it—it may have a small cairn, but don't count on it—and have reached a major intersection with a sign to Spaulding Reservoir, retrace your route 2.6 miles.) Park here.

Hike southeast (Rocky Canyon quad) on the way for 1.7 miles across the flat to Guano Rim. If you are backpacking, you may want to make camp at the base of the rim in the sandy flat. The next decent camping spot is The Potholes.

At the rim, the way turns into a jeep trail. Follow said jeep route 5.5 miles to the Sage Hen Canyon (Sage Hen Flats quad, after crossing Chimney Rock quad). Petroglyphs can be seen on many rims, especially next to an old cabin.

To see Indian Caves, tinajas (rocks with smooth holes in them formed by the water working little pebbles in a circle), and petroglyphs, explore The Potholes upstream 1.2 miles to a way crossing. Hike this way 1 mile northwesterly back to the cairn on the rim above the cabin. From here, retrace your steps on the jeep trail 2.1 miles to a very faint way that heads west 0.2 mile to an often dry lakebed (Rocky Canyon quad, after crossing Chimney Rock quad). Continue westward across or around the lakebed, to another sometimes dry lakebed, and then westward to a break in Guano Rim called Wagonslide (1.6 miles). From Wagonslide, head northerly to your camp at the base of the rim, or cross-country to your vehicle (3.3 miles).

PRONGHORN WILDERNESS (PROPOSED)

One of the largest concentrations of pronghorn in Oregon.

Location:	Harney and Lake Counties, 15 miles east-southeast of Adel
Size:	436 square miles (279,039 acres)
Terrain:	Huge gentle flats and gently rolling hills dissected by the occasional canyon and dotted with ephemeral lakes
Elevation Range:	4,586–6,185 feet
Managing Agencies:	Fish and Wildlife Service (Hart Mountain National Wildlife Refuge; some current and more proposed) and Lakeview and Burns Districts BLM (some current and less proposed)
Agency Wilderness Status:	10,350-acre wilderness study area; 0 acres recommended
Recreation Maps:	Southeast Quarter, South Half Lakeview Resource Area, Lakeview District BLM; South Half Burns District BLM

Situated on the eastern portion of the Hart Mountain National Wildlife Refuge and continuing east toward Beatys Butte and the Catlow Valley and south toward the Sheldon National Wildlife Refuge, the proposed wilderness is part of the critically important "biological unit" for the Hart Mountain–Sheldon pronghorn herd (see Hart Mountain National Wildlife Refuge Additions). It is also part of the Oregon Biodiversity Project's Hart Mountain Conservation Opportunity Area.

Most of the area is a classic sagebrush steppe ecosystem with big and low sagebrush/grasslands communities dominating the landscape. Juniper is found at higher elevations. Riparian vegetation is found along the few streams, such as Guano Creek and Guano Slough in Black Canyon. Water is usually seasonally available at several sink lakes.

Crosby's buckwheat (Erigonum crosbyae), a recently discovered species, is found on a unique soil type. This species is known to exist at only two Oregon locations.

A bit of badlands topography can be found in the lower Guano Creek area.

Raptor habitat is found in the rims and canyon edges along streams. Besides being critical habitat for the pronghorn herd, the area supports mule deer and, increasingly, Rocky Mountain elk. Canada geese and other waterfowl use the numerous ephemeral lakes. Sage grouse are also found in good numbers.

Pronghorn in the proposed Pronghorn Wilderness

The Sheldon tui chub is found in Guano Creek. Its most secure (continuously wet) habitat is on the Sheldon Refuge in Nevada. At times of high water in the Guano Creek system all the chub habitat is connected. The area includes the BLM's Guano Creek Wilderness Study Area.

22. Guano Creek

What to Expect:	A pleasant hike and swim in a desert canyon with running water and willow trees and perhaps seeing the Sheldon tui chub
Distance:	4 miles round trip
Elevation Range:	5,220–5,410 feet
Drinking Water:	Yes
Best Times:	Spring, summer, fall
USGS 7.5' Maps:	Alger Lake, Guano Lake
Oregon Map Starting Point:	Adel

Drive approximately 28 miles to an intersection with a stop sign (0.6 mile east of milepost 49). (Don't sucker for the sign to Guano Lake 1 mile west.) Drive northerly approximately 12 miles to the Shirk Ranch, keeping the Guano Valley and Guano Lake to your east and the low hills and rims to your west. North 0.8 mile from an intersection at some abandoned buildings is an unimproved way to the northwest. Park.

Begin hiking (Guano Lake quad) on the old way, which turns into a jeep trail (Alger Lake quad). Follow the jeep trail to the end and hike down into Guano Creek Canyon. Hike down the creek until intersecting a jeep trail. Return as you came.

PUEBLO MOUNTAINS WILDERNESS (PROPOSED)

A fascinating mix of scenery, geology, vegetation, and wildlife.

Location:	Harney County, 10 miles southeast of Fields
Size:	134 square miles (86,010 acres)
Terrain:	Deeply incised high mountain ridges and steep escarpments with a massive tilt
Elevation Range:	4,200–8,630 feet
Managing Agency:	Burns District BLM
Agency Wilderness Status:	72,090-acre BLM wilderness study area; 25,550 acres recommended (additional wilderness in Nevada)
Recreation Map:	South Half Burns District BLM

The geology is spectacular. The main ridgeline of the Pueblo Range and Pueblo Peak itself rise majestically above the valley floor and include metamorphic outcrops that are the oldest rock in southeast Oregon. The range has an enormous westward tilt along its 15 miles of ridgeline that has an average elevation of 7,300 feet.

Water is plentiful. Several streams dissect the area, including some with water-falls, including one 30 to 40 feet high.

Plant species diversity is uncommonly high for southeast Oregon. Twenty-three plants of special concern are found here in several interesting vegetative communities.

The dominant vegetation is big sagebrush overstory with bluebunch wheat-grass, Idaho fescue, Thurber's needlegrass, and bottlebrush squirreltail in the understory. Low sage can also be found.

A mixed shrub community on open slopes of the foothills features big sage-brush, budsage, shadscale, spiny hopsage, gray and green rabbit-brush, Nevada and green Mormon tea, shrubby buckwheat, winterfat, bitterbrush, purple sage, and little leaf horsebrush.

The higher, rockier talus and outcrops host land oceanspray and mountain snowberry.

Mountain mahogany and quaking aspen are found at higher elevations. Alder, narrowleaf cottonwood, willow, wild rose, and chokecherry occur along the creeks and near springs. Juniper is very rare, with only about ten trees having been sighted.

Alpine wetlands support iris, desert lilies, and marsh marigolds.

Wildflowers are in abundance, including waterleaf phacelia, agoseris, balsamroot, blue and yellow violets, Indian paintbrush, tiny stonecrop, and alpine saxifrage. Miniature pink carpets of filaree cling to the hillsides. Nodding melic, thick-leaved phacelia, two-stemmed onion, and red buttercup are of special concern.

The northern edge of the range of Mormon tea (a natural source of the noncaffeine stimulant ephedrine) is found here. The narrowleaf cottonwood/Mormon tea community is an ecosystem unique for Oregon.

The wildlife is an interesting mix as well.

Bighorn sheep were reintroduced in the 1980s and have thrived in the prime and secluded habitat. The interspersion of water, forage, and thermal cover provides good habitat for both mule deer and pronghorn.

Eighty species of birds, including a large variety of songbirds and raptors, have been recorded. The Pueblo Valley to the east is on a migratory bird flyway. Sage grouse, mourning dove, and valley quail are abundant.

Reptile species are also abundant and include the rare collared lizard.

Fish species include the redband trout and Alvord chub.

Other mammals include elk, beaver, fox, badger, porcupine, coyote, bobcat, mountain cottontail rabbit, black-tailed jackrabbit, bushy-tailed woodrat, canyon mouse, deer mouse, and the long-eared myotis. Cougar may also be present.

Lest we forget the invertebrates, the rare Riding's satyr butterfly (*Neominois ringsii*) has been reported.

The Desert Trail traverses the area (see Appendix E).

Pueblo Range in the proposed Pueblo Mountains wilderness

23. Pueblo Peak

What to Expect:	Great views of the Alvord Basin, Alvord Desert, Steens Mountain, Sheepshead Mountains, Trout Creek Mountains, and Pine Forest Range from the second highest point in southeast Oregon
Distance:	16 miles round trip
Elevation Range:	4,300–8,630 feet
Drinking Water:	Yes
Best Times:	Summer, fall
USGS 7.5' Maps:	Ladycomb Peak, Tum Tum Lake, Van Horn Basin
Oregon Map Starting Point:	Fields

Drive 8 miles south on OR 205 to the Whitehorse County Road. Continue south on OR 205 0.8 mile to an unimproved way to the west. Drive 0.2 mile across flat and park.

Hike (Tum Tum Lake quad) 4.9 miles up the unimproved way to the headwaters of Arizona Creek (Ladycomb Peak quad), crossing over to the headwaters of Cottonwood Creek and then south into Stergen Meadows. Campsites and springs are plentiful at Ten Cent Meadows to the south at the head of the Van Horn Basin. Climbing Pueblo Peak via the north shoulder is the least steep.

Return the way you came.

SHEEPSHEAD MOUNTAINS WILDERNESS (PROPOSED)

Many more people know of them than have been to them.

Location:	Harney and Malheur Counties, 10 miles west of Burns Junction
Size:	401 square miles (257,120 acres)
Terrain:	Mostly mountainous with some wide flats
Elevation Range:	3,920–6,294 feet
Managing Agencies:	Burns and Vale Districts BLM
Agency Wilderness Status:	245,167-acre BLM wilderness study area; 139,447 acres recommended
Recreation Maps:	South Half Burns District BLM; North Half Jordan Resource Area, Vale District BLM

The Sheepshead Mountains are mostly known to people who drive by them on their way elsewhere.

Looking south across the proposed Sheepshead Mountains Wilderness

The area has diverse topography: steep-faced ridgelines, plateaus, rolling hills, broad and gentle fans, low basins, and playa lakebeds. The views are terrific, especially from the summits, including incomparable views of Steens Mountain.

Vegetation is predominantly big sagebrush, low sagebrush, and salt desert scrub communities. A total of seven juniper trees have been counted.

The Oregon Biodiversity Project has included the Sheepsheads in their Crooked Creek–Alvord Basin Conservation Opportunity Area: "[T]he areas around the Sheepshead Mountains contain extensive areas of playa, salt desert scrub, and sand dune habitats. They provide habitat for several at-risk endemic fish species and a variety of reptiles, small mammals and insects."[8]

The area is crucial winter range for pronghorn and great habitat for bighorn sheep. It is also northern kit fox habitat.

The Mickey Basin has an abundance of springs, seeps, and wet meadows and contains species not found over most of the rest of this area. Common species include Townsend's pocket gopher, montane meadow mouse, common snipe, and killdeer. The playa is occasionally flooded during spring and is used by migrating waterfowl and shorebirds. Long-eared owls nest in buffalo berry found near springs.

Four plant species of special concern are found in the area. Cactus grows on Mickey Butte.

This proposal consists of six BLM wilderness study areas: Heath Lake, Palomino Hills, Sheepshead Mountain, Table Mountain, West Peak, and Wildcat Mountain.

24. Mickey Basin and Mickey Butte

What to Expect:	A wet oasis and the highest point in the range
Distance:	9-mile loop
Elevation Range:	3,920–6,294 feet
Drinking Water:	In Mickey Basin
Best Times:	Spring, fall
USGS 7.5' Maps:	Coffin Butte, Mickey Springs
Oregon Map Starting Point:	New Princeton

Drive 32 miles southeasterly on OR 78. Turn southwesterly on the Andrews–Folly Farm County Road. In approximately 26 miles, but precisely where the road begins a 90-degree turn to the west, head easterly 8.6 miles (past Mickey Hot Spring—see Steens Mountain National Conservation Area) and park at the intersection.

Hike (Mickey Springs quad) into the 4-mile-long depression that is Mickey Basin, exploring any springs, wet areas, and ruins that you fancy (also Coffin Butte quad). To get a workout and some great views, begin your climb of Mickey Butte at the middle of Mickey Basin's western edge. Walk up the lower part of the ridge that leads to the summit. Return as you came.

SHIFTING SAND DUNES WILDERNESS (PROPOSED)

The most unique addition possible to Oregon's wilderness system.

Location:	Lake County, 15 miles east-northeast of Christmas Valley
Size:	25 square miles (16,518 acres)
Terrain:	Mostly open sand and flats with a few minor hills
Elevation Range:	4,290–4,478 feet
Managing Agencies:	Lakeview District BLM (present); National Park Service (proposed)
Agency Wilderness Status:	16,440-acre BLM wilderness study area; 0 acres recommended
Recreation Map:	Northwest and Northeast Quarters, Lakeview Resource Area, Lakeview District BLM

Some ecosystems don't get any respect.

The area contains the largest inland moving sand dune system in Oregon, and possibly the Pacific Northwest. The dunes—because of the resulting hydrologic and soil conditions—are critical to the preservation of the adjacent Lost Forest, a disjunct stand of ponderosa pine, in a place where low rainfall alone would normally prohibit any forest from growing. (See Lost Forest–Shifting Sand Dunes National Monument.)

The proposed wilderness is more than just open sand. Because of the edge effect created between the sand, sagebrush, and forest, the area is excellent wildlife habitat. Predators with limited range in the desert, such as the cougar and bobcat, are found here. So too is the badger. Small mammals include the black-tailed mountain hare (jackrabbit), pygmy rabbit, least and yellow pine chipmunks, Townsend's and golden-mantled ground squirrels, and the northern grasshopper mouse. Bird species include the American avocet, sage thrasher, sapsucker, mountain bluebird, prairie falcon, and golden eagle. A large number of reptile species are also present.

Wildflower species include the sand lily, hairy evening primrose, paintbrush, and specklepod milk-vetch.

The seemingly endless combinations of form and light are remarkable. The solitude is outstanding. The shifting sand dunes encourages contemplation—when the all-terrain vehicles are not roaring around you.

Only small portions of this dunes system are closed to vehicles. Aesthetically and geologically, they are the least interesting. The most spectacular dunes are open to—and sometimes crawling with—off-road vehicles. Eight thousand people visit the sand dunes annually, the large majority of whom do so with an engine roaring in their ears.

Despite legal restrictions, vehicles routinely violate the Lost Forest Research Natural Area and other vehicle closures.

The proposed Shifting Sand Dunes Wilderness with Lost Forest at back

The dunes cover both paleontological and archaeological sites that can be uncovered by the wind. On such occasions, because of the motorized use, no protection exists for the fossil beds and lithic sites.

25. Nothing But Sand

What to Expect:	Sand dunes
Distance:	3-mile loop
Elevation Range:	4,303–4,360 feet
Drinking Water:	No
Best Times:	Winter, spring, summer, fall (but not on a weekend, especially the 3-day variety)
USGS 7.5' Map:	Fossil Lake
Oregon Map Starting Point:	Christmas Valley

Drive 2 miles due east, turn north on Lake County Road 5-14C, and follow the signs to the Lost Forest and/or Sand Dunes. In about 16 miles you'll be headed due east and cross under a high-tension powerline. Further east 5.1 miles is an unimproved way to the south (right). Park here.

Hike (Fossil Lake quad) southward through a little island of western juniper, into the open and soon onto the sand. Hike south and range east or west as far as you like.

If you catch the often-high afternoon winds, you'll really feel alone.

When it is time to leave, walk northerly in the direction you think your vehicle is. If you miss, you'll soon hit the east-west road you came in on.

STEENS MOUNTAIN NATIONAL CONSERVATION AREA (PROPOSED)

An ecological island in the sky.

Location:	Harney County, 60 miles south-southeast of Burns
Size:	1,221 square miles (903,759 acres)
Terrain:	A massive fault-block range, sculpted by Pleistocene glaciers and carved by streams with vast flats to the leeward
Elevation Range:	4,015–9,773 feet
Managing Agency:	Burns District BLM
Recreation Maps:	South Half Burns District BLM; Northeast Quarter, North Half Burns District BLM

Steens Mountain is a sky island. Rising over a mile above the surrounding landscape, the massive fault-block range makes its own precipitation. The result, according to the Oregon Biodiversity Project, is "some of the most ecologically diverse landscapes in the Basin and Range Ecoregion."

Steens Mountain is a glaciated fault block of uplifted volcanics that has had significant erosion, the evidence of which is equally obvious and beautiful.

Topographically, Steens Mountain can be divided into three major zones separated by cross faults (it was too big to rise as one): North Steens, High Steens, and South Steens. High Steens towers 2,000 feet above the others. All part of one large fault-block range, it slopes west, either to the Catlow Rim at the edge of the Catlow Valley in the south or to the Blitzen Valley in the north.

To the east on its leeward side, Steens Mountain casts a huge rain shadow across the Alvord Desert country—as ecologically interesting as Steens Mountain, though in very different ways.

"The Alvord Basin . . . contain(s) extensive areas of playa, salt desert scrub, and sand dune habitats. They provide habitat for several at-risk endemic fish species and a variety of reptiles, small mammals and insects," notes the Oregon Biodiversity Project.[9]

A story of Steens Mountain can be told through its vegetation.

The first chapter starts at the Catlow and Blitzen Valleys, at the Arid Sagebrush Zone, which is dominated by both big and low sagebrush, with only the occasional western juniper thrown in. The elevation band is 4,200 to 5,500 feet.

As elevation increases, so does precipitation. The next band is the Western Juniper Zone (5,000–6,000 feet). You'll still see sagebrush, but the juniper is dominant.

As elevation increases, so too does the harshness of the seasons. The Mountain Mahogany Zone (6,000–8,000 feet) is named for a species that favors poor soils and rocky ridges, so its occurrence is scattered.

The fourth zone is sagebrush again, only this time it is the Mountain Big Sagebrush Zone (6,500–8,500 feet). This species of sagebrush may reach 2 to 3 feet in height. In this zone you'll see an abundance of wildflowers during the spring and summer.

Notice the overlap in elevation ranges. This reflects other factors coming into play, such as soil depth and type, slope, aspect, and so forth. Nature is rarely discretely packaged.

Steens Mountain is unusual in that timber line is defined by nonconiferous species. (Isolated white fir trees and stands can be found on the mountain, but they are relics from a far different time.) The Quaking Aspen Zone (6,000–8,000 feet) is perhaps the most colorful zone. In the fall the leaves clothe the mountain in a crimson and gold mantle.

Ever upward and onward, the sixth band is the Subalpine Meadow Zone (7,000–8,400 feet), the meadows of which are found below large snowdrifts and along streams. Wildflowers dominate the view.

The next band is the Snow Cover Zone (8,000–9,700 feet). Drifts of snow remain until late summer. The soils—if they exist at all—are quite shallow and rocky. Vegetation is limited to colorful herbs.

Finally is the Subalpine Grassland Zone (9,000–9,700 feet). These grasslands are found where snow doesn't usually accumulate and the soil is very rocky. It is too harsh for shrubs, and other vegetation rarely exceeds a half foot in height.

These first eight zones are spread across a horizontal distance of 20 to 25 miles on the west slope of Steens. The next seven chapters are repeats of the first seven, though in reverse order and in a very compressed form. On the east face of Steens Mountain, the horizontal distance from the summit to the Alvord Desert Playa is 4 to 5 miles, five times as steep as the west side. Given this steepness, the manifestations of some of the zones are very scattered. Obviously, stream character is also extremely different than on the more gentle slopes of the west side.

The remaining three chapters of the story are not on Steens Mountain proper, but within its massive rain shadow to the leeward east. Coming down off the alluvial fans that support the Arid Sagebrush Zone, we now can see the Salt Desert Scrub Zone (3,900–4,200 feet). Because of the alkali and often coarse sandy soils, shadscale and greasewood are the dominate species.

In the same elevation band, but distinctly unique, is the Playa Zone. These large barren playas are sinks that fill with water in the winter and are mostly bone-dry in the summer.

Often to the east of the playas—due to the prevailing westerly winds—is a Sand Dune Zone. Some dunes are very open, others somewhat vegetated with salt desert scrub and big sagebrush.

As the elevation rises—perhaps as little as 20 feet—to the east, one starts to see a return of the Arid Sagebrush Zone. Along a rim, where soil and moisture accumulate in cracks, the western juniper can again be seen.

This story is not complete without sidebars. Where cold springs exist, so do oases. The Steens fault created several hot springs in the Alvord Desert, all of which have their ecological uniqueness. Certain areas have almost pure stands of winterfat (a very nutritious shrub) or Great Basin wildrye. Several rare plants are associated with the alkali soils.

Quaking aspen groves in the proposed Steens Mountain National Conservation Area

A diversity of vegetation on Steens Mountain means a diversity of wildlife. Most species associated with the Great Basin are here, as well as several more associated with mountainous forests. "Large portions of the area have barely been touched by development, and the area provides important habitat for a wide variety of wildlife, ranging from migratory birds and big game to rare and endangered mammals and fish," says the Oregon Biodiversity Project about the Steens Mountain Conservation Opportunity Area.[10] For example, the only populations of northern water shrew in eastern Oregon and pika in southeast Oregon exist on Steens Mountain. A subspecies of tiger beetle is found only on Steens, as are certain species of ants.

The riparian areas of Steens Mountain are a stronghold for redband trout, a species in serious decline. The mountain is also a haven for bighorn sheep, a species in serious recovery.

One species, no longer present, was the grizzly bear.

WHAT TO DO

Most people first experience Steens Mountain by driving the North Loop Road from Frenchglen to the summit. The road is usually open after the Fourth of July, but check with the Burns District BLM. It is about 30 miles to the summit. Take all day, explore Whorehouse Meadows (below), take in all the overlooks (each one is different). Walking 1/4 mile in any direction from along the loop road will yield you solitude. If you do take the hike (especially to the summit), remember the thinner air.

Most return the way they came, as the south Steens Mountain Loop Road is harder on vehicles. It is about as far back to Frenchglen, but it will be much slower.

Perhaps the Steens Mountain Loop Road should be called the Inner Loop. The Outer Loop circumnavigates the entire mountain.

Starting at the Diamond turnoff between mileposts 40 and 41 on OR 205 (measured from OR 78 near Burns), go east to Diamond (BLM has a brochure for the Diamond Loop National Backcountry Byway) and to Diamond Craters (see Diamond Craters National Monument) and Diamond. Continue northward to New Princeton and turn southeast on OR 78. In 32 miles turn southwesterly on the Andrews–Folly Farm County Road.

Where the county road bends 90 degrees to the west, go easterly 6 miles to Mickey Hot Springs (210 degrees Fahrenheit). The road goes just south of Mickey Butte (see exploration in Sheepshead Mountains Wilderness). Sometimes a tiny geyser is present; at all times the mud is boiling and steam is venting. Keep dogs on leash as many a canine has met a scalding end by jumping into the inviting, but deadly pools. These hot springs are not for soaking.

Back at the county road, go about 8 miles to Pike Creek (see exploration in Steens Mountain Wilderness). Note the juniper growing out of the huge boulder. Primitive campsites are plentiful both on some private land on the creek and on public land up the hill.

Continue southward on the county road from the turnoff to Pike Creek about 2 miles and take a bath at Alvord Hot Springs (the tin shack in the meadow east of the road). Don't let the bullet holes bother you, though some came in and some went out. These springs are on private land but are open to the public.

If you didn't walk out to the Alvord Desert playa during the last stop, then take the dirt way down to the playa's edge 2.5 miles south of Alvord Hot Springs. There is fresh water (untested) at Frog Spring. (See Alvord Desert exploration in Alvord Wilderness.)

At the intersection 1 mile north of Fields, hearty souls with hearty vehicles can take the powerline road east-northeast 2.1 miles and turn northerly on the first prominent way. In 1.8 miles you come the site of the first official Twenty Mule Team borax mine. More interesting is Borax Lake, home of the Borax Lake chub. Belly crawl up to the lake shore and you'll likely see some of the diminutive fish. The row of hot springs a ½ mile north of the lake is worth the walk. Borax Lake and vicinity is owned by The Nature Conservancy.

After Fields (best chocolate malts for hundreds of miles), pick up OR 205 westward through Long Hollow to the Catlow Valley, coming through a break in the Catlow Rim. Head northward past Home Creek (see exploration in Steens Mountain Wilderness) and past the Roaring Springs Ranch and the South Steens Mountain Loop turnoff and on to Frenchglen (best food and drink in Harney County). About 20 miles north of Frenchglen is where you started.

The elapsed distance is about 250 miles. It can be done in one day, but passengers may get quite cranky. Camp along the way to fully enjoy.

The Desert Trail traverses the area (see Appendix D).

26. Whorehouse Meadows

What to Expect:	Luscious mountain meadows and sensuous aspen groves
Distance:	4-mile loop
Elevation Range:	7,200–7,600 feet
Drinking Water:	Yes
Best Times:	Summer, fall
USGS 7.5' Map:	Fish Lake
Oregon Map Starting Point:	Frenchglen

Approximately 17 miles up the North Steens Mountain Loop Road from Frenchglen is the turnoff into Fish Lake Campground. Just 0.4 mile beyond the campground, as the road crosses a flat, and to the east, is Whorehouse Meadows. The meadows are privately owned. Traditionally, the owners have not sought to prevent public enjoyment. Park where safe. There is no set hike route. It is open meadows; just let yourself be drawn in.

The ladies and their house (actually camp wagons and tents) are long gone, having serviced sheepherders and other pioneers. In a prudish fit—from which they've both since recovered—BLM and the U.S. Geological Survey unilaterally changed the name to "Naughty Girl Meadows." The public furor caused the U.S. Board of Geographic Names to find for history and honesty. The "current" 1968 Fish Lake quad has the blasphemous aberration, but newer maps have it right.

Hike east to the head of McCoy Creek (Wildhorse Lake quad), where you may find evidence of beaver. Take your favorite lunch, libation, and lover.

STEENS MOUNTAIN WILDERNESS (PROPOSED)

The most diverse wildland in the Oregon Desert.

Location:	Harney County, 60 miles south-southeast of Burns
Size:	956 square miles (612,021 acres)
Terrain:	Rugged glacial cirques, precipitous rims, gently sloping plateaus, and deep river canyons
Elevation Range:	4,015–9,773 feet
Managing Agency:	Burns District BLM
Agency Wilderness Status:	257,390-acre BLM wilderness study area; 81,125 acres recommended
Recreation Maps:	South Half Burns District BLM; Northeast Quarter, North Half Burns District BLM

The proposed Steens Mountain Wilderness includes terrain from all parts of Steens Mountain. (For discussions of the topography, vegetation, and wildlife, please see the Steens Mountain National Conservation Area.)

Three units comprise the proposed wilderness: Alvord Peak, High Steens, and Little Blitzen.

Alvord Peak Unit

In the south Steens, the Alvord Peak unit is among the least visited portion of Steens Mountain. It is a series of ten volcanic peaks, the highest of which is Alvord Peak.

High Steens Unit and Little Blitzen Units

The Little Blitzen unit is separated from the High Steens unit by the Steens Mountain Loop Road. Its character, vegetation, wildlife, and other wilderness values are typical of the High Steens unit, which surrounds it on three sides.

These two units range from the highest to the lowest points on Steens Mountain and include some of the south Steens, much of the north Steens, and all of the high Steens, save the roads.

In the north Steens, most notable are the steep escarpments of the east face, with their variety of color. Moving westward, one finds rolling hills, canyons, and flat basins with small intermittent lakes.

In the high Steens, the rims still dominate, but Pleistocene glaciers came into play. Glacial cirques, talus slopes, hanging lakes (tarns), ponds and streams, and high-elevation fescue grasslands are great for wildlife. The High Steens unit contains much of the Catlow Rim, recognized for its high density of nesting raptors.

Big Indian Gorge in the proposed Steens Mountain Wilderness

The High Steens unit contains seven BLM wilderness study areas: Blitzen River, High Steens, Home Creek, Little Blitzen Gorge, Lower Stonehouse, South Fork Donner und Blitzen, and Stonehouse.

The Desert Trail traverses the area (see Appendix D).

27. Alvord Peak Summit (Alvord Peak Unit)

What to Expect:	Rugged volcanic peaks and bighorn sheep
Distance:	6.8-mile loop
Elevation Range:	4,145–7,132 feet
Drinking Water:	Yes
Best Times:	Summer, fall
USGS 7.5' Map:	Fields
Oregon Map Starting Point:	Fields

Go 1 mile north on OR 205 to the intersection with the Andrews–Folly Farm County Road. Proceed north 2.3 miles to an unimproved way that heads westerly. Park.

Walk the way 1.8 miles to Burke Spring. From Burke Spring climb steeply to "The Peaks." If you are backpacking, a little bench just north of Alvord Peak has water and can serve as camp. Hike the eastside of Alvord Peak to Buckwilder Pass, then down to the spring 1 mile east of Alvord Peak, and finally cross-country back to your vehicle.

28. Bridge Creek (High Steens Unit)

What to Expect:	Deep and colorful canyons dissecting a broad plateau
Distance:	8- or 10.1- mile loop
Elevation Range:	4,200–5,040 feet
Drinking Water:	Yes
Best Times:	Spring, fall
USGS 7.5' Map:	Page Springs
Oregon Map Starting Point:	Frenchglen

Drive easterly 3 miles from OR 205 toward Page Springs Campground. After crossing the Donner und Blitzen turn north onto the East Canal Road (west of East Canal). If this refuge road is open, drive 2.2 miles and park. (If not, park and walk 2.2 miles to a point near the mouth of Bridge Creek.) Cross the canal (head gates provide dry-footed crossings) and hike into Bridge Creek Canyon. Fisherpeople and game trails exist for a while. At 3.4 miles into the canyon, a break in the south rim with a usually dry stream channel is your escape route to the rim. Other earlier escapes are possible if you get tired of hiking in the canyon (or over those very large fields of very large boulders). Set a course back to your vehicle.

29. Home Creek Butte (High Steens Unit)

What to Expect:	Bighorn sheep in the spring, great views, and ancient junipers anytime
Distance:	6.2 miles round trip
Elevation Range:	4,605–6,006 feet
Drinking Water:	No
Best Times:	Spring, fall
USGS 7.5' Map:	Home Creek Butte
Oregon Map Starting Point:	Frenchglen

Drive approximately 24 miles south of Frenchglen on OR 205 (8 miles south of Roaring Springs Ranch). Park at Home Creek Canyon, the obvious break in the Catlow Rim.

Two hikes exist. The first option is a mile or so of good birding and scenery and possibly seeing some bighorn sheep from below on an easy former cattle trail on the north side of the creek. Follow the old irrigation ditch that turns into the trail. Great Basin redband trout may be seen in the creek.

It is possible to continue up the creek to the destination of the second option, but it is not recommended without a guide (seriously).

The second option is to hike directly up the north side of Catlow Rim where it breaks for Home Creek. (Yes, it is 1,401 feet in 0.8 mile, but it is at the beginning of the hike.) The ultimate objective is Home Creek Butte 2.3 miles by rim to the east. After reaching the plateau, slowly and quietly work your way along the north rim of Home Creek. Keep looking down, and if it is April or May, you'll almost undoubtedly see bighorn sheep, including lambs.

Return the way you came.

30. Little Blitzen River (Little Blitzen Unit)

What to Expect:	A gentle glacial valley in the high Steens and outstanding near-summit views
Distance:	17.8 miles round trip
Elevation Range:	5,300–9,100 feet
Drinking Water:	Yes
Best Times:	Summer, fall
USGS 7.5' Maps:	Fish Lake, Wildhorse Lake
Oregon Map Starting Point:	Frenchglen

Go 10 miles south of Frenchglen on OR 205. Turn east onto the South Steens Mountain Loop Road. At approximately 20 miles is South Steens Campground. East of the campground entrance 0.2 mile is a parking area on the south side of the loop road.

Farther east 0.2 mile is a BLM sign noting a trail starting on the north side of the road by a big boulder. Follow the trail 0.6 mile to cross the Little Blitzen River (Fish Lake quad). Pick up a very nice trail on the north side of the river. Approximately 7 miles upriver a major tributary enters through a break in the north rim (Wildhorse Lake quad). Camping is nice.

You have two options. The first is continue upriver into the glacial cirque for 2 miles and 1,000 feet elevation gain. The second is to hike the next day 3 miles to the east rim of Steens Mountain. This elevation gain is 2,300 feet, but the views and the exaltation are worth it!

Start early up the west side of the creek. It gets less steep in about a mile (don't miss the waterfall). Hike your way eastward to the point where Kiger Gorge cuts into the Steens Mountain rim (you do have to cross the South Steens Mountain Loop Road). A great place for lunch.

Return to camp and hike out the next day.

31. Pike Creek (High Steens Unit)

What to Expect:	A rugged canyon on the east face of the Steens
Distance:	4 miles round trip
Elevation Range:	4,800–6,102 feet
Drinking Water:	Yes
Best Times:	Spring, summer, fall
USGS 7.5' Map:	Alvord Hot Springs
Oregon Map Starting Point:	Andrews

Drive approximately 10 miles north of Andrews on the Andrews–Folly Farm County Road. At the Alvord Hot Springs (the tin shack in the meadow east of the road) go 1.8 miles and turn westward onto an unimproved way. After 0.8 mile, park 50 yards north of the rock with a juniper growing out it. Several good car campsites, both on private lands near the creek and uphill on public land, are available.

Begin your hike by walking the old mining "road" on the south side of the creek. The "road" (though not shown on the quad map) crosses the creek and continues uphill. On north side, the "road" goes consistently up, then a little bit of down, then up, and then down under a large boulder, beyond which is a path taking off uphill, marked with use. The trail moves ever upward into the head-waters of Pike Creek. Eventually you'll be cross-country hiking. An objective is the rocky point (elevation 6,102 feet) between the two major forks of Pike Creek. It is rough, but doable.

Return as you came.

TROUT CREEK MOUNTAINS WILDERNESS (PROPOSED)

Two ranges of desert mountains with deeply incised canyons and stands of aspen and willow among the sagebrush and plentiful water.

Location:	Harney and Malheur Counties, 20 miles east of Fields
Size:	412 square miles (263,799 acres)
Terrain:	Gentle plateaus dissected by very steep and rugged canyons
Elevation Range:	4,230–8,264 feet
Managing Agencies:	Burns and Vale Districts BLM
Agency Wilderness Status:	217,330-acre BLM wilderness study area; 164,070 acres recommended (additional wilderness in Nevada)
Recreation Maps:	South Half Jordan Resource Area, Vale District BLM; South Half Burns District BLM

The topography ranges from the nearly flat to the nearly vertical. Rugged and dramatic canyons (often in excess of 1,000 feet), scree and talus slopes, extensive spires and badlands, high plateaus, distinctive buttes, and broad valleys all combine to make a terrain that is as diverse as the views are striking.

The area actually consists of two major mountain ranges: Trout Creek Mountains and Oregon Canyon Mountains. Little Whitehorse Creek, which coincidentally and generally parallels the Harney-Malheur county line, separates the ranges.

According to the Oregon Biodiversity Project, "This remote area has a number of features that are priorities for conservation: high-quality streams, woody riparian habitats, and significant aspen and mountain mahogany woodlands. The area also supports a half-dozen at-risk plant species."[11] The diverse array of habitats supports over 225 species of plants.

Tree species include quaking aspen, willow, thin leaf alder, black cottonwood, bittercherry, and common chokecherry. Pockets of curlleaf mountain mahogany abound in higher areas. Western junipers grow below rims.

Plant communities include big sagebrush/bluebunch wheatgrass, low sagebrush/bluebunch wheatgrass, low sagebrush/Idaho fescue, and mountain mahogany types. In the lower and much drier elevations to the west in the Pueblo

Endangered Lahontan cutthroat trout in Willow Creek within the proposed Trout Creek Mountains Wilderness

Valley, desert shrub species predominate, such as shadscale, bud sage, and spiny hopsage. Big sagebrush (sometimes 8 to 10 feet tall) is found in the lower elevations and deeper soils, and dwarf sage is at higher elevations. Also present is the rare three-tip sage (*Artemisia tripartita*).

"The Trout Creek Mountains include some of the most outstanding and diverse desert wildlife habitat in Oregon," notes the Oregon Biodiversity Project. "Lahontan cutthroat trout populations represent two of the last genetically pure strains of native trout in the Pacific Northwest."[12]

The Willow/Whitehorse trout is a unique and very endangered species. The Trout Creek Mountains are the northern extent of the range of the Lahontan redside shiner.

When the Fish and Wildlife Service listed the Lahontan cutthroat trout as a threatened species under the Endangered Species Act, it didn't know that some were Oregonians. Native populations exist in the Sage Creek and Line Canyon drainages.

Bighorn sheep were successfully reintroduced into the Oregon Canyon Mountains in 1987. Both mountain ranges provide some of the best-quality mule deer habitat in Malheur County. Pronghorn are also present in large numbers.

Beaver can be found in most streams. The northern kit fox may inhabit the desert scrub in the western edge of the area. Large numbers of sage grouse can be found summering and nesting at the higher elevations and wintering at the lower elevations. Raptors on the large cliff faces are common as are songbirds in riparian areas. Cougar and bobcat—species with restricted ranges in the desert—are notable predators.

Cultural inventories have discovered over one hundred archaeological sites documenting use for the last seven thousand years by Northern Paiute Indians.

The proposal is in two units (Oregon Canyon Mountains and Trout Creek) and includes seven BLM wilderness study areas: Disaster Peak, Fifteenmile Creek, Mahogany Ridge, Oregon Canyon, Red Mountain, Twelvemile Creek, and Willow Creek.

32. Little Whitehorse Creek (Oregon Canyon Mountains Unit)

What to Expect:	A pilgrimage to a beautifully recovering stream where livestock have been excluded for two decades
Distance:	12 miles round trip
Elevation Range:	4,520–4,954 feet
Drinking Water:	Yes
Best Times:	Late spring, summer, fall
USGS 7.5' Maps:	Little Whitehorse Creek, Red Mountain, Whitehorse Ranch
Oregon Map Starting Point:	Fields

Go 8 miles south on OR 205 and turn easterly on the Whitehorse Ranch Road. After approximately 24 miles you are proceeding north-northeasterly. The road bends to the northeast, crosses Willow Creek, and immediately resumes its north-northeast direction. A small unnamed butte, approximately 100 feet high, is to the east. At 1 mile after crossing the creek, turn due south on a dirt road. (If you overshoot, the turn is 2.2 miles back, or southwesterly, from the bridge on Whitehorse Creek, just south of the Whitehorse Ranch main buildings.) After 2.4 miles turn west into the hot springs and park.

Hike south on the unimproved "road" that parallels Willow Creek (Red Mountain quad). In about 3 miles you'll come to an intersection (Little Whitehorse Creek quad). Bear southeasterly (left). In 0.4 mile is another intersection. Again bear southeasterly. In 2.2 miles you reach Little Whitehorse Creek. The exclosure is 100 yards upstream. Notice the wild rose, alder (not aspen), willows, wild mint, and well-developed stream channel.

Return as you came or set your own route cross-country.

33. Mud Spring Base Camp (Oregon Canyon Mountains Unit)

What to Expect:	An easy walk to an aspen camp, from which one can range in all directions
Distance:	12.2-mile loop
Elevation Range:	5,600–6,880 feet
Drinking Water:	Yes
Best Times:	Summer, fall
USGS 7.5' Maps:	Doolittle Creek, Dry Creek Bench
Oregon Map Starting Point:	Fields

Go 8 miles south on OR 205 and turn easterly on the Whitehorse Ranch Road. Approximately 27 miles east of OR 205 on the Whitehorse Ranch Road is a cattle guard (in front of the Whitehorse Ranch entrance). Go northeast 3.8 miles and cross under a three-strand, two-pole powerline. Continue 0.3 mile and turn south onto Mud Spring Road (unsigned). Go 4.7 miles south to a minor intersection. You'll pass through several gates. Take the left fork (southeast). Go 0.4 mile through a fence. Continue southeast 1.8 miles to a fence that separates the crested wheatgrass seeding from the native vegetation (Dry Creek Bench quad). Park on the crested wheatgrass seeding.

Hike southeast 4.3 miles to Buckaroo Corral Spring. Ignore any minor ways and jeep trails leaving the main way. As you walk the "road" (BLM is recommending closure to improve wilderness integrity) you'll see an occasional clump of crested wheatgrass that has invaded the wilderness. Destroy it.

At the Buckaroo Corral Spring intersection, continue southeasterly 0.6 mile to a way intersection. Continue east 0.2 mile to Mud Spring. Tank up on water and continue easterly on a "road" 1 mile to quaking aspen campsites.

From camp, you can range in any direction. The country is open and the canyons distinct enough to make map reading relatively easy. East is Oregon Canyon (see exploration later), south is Whitehorse Creek Canyon, and north are Twelvemile and Dry Creek Canyons.

Return the way you came, or venture westward through the Fish Creek Breaks to a fence and back to your vehicle.

34. Oregon Canyon (Oregon Canyon Mountains Unit)

What to Expect:	Water, trees, sage, colorful lichen, wildlife, flowers, rock formations, and more
Distance:	8 miles round trip (from Mud Spring Base Camp)
Elevation Range:	5,500–7,000 feet (from Mud Spring Base Camp)
Drinking Water:	Yes
Best Times:	Summer, fall
USGS 7.5' Map:	Oregon Canyon
Oregon Map Starting Point:	Fields

Follow driving and hiking directions to Mud Spring Base Camp (above). Backpack into the depths of Oregon Canyon by hiking 2.6 miles south to the head of

Oregon Canyon in the proposed Trout Creek Mountains Wilderness

the Mahogany Spring drainage. What's ahead is so inviting that you won't worry much about how steep it is going down (let alone returning). Before you is the incomparable Oregon Canyon. Return as you came.

35. Little Trout Creek (Trout Creek Unit)

What to Expect:	A one-night backpack along a pretty ridge and beautiful creek
Distance:	13.4-mile loop
Elevation Range:	5,160–7,000 feet
Drinking Water:	Yes
Best Times:	Spring, fall
USGS 7.5' Maps:	Pole Canyon, The V
Oregon Map Starting Point:	Fields

From Fields, go 8 miles south on OR 205 to the Whitehorse Ranch Road. Go east approximately 14 miles until you cross a very small white bridge. You are traveling northeast. From this bridge go 0.7 mile to the Trout Creek Mountain Loop Road (unsigned). Turn east and go 2.3 miles to a sharp turn through a cattle guard. Go 0.2 mile and park near the BLM information sign.

Hike 0.2 mile down a way to Little Trout Creek (Pole Canyon quad). Cross the creek at the ford and continue up the way. In 0.1 mile the way leaves the creek and continues west up a side canyon. At this point, do not take the lesser way to the northwest, but continue southwest into a broad valley. At 0.9 mile the way turns to a jeep trail as it steeply climbs onto the gentle Center Ridge. Continue south-southeast along Center Ridge until you come to a gate and fence in 2.4 miles, just before a mahogany grove. Camp either at Little Table Seep to the east (water) or in the mahogany grove.

Continue southerly 3.2 miles up Center Ridge to Amos Spring (The V quad). Walk down the draw below Amos Spring into Little Trout Creek Canyon. It is a great walk with a good trail and magnificent vegetation. The wild roses are lush and tall, and a nice aspen-shaded waterfall comes in from the east.

The trail crosses the creek countless times. Resign yourself to wet feet. Walking down Little Trout Creek 6.4 miles will return you to your first crossing. After reaching the first way, continue 0.2 mile up to your vehicle.

BLUE MOUNTAINS
ECOREGION

Though they give the ecoregion its name, the Blue Mountains, as the headwaters of the Malheur, John Day, and Umatilla Rivers, are only a part of it. Also included are Hells Canyon, the Wallowa Mountains, and the Powder and Grande Ronde river valleys. Ecologically, the ecoregion extends into Washington and Idaho.

The Blues run generally northeast-southwest. Major appendages to the main spine (albeit a rather broken one) of the Blue Mountains are usually given other names: the Ochoco, Aldrich, Strawberry, Greenhorn, and Elkhorn Ranges.

According to the Oregon Biodiversity Project, sharp elevational diversity causes climate differences over broad temperature and precipitation ranges. While more than half of the region is forested, vast portions are dominated by treeless ecosystems. The ecoregion has two distinct timberlines: the upper one we usually think of first that gives way to alpine habitat, but also a lower timberline that gives way to grasslands and steppes.

Fescue bunchgrass once was the most common grassland, of which agricultural development has taken half. Sagebrush and grassland steppes dominate the eastern portion of the ecoregion, while western juniper dominates the southern sections. The lower elevations also often had wetlands, again decimated by agriculture.

The summers are short and dry, the winters long and cold.

Fire dominated this ecoregion, both in the forest and the steppe. Suppression of fire in the forested regions and excessive fire in the cow-bombed grasslands—the latter of which have been overtaken by the highly flammable exotic cheatgrass—have significantly changed the landscape.

The Columbian sharp-tailed grouse was once common in prairie areas but was extirpated by the 1970s. Reintroduction efforts are underway.

The Oregon Biodiversity Project has estimated that 6.9 percent of the ecoregion is adequately protected to conserve and restore biodiversity. These areas are in mostly the forested portions.

HOMESTEAD ADDITION (PROPOSED) TO THE HELLS CANYON WILDERNESS

Ten miles of a very rugged and knifelike ridge descending from forest to desert.

Location:	Baker County, 2 miles west of Homestead
Size:	24 square miles (15,546 acres)
Terrain:	Extremely rugged, though nonetheless quite gorgeous and inviting
Elevation Range:	2,000–5,200 feet
Managing Agencies:	Vale District BLM, Wallowa-Whitman National Forest
Agency Wilderness Status:	7,001-acre BLM wilderness study area; 0 acres recommended
Recreation Map:	North Half Wallowa-Whitman National Forest

Getting to the area is easy, as good roads bound all sides. Once in the area, travel is rugged and often difficult. However, the wildness and the solitude are well worth the sweat.

There is not 1 foot of maintained hiking trail, even though half the area is Forest Service land and part of the Hells Canyon National Recreation Area. The 10-mile-long north-south knifelike ridge that dominates the area is a perfect location for the Desert Trail (see Appendix E). But until it is constructed, travel is difficult. If you do backpack the ridge, plan to spend three times longer than you'd imagine and plan to drop down into steep side canyons for water.

The ridge begins in forests of beautiful old-growth ponderosa pine and Douglas-fir in the north. It descends southward through a decreasing forest and increasing grassland to the tree-free arid grassland. Vegetation includes bunchgrass, big sagebrush, elderberry, hawthorn, poison ivy, and snowberry.

Wildlife includes mule deer, elk, cougar, black bear, and blue grouse. It is also habitat for Rocky Mountain bighorn sheep. Up to seventy bald eagles use the Snake River directly to the east.

The grizzly bear is officially extirpated in Oregon (the last having been shot on September 14, 1931, in Chesnimnus Creek 70 miles to the north in Wallowa County), but a reliable sighting of a griz heading east up Steep Creek into the Homestead Ridge area (and from the Lake Fork Roadless Area, which is separated by a mere road from the Eagle Cap Wilderness) in 1979 suggests that the grizzly bear is not yet done with Oregon.

The views from the high ridge are spectacular, both near and far. To the west, the Wallowa Mountains and Lake Fork drainage dominate. To the east, the Seven Devils Mountains in Idaho are dominant. One needs to try to ignore the butt-ugly Snake River reservoirs behind Hells Canyon and Oxbow dams.

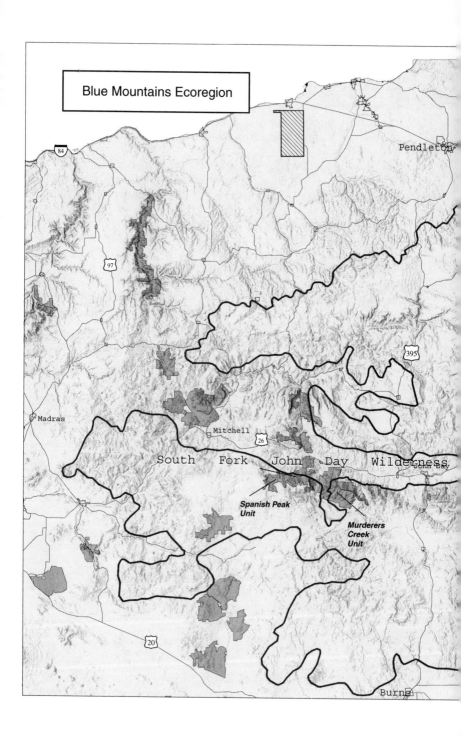

Blue Mountains Ecoregion

Pendleton

Madras

Mitchell

South Fork John Day Wilderness

John Day

Spanish Peak
Unit

Murderers
Creek
Unit

Burns

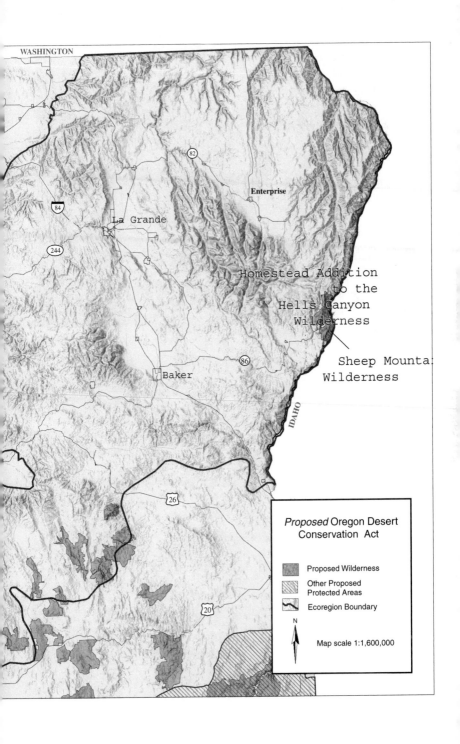

WASHINGTON

82

Enterprise

84

La Grande

244

Homestead Addition
to the
Hells Canyon
Wilderness

86

Sheep Mountai:
Wilderness

Baker

IDAHO

26

20

Proposed Oregon Desert
Conservation Act

Proposed Wilderness

Other Proposed
Protected Areas

Ecoregion Boundary

N

Map scale 1:1,600,000

Black bear (this one is actually cinnamon colored) in the proposed Homestead Addition to the Hells Canyon Wilderness

Prehistoric rock cairns can be found in the area, and an old Indian trail traverses the ridge from the Snake River to Pine Creek.

The Hells Canyon Preservation Council advocates the relocation of the powerline that separates Homestead Ridge and the larger Hells Canyon Wilderness to the north. Private lands along the lower edges and inholdings should be acquired to give full integrity to the area. BLM and the Forest Service did not recommend wilderness designation because they respectively favor mining and logging of the area.

36. McLain Gulch

What to Expect:	An extremely rugged climb to a spectacular canyon overlook and pristine basin
Distance:	4 miles round trip
Elevation Range:	2,861–4,961 feet
Drinking Water:	Yes
Best Times:	Summer, fall
USGS 7.5' Map:	McLain Gulch
Oregon Map Starting Point:	Halfway

From Halfway, drive 9 miles east on OR 86 to North Pine Creek Road. Drive north 5.6 miles to North Pine Rest Area (Roadside Park on quad map). At the restroom, a dirt way goes east 0.1 mile to the creek, a good car campsite. Park between the road and the creek and out of sight of both. Wade the creek (summer is better as the roaring spring flow has diminished) and walk northeasterly 0.5 mile on an unimproved ex-road. It then turns southeast into an ex-four-wheel-drive trail that follows the stream bottom and peters out after 0.6 mile. Continue cross-country due eastward and ever upward 0.5 mile on open slopes to the saddle at Homestead Ridge at 4717T on the quad map. Down and to the east is upper McLain Gulch, which has a fine riparian area of rushes, sedges, rose, and willows. It is so steep that no livestock have ever defiled it. Camping sites are available, or this can be done as a long day hike. It is not that long a distance, but it is extremely steep.

SHEEP MOUNTAIN WILDERNESS (PROPOSED)

A wildlife wonderland known of by few and visited by fewer.

Location:	Baker County, 4 miles south of Homestead
Size:	15 square miles (9,769 acres)
Terrain:	A large plateau surrounded by steep slopes
Elevation Range:	1,830–4,935 feet
Managing Agency:	Vale District BLM
Agency Wilderness Status:	7,040-acre BLM wilderness study area; 7,040 acres recommended
Recreation Map:	North Half Wallowa-Whitman National Forest

There are many surprises, most pleasant, in the area.

Sheep Mountain (4,310 feet), though a prominent feature from within and without the area, is not the highest point. The plateau to the west and south is higher.

The bighorn sheep, which often winter on the lower slopes near the river, are the Rocky Mountain subspecies, not the California subspecies common to most of the desert.

There is sagebrush, but the large native grouse here is not the sage grouse but the Columbian sharp-tailed, which had been extirpated from Oregon. Reintroduction efforts are underway.

A designed and constructed (mostly cairns) 3-mile hiking trail actually exists on Oregon BLM desert lands.

Black Canyon Creek has a pristine riparian zone, as cliffs have prevented invasion by livestock. Steep slopes elsewhere have discouraged livestock from munching riparian zones. Well-developed woody species are common.

The only unpleasant surprise is a small radio repeater building atop the plateau. However, it is small and painted a neutral color.

The Snake River Canyon is thought to be a center of evolution for many groups of species that link the Pacific Northwest with such far-off and different places as the Mojave Desert. Rare plant species include Cusick's camas (*Cammasia*

The proposed Sheep Mountain Wilderness across the Powder River

Cusickii), thyme-leafed buckwheat (*Eriogonum thymoides*), and swamp onion (*Allium madidum*).

The grassy slopes to the south and west are stands of Idaho fescue and bluebunch wheatgrass. Old-growth ponderosa pine and Douglas-fir are found in the flatter areas of steep draws. On the top of the plateau, big sagebrush, squaw currant, snowberry, buckwheat, and bluebunch wheatgrass dominate.

Other notable wildlife species include elk, mule deer, black bear, cougar, bobcat, red-tailed hawk, kestrel, numerous kinds of songbirds, and blue grouse. Two bald eagle wintering roosts are located in the area, supporting approximately seventy-five individuals.

Undeveloped private lands adjacent to Pine Creek should be acquired and added to the area. BLM is recommending acquiring a 200-acre inholding if the seller is willing.

37. Black Canyon Headwaters

What to Expect:	A very steep beginning to a large high-mountain plateau
Distance:	8 miles round trip
Elevation Range:	3,600–4,868 feet
Drinking Water:	No
Best Times:	Summer, fall
USGS 7.5' Maps:	Brownlee Dam, McLain Gulch, Oxbow
Oregon Map Starting Point:	Pine

From the OR 86 turnoff (either one), go to downtown Pine. In Pine you are on Pine Town Lane. Continue 1 mile east-southeast where road turns sharply to north-northeast for 0.1 mile (crossing Pine Creek) before turning east. In 2 miles (you're on Gulick Road) the pavement ends and the road turns southeasterly for 3 miles. It then heads due east. In 1.2 miles cross under a big powerline, again in another 1 mile, again in 0.1 mile, and again in 0.8 mile.

(Notice the several livestock exclosures along the route. Different people see different things. The rancher obviously is proud of all the forage he's prevented from going to waste outside the exclosures. Conservationists are appalled.)

The road deteriorates as it nears the rim above Brownlee Dam. You may want to stop somewhere along the rim (great dry car camp) and walk the remainder. If you have four-wheel drive, you can make the "trailhead" north 2 miles after going under the powerline for the last time. Otherwise, it is a pleasant enough walk.

The unmarked "trailhead" (we'll eventually find those cairns) is where the road obviously crosses from one drainage to another. Park. Take the unmapped four-wheel-drive track east 0.4 mile up and over the ridge and down and across the little valley. Follow the east-west fence that demarcates private land to the fence corner. Continue north on a well-defined cattle trail along the fence. After crossing a small creek channel, hike up the very steep ridge directly north. Follow this ridge, which is the west side of Black Canyon. You'll eventually see infrequent and short cairns, useful for little more than confirming you are on your correct northward course. The steep ridge soon gets gentle at the 4404 and 4408 elevations on the USGS 7.5' quad map, and near the radio repeater at 4868T (you're now 2.5 miles from the fence corner). The trail continues northeast along the edge of the plateau 1.1 miles downward toward Sheep Mountain (Oxbow quad).

Views are of the Wallowa Mountains to the northwest, Homestead Ridge to the north, and the Seven Devils to the northeast. You can camp on top of the plateau or in some trees and explore more later. This can also be done as a long day hike.

Return the way you came.

SOUTH FORK JOHN DAY WILDERNESS (PROPOSED)

*Stark natural beauty with a great diversity of vegetation
from large conifers to tiny flowers.*

Location:	Grant County, 4 miles South of Dayville
Size:	120 square miles (76,588 acres)
Terrain:	Steep rocky slopes and rims with more gentle foothills
Elevation Range:	2,520–6,987 feet
Managing Agencies:	Prineville District BLM, Malheur and Ochoco National Forests, Oregon Department of Fish and Wildlife
Agency Wilderness Status:	9,395-acre BLM wilderness study area; 0 acres recommended
Recreation Map:	South Half, Upper John Day River, Prineville District BLM

Like the multi-unit North Fork John Day Wilderness, this proposed counter-part in the South Fork Basin is comprised of several wilderness units. The Spanish Peak and Murderers Creek units contain both forest and desert lands. The remaining units are primarily forested and are not further described here.

The open and rocky terrain makes for a highly scenic and varied landscape.

The area is a great place to view, photograph, and/or hunt charismatic megafauna. It is pronghorn summer range, mule deer and elk winter range, and year-round bighorn sheep range—all of it crucial habitat.

Other wildlife of note includes sage grouse, beaver, mink, weasel, raccoon, black bear, cougar, and bobcat. Numerous raptors and songbirds are common because of the diverse habitat. The spotted bat, perhaps America's rarest mammal, is found here.

The upper reaches of the area are Forest Service lands, while BLM and Oregon Fish and Wildlife control the lower reaches. The Phillip W. Schneider (formerly known as the Murderers Creek) Wildlife Management Area was established to protect deer winter range but obviously has additional key values.

The upper slopes are forested with ponderosa pine, mountain mahogany (south faces), and Douglas-fir and grand fir (north faces). In the open areas below rims, sagebrush and grass are found. Downslope the vegetation changes to sagebrush and grassland communities. Western juniper occurs throughout. The South Fork John Day milk-vetch (*Astragalus diaphanus* var. *diurnus*) occurs only in loose and exposed soils and riparian habitats. Hardwood riparian communities are found in the lowest reaches of the many tributary streams to the South Fork John Day River, a unit of the national wild and scenic rivers system.

The Oregon Biodiversity Project's South Fork John Day Conservation Opportunity Area was recognized because of the critical habitat for anadromous fish (fish that ascend rivers from the sea to breed—here, salmon and steelhead) and redband trout. The lower elevations are actually in the Lava Plains ecoregion.

The BLM's rationale for not recommending wilderness designation:

> *Although the study area contains a number of wilderness values, including naturalness, outstanding opportunities for solitude and recreation, as well as scenic and wildlife values, the benefits of preserving those values are outweighed by the benefits of developing the area's resources through intensive management practices.*[1]

They want to seed exotic species for another sixty animal-unit months of livestock and to log an average of fifteen truckloads annually.

Aldrich Mountain and South Fork John Day River in the proposed South Fork John Day Wilderness

38. Smokey Creek (Murderers Creek Unit)

What to Expect: A very rugged, but highly scenic cross-county excursion
Distance: 4–10 miles round trip
Elevation Range: 2,650–6,987 feet
Drinking Water: No
Best Times: Spring, summer, fall
USGS 7.5' Maps: Dayville, Aldrich Mountain North
Oregon Map Starting Point: Dayville

From Dayville, drive south up the South Fork John Day River Road 4.2 miles where the road crosses to the east bank of the South Fork John Day River (you've left the open valley and are going into the canyon). Continue south 0.5 mile to the intersection of a side road just south of the Smokey Creek crossing (unnamed). Drive (or park here if you don't like the road) east 0.2 mile and park at creek ford (Dayville quad).

Your hike is at least 2 and up to 5 miles one way. How long is up to you, and you don't need to choose now. If you do plan to do the summit of Aldrich Mountain (worth the view!), make it a backpack in the summer or early fall. The route is up the ridge southwest of Smokey Creek. From your camp, day hike to the summit. If you're too tired, turn around.

Proceed due south and steeply up the ridge to skirt the posted private property along Smokey Creek. Once on the ridge, walk southeast along 3768, 3603, Bottle Rock, 4363, 4905, and (Aldrich Mountain North quad) 5201. You're now entering forest for the final 2 miles to the summit of Aldrich Mountain.

Return the same way.

A shuttle alternative is to start at Aldrich Mountain Lookout and walk this route down (you could also do it uphill if you're nuts).

If you're lucky, quiet, and observant, you should see lots of big game.

COLUMBIA BASIN
ECOREGION

The ecoregion has been greatly affected by water, though it doesn't have much now. The great floods of the Columbia River, the wind-blown sand and silt from the river (loess), and the carving action of the Deschutes, John Day, and other streams that created basalt canyons surrounded by lava plateau—all are water's work.

Winters are cold and summers hot. Most of the ecoregion gets less than 15 inches of precipitation annually. In many areas, it is less than 8 inches, mostly falling as snow.

The basin was once a vast sagebrush steppe and bunchgrass prairie, often called palouse. (Palouse is the name botanists and ecologists give to the kind of grassland that grows on loess—a windblown deposit of fine-grained calcareous silt or clay—common to eastern Washington where the Palouse Indians once lived. The grassland is extremely rare because most of it was on gentle enough slope to grow wheat, and the loess soil grows lots of wheat.)

According to the Oregon Biodiversity Project, several unique habitats exist: dunes along the Columbia, oak woodlands near the Cascades ecoregion, and mounded prairie. Much of the wetlands have been lost to Columbia River reservoirs.

The best potential lands for conservation and restoration are associated with the military-industrial (as opposed to the agriculture-industrial) complex. A corridor of high-quality bunchgrass and steppe exists along the reservoirs because it is Umatilla Army Depot land. Navy bombing of their Boardman range had less ecological impact than cow bombing.

In 1962, Oregon leased—until 2032—tens of thousands of acres of state lands to Boeing to develop a spaceport. While Boeing has subleased much for agriculture, much remains in good condition (last Oregon holdout for the Washington ground squirrel).

The Oregon Biodiversity Project has estimated that 1.9 percent of the ecoregion is adequately protected to conserve and restore biodiversity.

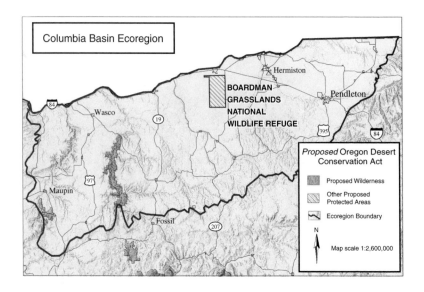

BOARDMAN GRASSLANDS NATIONAL WILDLIFE REFUGE (PROPOSED)

The Navy is abandoning its bombing range, which contains one of the best remaining blocks of native grasslands on the Columbia Plateau.

Location:	Morrow County, 3 miles south of Boardman
Size:	74 square miles (47,627 acres)
Terrain:	Flat prairie to gentle valleys
Elevation Range:	395–971 feet
Managing Agencies:	U.S. Navy (present); Fish and Wildlife Service (proposed)
Recreation Map:	Hermiston, OR-WA, 1:100,000 topographic (BLM surface management edition best; otherwise get USGS edition)

The practice of livestock grazing is more damaging to nature under the jurisdiction of the U.S. Department of the Interior than is practice bombing by the U.S. Department of Defense. It would be worse than livestock if live ordnance were used (but only by degrees). The dummy ordnance used sometimes caused range fires, which are beneficial to the grassland, as they mimic natural wildfires that have historically been suppressed.

From 1943, when the U.S. Army Air Force took charge (the navy took over in 1960), until 1963, no livestock grazing occurred on the bombing range. Since then, lands outside the core "octagon" have been leased to local ranchers. Competitive bids have reached $18 per animal-unit month (BLM charges $1.35), and the navy does nothing for the ranchers, making them haul their own water, maintain fences, and so forth. It makes perfect sense, really—the Department of Defense, renowned for $200 hammers and $400 toilet seats, doesn't consider the livestock industry its constituency.

In 1978, a research natural area was established, including lands at ground-zero of the bombing range, totaling 5,176 acres.

Despite the rusted military tanks, fake towns (both targets for jets from Whidbey Island Naval Air Station in Puget Sound), service roads, and widely littered plastic bullets, the bombing range contains some of the largest and best remnants of native grassland and shrub steppe left on the Columbia Plateau of Oregon.

Despite the relative lack of habitat diversity, the area is abundant with sagebrush steppe wildlife species. Forty-three bird, thirty-two plant, fourteen mammal, six reptile, and one amphibian species are known to inhabit the range, including the at-risk Washington ground squirrel, western burrowing owl, grasshopper sparrow, Robinson's onion, Laurence's milk-vetch, and gray cryptantha.

The range also contains some of the best desert crust (see Natural History chapter) remaining anywhere.

Badger, bobcat, and the ubiquitous coyote are the top predators. The area is thick with long-billed curlews. Bald eagles can be seen at the northern end of the range near the Columbia River. Also on the north end are spectacular white sand dunes.

Needle-and-thread grass and Indian rice grass in the proposed Boardman Grasslands National Wildlife Refuge (Photo by Berta Youtie)

While controlled by the navy, some of the land actually belongs to BLM. When it will be declared military surplus is unsure.

The Oregon Biodiversity Project has identified the bombing range, the adjacent Boeing state lands lease, and the state's Willow Creek Wildlife Management Area as Boardman–Willow Creek Conservation Opportunity Area and urges that "long-term protection and management of these native habitats for biodiversity values should be a top conservation priority in this ecoregion."[1]

Pronghorn reintroduction is likely quite feasible, and the establishment of a Boardman Grasslands National Wildlife Refuge (managed by the U.S. Fish and Wildlife Service) would provide part of an important ecological linkage between the heart of the Oregon Desert and the Washington portion of the Columbia Basin, including the Arid Lands Ecology Reserve on the Hanford Nuclear Reservation.

WHAT TO DO

No exploration is described, as the area is closed to the public. Trespassers may be shot.

KLAMATH MOUNTAINS ECOREGION

The Klamath Mountains ecoregion is not considered desert, nor should it be. It is west of the Cascade crest, and annual rainfall ranges from 20 to 120 inches. Elevations range from 100 to 7,500 feet. The Klamaths, Siskiyous, and several other mountain ranges that comprise the ecoregion are generally forested and include the most diverse conifer forests in the world (thirty species). The wide valleys of the Klamath, Rogue, and Umpqua have a drier feel to them, as do the savanna-like foothills, but these are far from desert conditions.

Yet, the ecoregion possesses some elements of the Oregon Desert. For example, in parts of the Rogue and Klamath Basins, one finds sagebrush and western juniper. Amazingly, pronghorn used to inhabit the Rogue Valley, moving to the high Cascades in the summer.

In the words of the Oregon Biodiversity Project, the Klamath Mountains are a "floristic crossroads" where species of the Sierra Nevada, Sacramento Valley, California Coast Range, Washington and Oregon Cascades, *and* the Great Basin all converge.[1] This is starkly obvious, even to the botanically challenged, in places like Soda Mountain.

The very diverse habitat is a focal point of biodiversity. The ecoregion is a major center of species endemism and diversity. Of the four thousand native taxa in Oregon, one-half are in the Klamath Mountain ecoregion, and one-quarter of these are found only in the ecoregion.

That makes sense in this oldest part of Oregon. Unlike much of the rest of the state, this ecoregion is not largely influenced by volcanism. The rock is more metamorphic and sedimentary than igneous.

The Oregon Biodiversity Project has estimated that 16.2 percent of the ecoregion is adequately protected to conserve and restore biodiversity.

SODA MOUNTAIN WILDERNESS (PROPOSED)

Multiple collisions at an ecological crossroads.

Location: Jackson County, Oregon, and Siskiyou County, California, 18 miles southeast of Ashland
Size: 59 square miles (38,000 acres)
Terrain: Deeply incised canyons and high ridges
Elevation Range: 2,355–6,089 feet
Managing Agencies: Medford BLM, Ukiah (California) BLM, California Fish and Game
Agency Wilderness Status: 5,895-acre BLM wilderness study area; 5,867 acres recommended
Recreation Map: East Half Medford District BLM (Oregon portion)

Ecologically, this is truly where east meets west meets north meets south.

One finds the western limits of the arid and sunny Oregon Desert; the intermixing of the wet temperate forests of the Cascade and Klamath mountain ranges; the eastern limit of the plants of the moist and cool Pacific Ocean; and the northern limits of drier, sunnier California chaparral.

Depending on the aspect, elevation, and soil, you may be in a true fir forest, a montane wildflower meadow, a pine-oak/fescue grassland, a maple–black oak riparian forest, a California white oak savanna, a juniper-cedar/bunchgrass bald, or a chaparral brushland.

The proposed Soda Mountain Wilderness is a mosaic of diverse ecosystems.

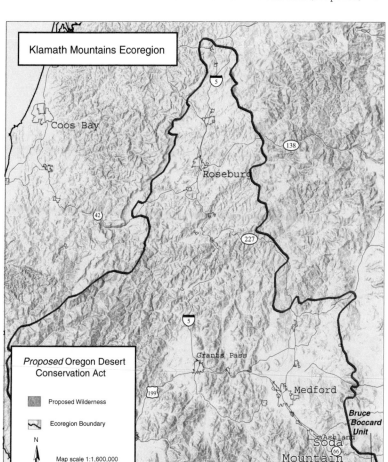

Klamath Mountains Ecoregion

Proposed Oregon Desert
Conservation Act

Proposed Wilderness

Ecoregion Boundary

N

Map scale 1:1,600,000

Coos Bay

Roseburg

Grants Pass

Medford

Ashland

Bruce
Boccard
Unit

Soda
Mountain
Wilderness

Pilot Rock Unit

CALIFORNIA

The east-west Siskiyou ridge connects the Cascade and Klamath Mountains, allowing for easy species migration. Ten rare, threatened, or endangered species have been identified in this mosaic. The lower elevations are critical black-tailed deer winter range. Roosevelt elk, mountain quail, cougar, black bear, bobcat, golden eagle, goshawk, and prairie falcon are present.

The desert influence is obvious: big sagebrush, low sagebrush, Idaho fescue, bluebunch wheatgrass, western juniper, lupine, rabbit-brush, desert parsley, Indian paintbrush, and wild rose are all present. In late summer those flowers are visited by clouds of butterflies.

At Agate Flat lie deposits of petrified wood and many colors of agate. Pilot Rock, the most prominent feature of the area, is a volcanic plug of columnar basalt (visible from Interstate 5).

During the last-minute deliberations on the president's Northwest Forest Plan, the Soda Mountain Wilderness Council convinced the White House to create the Cascade Siskiyou Ecological Emphasis Area, which includes the wilderness proposal. Logging is prohibited until 2005, when a new management plan will be completed.

The area consists of two units: Pilot Rock and Bruce Boccard.

39. Pacific Crest Trail: Soda Mountain–Pilot Rock (Pilot Rock Unit)

What to Expect:	A long, gentle walk on a real trail
Distance:	24 miles round trip
Elevation Range:	4,700–5,260 feet
Drinking Water:	Yes (always at Bean Cabin on the Pacific Crest Trail)
Best Times:	Summer (wildflowers peak in June and July)
USGS 7.5' Maps:	Soda Mountain, Siskiyou Pass
Oregon Map Starting Point:	Ashland

From Ashland travel 16 miles east on OR 66 to Greensprings Summit. Go south on Soda Mountain Road (BLM Road 39-3E-32.3). After 3.8 miles (having gone under powerlines twice) is the Pacific Crest Trail trailhead.

Southwest 12 miles on the well-marked Pacific Crest Trail is Pilot Rock, where camp spots can be found.

40. Boccard Point (Pilot Rock Unit)

What to Expect:	Excellent views
Distance:	5 miles round trip
Elevation Range:	5,260–5,720 feet
Drinking Water:	No
Best Times:	Summer (wildflowers peak in June and July)
USGS 7.5' Map:	Soda Mountain
Oregon Map Starting Point:	Ashland

At the Pacific Crest Trail trailhead (above), map your own route to Boccard Point and back (the newly official name isn't on the USGS 7.5' quad map and honors the late great conservationist Bruce Boccard). Boccard Point is the prominent ridge straddling the boundary line between sections 32 and 33 on the northwest-southeast divide between Camp and Dutch Oven Creeks. Use the Pacific Crest Trail, the ex-unimproved roads, and ex-four-wheel-drive trails. Go cross-country, as the forest is often open. Views from the Soda Mountain summit are nice if you ignore the abominably growing antenna farm.

41. Dutch Oven and Camp Creeks (Pilot Rock Unit)

What to Expect:	A very rugged cross-county backpack
Distance:	8.3-mile loop
Elevation Range:	3,200–5,400 feet
Drinking Water:	Yes
Best Times:	Summer (wildflowers peak in June and July)
USGS 7.5' Map:	Soda Mountain
Oregon Map Starting Point:	Ashland

At the Pacific Crest Trail trailhead (earlier), continue driving southeasterly 2.4 miles (cross under powerlines three more times) to a ridge-top intersection near a horse corral. Park. Get an early start to make a nice camp. Walk 1.2 miles southwesterly on an ex-unimproved road that turns into an ex-four-wheel-drive track across the south slope of Soda Mountain. Follow the ridge south 0.5 mile to Boccard Point (see earlier).

Drop west down into Dutch Oven Creek and follow it to the confluence of Dutch Oven Creek and Camp Creek (this will take the rest of the day, though it is just 2.5 miles). Camp at the confluence with Camp Creek.

The next day explore the cliffs 1 mile down Camp Creek from its confluence with Dutch Oven Creek.

To return, start early. Go north up Camp Creek to the confluence with the unmapped East Fork Camp Creek (0.2 mile from the confluence of Camp Creek with Dutch Oven Creek). Bushwhack your way 2 miles up the East Fork to catch the end of an ex-unimproved road. Follow this route 2.1 miles back to your vehicle.

Have a beer.

LAVA PLAINS
ECOREGION

The Lava Plains ecoregion is basically a big plateau that has been carved up by the Deschutes, Crooked, and John Day Rivers and other streams. The elevations range from 1,400 to 6,500 feet. Precipitation ranges from 10 to 20 inches annually. There are—and were—very few natural lakes and wetlands, as the source for much of the water affecting the bioregion comes from conifer forests at higher elevations.

Big basin sagebrush and native grasslands were widespread. Seventy-five percent of the former and 80 percent of the latter have been converted to agriculture and urbanization, and much of the remainder is in a degraded state because of livestock and off-road vehicles. Riparian woodland communities were also once common but have been hammered here as they have been everywhere else by dams, irrigation diversions, and so forth.

Western juniper is found in the greatest concentrations and diversity in the Lava Plains. Juniper is associated with thirty different plant communities. Fire suppression and livestock grazing have allowed juniper to expand into sagebrush country.

The unique ash deposits in the Middle John Day country and east of Post are quite diverse and support several endemic plant species. Adjacent to the ash deposits one can often find salt desert scrub types, such as the shadscale and black greasewood communities. The ash deposits came from several sources, but the influence of Mount Mazama (known now as Crater Lake Caldera) ash falls was very significant.

The Oregon Biodiversity Project reminds us to sweat both the large and the small stuff. Consider the arrow-leaf thelypody (*Thelypodium eucosmum*). Its range is restricted to western juniper communities and is generally adjacent to seasonal springs. This purple-flowered, tall, and showy mustard is found only in Grant and Wheeler Counties, mostly near Mitchell and Kimberly, mostly on BLM holdings, and it is threatened by livestock grazing.

The Oregon Biodiversity Project has estimated that 1.9 percent of the ecoregion is adequately protected to conserve and restore biodiversity.

BADLANDS WILDERNESS (PROPOSED)

Striking volcanic outcrops covered by juniper and a dry river canyon with polished lavas.

Location:	Deschutes and Crook Counties, 9 miles east of Bend
Size:	46 square miles (30,463 acres)
Terrain:	Volcanic flows and outcrops with sandy basins in between
Elevation Range:	3,368–3,900 feet
Managing Agency:	Prineville District BLM
Agency Wilderness Status:	32,221-acre BLM wilderness study area; 32,030 acres recommended
Recreation Map:	West Half Central Oregon Public Lands, Prineville District BLM

The dictionary defines badlands as "barren land characterized by roughly eroded ridges, peaks, and mesas." Oregon's badlands are a little different. There aren't many peaks and the edges are rough, not from erosion, but the lack thereof. Geologically, the flows are relatively new, and erosion has been slight.

The dominant geology is rolling hills comprised of ragged dark reddish brown and black basalt outcroppings and escarpments. The light tan sand brought into the area by wind fill countless small irregularly shaped basins and valleys.

The Badlands consist of two groups of volcanics, roughly divided by the Crook-Deschutes county line. The western flows are recent to 1 million years and are basalt to basaltic andesite in composition. The eastern flows are 2 to 5 million years old and consist of basalt.

There are numerous very large pressure ridges that were formed by slowly moving subcrustal lava. Some of these took the shape of muffins and bread loaves and have the same characteristic cooling cracks as baked goods.

The Dry River is a prehistoric river channel. It was formed during the Pleistocene epoch when the Millican Valley to the east drained into the Crooked River. It is now a part of the Great Basin. Erosion from this massive water drainage is evident in polished lava rock and tinajas (rocks with smooth holes in them formed by the water working little pebbles in a circle). Some tinajas here are up to 3 feet deep.

The juniper is all ages from young to old growth. Understory species include big sagebrush, gray and green rabbit-brush, bitterbrush, Idaho fescue, bluebunch wheatgrass, squirrel-tailed needlegrass, and phlox.

The area provides critical mule deer winter range and also supports pronghorn and a hundred other species of wildlife.

Several prehistoric and historic sites are located in the area. It served as a bombing range during World War II, but no ordnance has been found.

The numerous small, sheltered basalt-rimmed sandy basins scattered throughout the area make it easy to be alone and lost. Figure on it. To get your

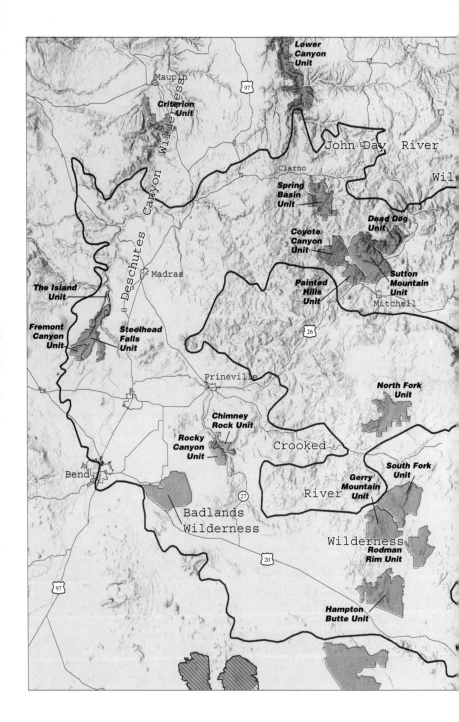

Lower
Canyon
Unit

Maupin

97

Criterion
Unit

Canyon Wilderness

John Day River

Clarno

Wil

Spring
Basin
Unit

Dead Dog
Unit

Coyote
Canyon
Unit

Sutton
Mountain
Unit

Deschutes

Madras

Painted
Hills
Unit

Mitchell

The Island
Unit

26

Fremont
Canyon
Unit

Steelhead
Falls
Unit

Prineville

North Fork
Unit

Chimney
Rock Unit

Rocky
Canyon
Unit

Crooked

South Fork
Unit

Bend

River

Gerry
Mountain
Unit

27

Badlands
Wilderness

Wilderness

Rodman
Rim Unit

20

97

Hampton
Butte Unit

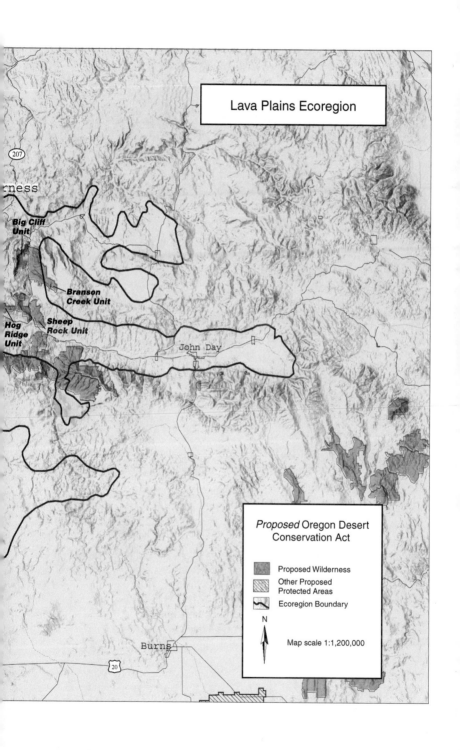

Lava Plains Ecoregion

(207)

rness

Big Cliff
Unit

Branson
Creek Unit

Hog
Ridge
Unit

Sheep
Rock Unit

John Day

Burns

(20)

Proposed Oregon Desert
Conservation Act

Proposed Wilderness

Other Proposed
Protected Areas

Ecoregion Boundary

N

Map scale 1:1,200,000

Pressure ridge and western juniper in the proposed Badlands Wilderness

bearings, climb a pressure ridge (and also take in views of several Cascade peaks, Smith Rocks, West Butte, and Horse Ridge).

The Badlands geology and juniper cover are a type not represented in the national wilderness system.

42. Badlands Rock

What to Expect:	Pressure ridges and old-growth juniper
Distance:	7.9 miles loop
Elevation Range:	3,591–3,656 feet
Drinking Water:	No
Best Times:	Spring, summer, fall
USGS 7.5' Map:	Horse Ridge
Oregon Map Starting Point:	Bend

From Bend drive east on US 20 to 0.9 mile east of milepost 16. Turn north onto the paved road. Go 0.9 mile and park at a small cattle loading chute.

Walk north on a way 0.2 mile to the intersection of two ways ("The Crossways"). The way from the west is the end of this loop exploration. Continue northerly 2.6 miles to Badlands Rock.

It is a short scramble to the top. Note the pressure ridge 1/2 mile west and a bit south. This is the next destination.

Take the unmapped way going west by the south end of Badlands Rock. Walk 0.7 mile (the way meanders) to the north side of the pressure ridge. As the pool of lava cooled, it cracked with a ring fracture along the edge. Circumnavigate the pressure ridge by walking the crack. Climb up into the center and see pristine grass.

Continue walking on the unmapped way westward for 0.4 mile. It dead-ends into a mapped north-south way at the base of yet another pressure ridge.

Go south on the way 3.8 miles to return to the originating intersection. Numerous unmapped and unmarked ways take off from your way of choice. Bear east when you have a choice.

At the Crossways go south 0.2 mile to return to your vehicle.

Easily done as a day hike, or make it an overnight.

43. Dry River Canyon

What to Expect:	Indian rock painting and tinajas
Distance:	2.5-mile loop
Elevation Range:	3,540–3,591 feet
Drinking Water:	No
Best Times:	Spring, summer, fall
USGS 7.5' Map:	Horse Ridge
Oregon Map Starting Point:	Bend

From the cattle loading chute (Badlands Rock exploration), walk north into the proposed wilderness on the way 0.2 mile to the Crossways.

The Dry River channel flows eastward at the point a few feet south of the Crossways. The river "channel" is quite broad, and no banks are discernible. Since water hasn't flowed for several thousand years, the vegetation in the channel is no different from that on the "banks" or "uplands."

Walk 0.5 mile north-northeast on the way. Continue 0.4 mile easterly, passing two ways to the south. As the way approaches the Dry River channel, walk south 0.1 mile into the channel. You'll come a barricade to keep vehicles from violating the channel. Walk the channel westward ("upstream") 0.9 mile back to the Crossways.

As you enter the channel, note the lava rocks polished by the water flow. Look for tinajas. Search carefully for Indian paintings and other artifacts. The canyon has nice stands of Great Basin wildrye and some currant.

After reaching the Crossways, walk south 0.2 mile to the cattle chute.

CROOKED RIVER WILDERNESS (PROPOSED)

Seven jewels representative of the ecological diversity of the Crooked River Basin.

Location:	Crook and Deschutes Counties, 12 miles south of Prineville (Rocky Canyon and Chimney Rock units); 8 miles northwest of Paulina (North Fork unit); 3 miles north of Hampton (Hampton Butte unit); centered about 15 miles south-southwest of Paulina (Rodman Rim, South Fork, and Gerry Mountain units)
Size:	213 square miles (136,584 acres)
Terrain:	Rugged river canyons, gentle buttes, big flats, and steep rims
Elevation Range:	2,994–4,800 feet
Managing Agencies:	Prineville District BLM, Ochoco National Forest (North Fork unit only)
Agency Wilderness Status:	101,971-acre BLM wilderness study area; 40,420 acres recommended
Recreation Map:	West and East Halves Central Oregon Recreation Lands, Prineville District BLM

The Crooked River Basin is quite large, and some of the wilderness units are widely separated. Each stands alone as a wilderness proposal, but also complements the wilderness and natural values of the others.

The wilderness proposal consists of six BLM wilderness study areas: North Fork, South Fork, Sand Hollow, Gerry Mountain, Hampton Butte, and Cougar Well.

Chimney Rock and Rocky Canyon Units

Neither are very big, but don't let that stop you. There's a lot of wildness and solitude packed in these units.

Both contain spectacular rim frontage along the wild and scenic Crooked River, designated by Congress in 1988. This protection only extends an average of 1/4 mile on each side of the river, so these wilderness units add some valuable depth to the natural river and associated values. They are Prineville's backyard wilderness.

Juniper, big sagebrush, and native grasses slope gently toward the Crooked River until the precipitous canyon rims. A few gaps in the rim, such as Rocky Canyon, break up the otherwise solid fortress of the basalt walls.

You can find a few big ponderosa pines along the banks of the Crooked River, but the dominant tree in the units is western juniper.

North Fork unit of the proposed Crooked River Wilderness

The Oregon Biodiversity Project has designated the Badlands Conservation Opportunity Area that includes the Badlands and Horse Ridge to the south, and all land north to and including the Rocky Canyon and Chimney Rock units. From *Oregon's Living Landscape:*

> *This area includes what is probably the largest block of high-quality old-growth juniper habitat in Oregon, and perhaps anywhere. The area's mosaic of sandy soils, Mt. Mazama ash, windblown loess, silts and volcanic clays support an impressive diversity of juniper communities, which in turn, provide important habitat for a variety of birds and other wildlife.[1]*

Sitting on the rims, you can look down on raptors that use the habitat along the cliffs above the Crooked River. There are also several small caves in the cliffs below the rims that serve as valuable habitat. The high flats are important deer and pronghorn habitat.

Camp in one of the several BLM campgrounds along the river and day hike into the area. The Crooked River Road, which separates the two units, is a BLM national backcountry byway.

BLM is not even considering these units for wilderness designation.

North Fork Unit

Here the forest transitions first to woodland and then desert, or from desert to woodland, depending on your point of view.

The unit contains 7 miles of the meandering North Fork Crooked River, which has downcut basalt in some places as much as 800 to 900 feet deep. Two small waterfalls can be found. Above the canyon walls are grassy plateaus. A total of 12.5 miles of the river is part of the national wild and scenic rivers system. Rainbow trout inhabit the river. The riparian zones are healthy grasses, rushes, dogwood, and willow.

Higher up, where there is enough precipitation, large Douglas-fir and ponderosa pine trees dominate the scene. In between one finds big and low sagebrush, bunchgrass, and many springs, seeps, and small tributaries to the river.

The unit is crucial winter range for both elk and mule deer, as well as home to pronghorn, golden eagles, bald eagles, Canada geese, bobcat, Lewis' woodpecker, and California quail.

A prehistoric trail reportedly exists in the unit.

BLM is not recommending the unit for wilderness designation because it favors oil and gas development, livestock grazing increases, and logging. This unit is actually in the Blue Mountains ecoregion.

South Fork Unit

Dominating the unit is the South Fork Crooked River Canyon, a beautiful assemblage of numerous combinations of reddish tan, dark brown, and black columns along with gigantic irregular blocks of basalt. Much of the rest of the unit consists of rolling hills and a desert plateau, often covered with western juniper. Parts of the canyon are 700 to 800 feet deep.

Habitat along the river is quite diverse and productive, supporting beaver, many songbird species, some waterfowl species, and rainbow trout.

Ferruginous and Swainson's hawks, both of which are candidates for the endangered species list, are found in the unit (also in the adjacent Gerry Mountain unit).

Besides being important mule deer winter range, the area also has important sage grouse habitat.

BLM is recommending most, but not all, of the unit for wilderness designation. They recommend closing a primitive road that separates their two wilderness study areas.

South Fork unit of the proposed Crooked River Wilderness

Gerry Mountain, Hampton Butte, and Rodman Rim Units

Much of these units is covered by dense stands of western juniper with an understory of bunchgrass, rabbit-brush, and sagebrush. Gerry Mountain is the highest of the many juniper-covered buttes, rising 1,100 feet above the surrounding lands to dominate the landscape. On the extensive flats, one finds Thurber's needlegrass and bluebunch wheatgrass.

The units contain much crucial range for pronghorn, mule deer, elk, and sage grouse.

Flowing water is nonexistent, but springs can be found. Some dry lakes exist.

BLM prefers that the units be developed for oil and gas and more livestock grazing.

44. Chimney Rock (Chimney Rock Unit)

What to Expect:	A steep but short hike to a rim with Cascade peak views
Distance:	5.2 miles round trip
Elevation Change:	3,100–3,300 feet
Drinking Water:	No
Best Times:	All year
USGS 7.5' Map:	Stearns Butte
Oregon Map Starting Point:	Prineville

Go south on OR 27 approximately 16 miles to Chimney Rock Campground. Park at the trailhead on the rim side of the road. The trail is constructed; it rises quickly to the rim and ends at Chimney Rock. The area is cow-free, so note the desert crust.

45. Crooked River Overlook (Rocky Canyon Unit)

What to Expect:	A moderate day hike or easy overnight to a rim overlook
Distance:	6 miles round trip
Elevation Change:	3,600–3,960 feet
Drinking Water:	No
Best Times:	Spring, summer, fall
USGS 7.5' Map:	Bowman Dam
Oregon Map Starting Point:	Prineville

South 20.4 miles from Prineville on OR 27 is the end of the pavement. Continue on Oregon's only unpaved state highway 2.6 miles to the Bear Creek County Road. Turn west (toward Alfalfa) and drive 0.8 mile to a cattle guard and a "Road Closed" sign at the hill crest. Continue west 0.3 mile and park at a primitive way on the north.

Walk north, first on the way, then along the rim 3 miles until you find a view you like. A major obscenity in your view will be Bowman Dam and Prineville Reservoir. Downstream, it's a federal wild and scenic river. Think free-flowing thoughts.

Return the way you came or make a western arc on your return, including, if you're ambitious, to the head of Rocky Canyon.

46. Gerry Mountain Summit (Gerry Mountain Unit)

What to Expect:	A hike a through a juniper woodland
Distance:	9 miles round trip
Elevation Change:	4,496–5,392 feet
Drinking Water:	No
Best Times:	Spring, fall
USGS 7.5' Map:	Gerry Mountain
Oregon Map Starting Point:	Post

Upon reaching Buck Creek Road (see Pickett Canyon exploration), go south 1.5 miles to a dirt road to the southwest (you're driving northeast). Park. The summit is 4.5 miles south at elevation 5392T. Follow the ex-unimproved road, which turns into an ex-four-wheel-drive trail, which peters out. Continue cross-country. The thick juniper and rolling terrain are a good test of your orientation skills.

Return as you came.

47. Pickett Canyon (South Fork Unit)

What to Expect: River canyon, steep walls, and gentle benches
Distance: 13-mile loop
Elevation Change: 3,940–4,700 feet
Drinking Water: In river
Best Times: Spring, fall
USGS 7.5' Map: Sand Hollow
Oregon Map Starting Point: Post

From Post drive 18 miles east on the Post-Paulina Road to milepost 43.4. Turn south on Camp Creek Road and drive 11.4 miles to the intersection with another county road. Continue south 5.3 miles on Buck Creek Road to a dirt road (BLM Road 6575) to northeast (you're driving southeast). Drive 0.2 mile to public land and park.

This is the road BLM is proposing to close to make a larger wilderness unit. Walk north 2.6 miles to Furnace Waterhole. Follow the fence line east-north-east and then drop into the head of Pickett Canyon. After 1.4 miles you'll reach the South Fork Crooked River with a nice camp spot.

It's easy walking downriver 2.4 miles to Soda Spring, with numerous camp spots along the way. The easiest canyon exit is an unnamed tributary canyon entering from the west 0.7 mile downstream of Soda Spring. Climb westerly and upwardly out of the canyon 1.3 miles, where you break out of the juniper into the open flat. Set a southwesterly course 2 miles back to Furnace Waterhole. Return the same 2.6 miles to your start.

48. River Mile 14 Island (North Fork Unit)

What to Expect: A gentle walk to a wild river
Distance: 3.2 miles round trip
Elevation Change: 4,000–4,349 feet
Drinking Water: In the river
Best Times: Spring, summer, fall
USGS 7.5' Maps: Committee Creek, Rabbit Valley
Oregon Map Starting Point: Post

From Post drive east 9 miles (milepost 34.8) to a major BLM road, number 6578. Ignore signs designed to discourage your travel on this very public road. Stay on 6578 for approximately 17.5 miles until you reach a four-wheel-drive track 0.2 mile northeast of Cabin Spring on the south side of Cabin Butte. Park.

Walk the jeep trail 1.6 miles down to the North Fork Crooked River. At the bottom is a small island. Explore upstream and/or downstream.

Return the same way.

DESCHUTES CANYON
WILDERNESS (PROPOSED)

The meeting of the Cascade and desert ecosystems provides an unusually rich natural diversity.

Location:	Deschutes, Jefferson, and Wasco Counties, 15 miles northeast of Redmond (Steelhead Falls and The Island units); 10 miles south of Maupin (Criterion unit)
Size:	51 square miles (32,864 acres)
Terrain:	The plateau is quite gentle and flat, the canyons definitely not
Elevation Range:	1,000–3,180 feet
Managing Agencies:	Prineville District BLM, Crooked River National Grassland (Ochoco National Forest)
Agency Wilderness Status:	3,240-acre BLM wilderness study area; 0 acres recommended
Recreation Maps:	South Half Lower Deschutes River Public Lands; West Half Central Oregon Public Lands; both Prineville District BLM (the best map for upper units is the Crooked River Grassland Map on the Ochoco National Forest Map)

The area consists of four units: Criterion, Fremont Canyon, Steelhead Falls, and The Island.

The canyon is a study in the merging of several geologic strata. The wildness and scenic wonder is proportional to the elevation change. The roar of the rapids in the canyon bottom, the rich green and red hues of the streamside vegetation, and the towering canyon walls all compete for attention.

Basalt and sedimentary-layered rock formations are of varying textures, thicknesses, and colors, including reddish brown, white, light gray, dark gray, and light tan. The rivers have bisected these formations for the last several thousand years. Basalt formations rise steeply from the canyon floors and form small plateaus in several locations.

Because of the warmer, sheltered conditions in the canyons, many species bloom up to a month earlier than in exposed desert ecosystems. Upland vegetation includes western juniper clusters with an understory of big sagebrush, green rabbit-brush, bitterbrush, Idaho fescue, and bluebunch wheatgrass. Canyon bottom vegetation includes red alder, red-osier dogwood, wax currant, spirea, wildrose, penstemon, and sedges.

On side hills one finds clusters of western juniper and the occasional ponderosa pine with an understory of big sagebrush, bitterbrush, bluebunch wheatgrass, Idaho fescue, green rabbit-brush, buckwheat, wildrye, milkvetch, yarrow, gold balsamroot, and sunflowers.

Fish species include bull trout, rainbow trout, brown trout, kokanee (land-locked sockeye salmon), squawfish, and sucker.

Peregrine falcon and bald eagle winter in the canyons. Several species of owls and waterfowl, swallows, hawks, osprey, golden eagles, and two hundred other species of birds are present.

Mule deer, coyote, cottontail jackrabbit, porcupine, beaver, river otter, and badger are common.

Rattlesnakes are in high densities. The desert night snake is also reported to be in the area.

Numerous Native American and historical sites cover the area.

The Island unit is among the best undisturbed grasslands (great desert crust) left anywhere in the Columbia Basin. It is both a research natural area and closed to the public. Because of the topography, it has never been grazed, save for some sheep that served as a cover for a still during Prohibition.

49. Steelhead Falls (Steelhead Falls Unit)

What to Expect:	A steep, but short drop into a spectacular and colorful river canyon with rock spires, old-growth juniper, and more
Distance:	3.8 miles round trip
Elevation Range:	2,250–2,540 feet
Drinking Water:	Yes
Best Times:	All year
USGS 7.5' Map:	Steelhead Falls
Oregon Map Starting Point:	Terrebonne

On US 97 at the north end of Terrebonne turn west (follow the signs to the Crooked River Ranch) onto Lower Bridge Drive. In 2.1 miles turn north (right) on 43rd Street. In 1.8 miles turn west (left) on Chinook Drive. Chinook turns to the north. In 1.1 miles turn west (left) on Badger Drive. Go on Badger (*don't* take Steelhead Drive) 0.4 mile, then turn south (left) on Rainbow Drive for 0.25 mile. Turn west (right) onto Parkey Drive (not signed at this right turn, but later signs will so confirm). At 0.1 mile after this curve, Rainbow Drive continues to the south and Parkey Drive continues west. Go west on Parkey (it meanders a bit). In 0.8 mile Parkey Drive dead-ends into a curving 77th. Go northward (right) on 77th. In 0.2 mile you reach a **Y**. Northwest 81st takes off 77th. Stay to the right. Seventy-seventh meanders northward and turns into Quail (Parkey reappears as a road to the west) in 0.2 mile. In another 1 mile is an unsigned intersection with a road to the east. Continue north on Quail. In 0.3 mile turn west (left) onto River Road. Generally head west (straight). In 0.5 mile you will reach an intersection with Folly Water Road and Canyon View Place. Go straight (generally west). Continue downhill 0.3 mile to an unmarked intersection. Continue downhill to the west. In 0.1 mile you reach the trailhead/campground.

The main trail heads down-canyon to the north. In 0.3 mile you'll reach Steelhead Falls. The falls are scenic (presently lacking any steelhead, as Portland General Electric dams downstream have blocked all fish passage). The trail continues down-canyon but peters out within a mile. Return to your vehicle by the same route.

Steelhead Falls in the proposed Deschutes Canyon Wilderness (Mount Jefferson at back)

JOHN DAY RIVER WILDERNESS (PROPOSED)

A spectacular river, linking equally spectacular cliffs, canyons, habitats, and scenery.

Location:	Jefferson, Gilliam, Grant, Sherman, Wasco, and Wheeler Counties, 16 miles west of Condon (Lower Canyon unit); 15 miles southwest of Fossil (Spring Basin unit); clustered about 10 miles north of Mitchell (Sutton Mountain vicinity units: Sutton Mountain, Coyote Canyon, Dead Dog, and Painted Hills); clustered about 15 miles northwest of Dayville (upper river units: Big Cliff, Branson Creek, Hog Ridge, and Sheep Rock)
Size:	313 square miles (200,083 acres)
Terrain:	Flat river bottoms, vertical cliffs, steep canyons, and gentle plateaus
Elevation Range:	560–5,012 feet
Managing Agencies:	Prineville District BLM, National Park Service
Agency Wilderness Status:	81,299-acre BLM wilderness study area; 39,978 acres recommended; 38,940 acres no recommendation
Recreation Maps:	North and South Halves BLM Lower John Day River; North Half BLM Upper John Day River; both Prineville District BLM

These ten wild places are connected by the federal- and state-protected wild and scenic John Day River. The units are Big Cliff, Branson Creek, Coyote Canyon, Dead Dog, Hog Ridge, Lower Canyon, Painted Hills, Spring Basin, Sutton Mountain, and Sheep Rock.

The protected river corridor averages just 1/2 mile in width and is inadequate to fully protect this highly scenic and naturally diverse region. Three very small areas (Clarno, Painted Hills, and Sheep Rock) along the river comprise the John Day Fossil Beds National Monument, managed by the National Park Service. All are unique and are worth visiting (contact NPS for more information).

Because of its seasonal snowpack and water diversions for irrigation, the streamflow in the Lower Canyon unit varies from an average of 10,000 cubic feet per second in the spring runoff to a mere 100 cubic feet per second in the late summer. The stark contrast of sheer wildness beside severely degraded landscapes is common.

Columnar basalt in the proposed John Day Wilderness

Basalt defines the John Day Basin. It is everywhere in varied colors, textures, and forms. Several rare and endemic plant species are found in the basin on undisturbed lands, especially on the numerous unusual soil types.

The Oregon Biodiversity Project has identified two conservation opportunity areas in the basin: Clarno and Picture Gorge. Both were recognized as important corridors for migration of salmon and steelhead and as important habitat for the declining redband trout.

California bighorn sheep can be found in many of the units, and could be reintroduced into the rest. Other wildlife of note includes both golden and bald eagles, prairie falcon, tree and cliff swallows, long-eared owl, Canada geese, duck, red-winged blackbird, beaver, and mink. Other fish species include northern squawfish, brown bullheads, rainbow trout, and smallmouth bass.

Lower Canyon Unit

Deep river canyons, often 1,000 and occasionally 1,600 feet deep, characterize this unit. The reddish brown Columbia River basalt dominates the view from the river. Above the canyons are rolling hills and plateaus. This unit is actually in the Columbia Basin ecoregion.

Lush riparian vegetation can be found in many of the numerous side canyons that enter the river. Species include chokecherry, red-osier dogwood, mock orange, poison ivy, wild rose, blackberry, and water birch. Scattered juniper are also present on the slopes that are mainly bluebunch wheatgrass or big sagebrush/Idaho fescue communities.

Spring Basin Unit

The high points that give views of the John Day Basin are well worth the climb. Numerous canyons, both large and small, offer great solitude and scenery. Be-

Painted hills in the Sutton Mountain unit of the proposed John Day Wilderness

Petroglyphs in Lower John Day unit of the proposed John Day River Wilderness

sides the wildlife common in the Lower Canyon unit, bobcats, meadowlarks, and mountain bluebirds are in abundance. The area is an excellent example of palouse grassland, with outstanding stands of bluebunch wheatgrass and sagebrush steppe. (Palouse is the name botanists and ecologists give to the kind of grassland that grows on loess—a windblown deposit of fine-grained calcareous silt or clay—common to eastern Washington where the Palouse Indians once lived. The grassland is extremely rare because most of it was on gentle enough slope to grow wheat, and the loess soil grows lots of wheat.)

Sutton Mountain Vicinity Units

Sutton Mountain has an abrupt and colorful 2,000-foot precipice on the west and a gently sloping plateau to the east. The units are uplifted basalt formations on top of the same ash layer as the Painted Hills unit of the John Day Fossil Beds National Monument. Numerous high points offer outstanding views. Cascades and waterfalls (including one 60 feet high) are present when water is running in the spring.

Vegetation is predominantly sagebrush steppe with some Douglas-fir and ponderosa pine in the canyons and juniper scattered across the slopes. The hedgehog cactus makes for a nice spring display. Paleontological resources are also present.

Upper River Units

BLM discounted these units because of the lack of river frontage and/or public access. The Big Cliff unit has a 3,200-foot elevation change in 2.5 miles. This

198 Lava Plains Ecoregion

unit is *very* rugged and has very pretty reddish brown cliffs as well. The units are covered with scattered juniper, an occasional pine, and stands of mountain mahogany. Big sagebrush and Idaho fescue are common in the open areas, along with Sandberg's bluegrass. Mule deer are common, and the rare wolverine can be found here.

50. Clarno to Cottonwood (Lower Canyon Unit)

What to Expect:	A very easy float through spectacular basalt canyons
Distance:	69-mile river trip
Elevation Range:	569–1,190 feet
Drinking Water:	Yes
Best Times:	Late spring, early summer
USGS 7.5' Maps:	Bath, Chimney Springs, Clarno, Esau Canyon, Harmony, Horseshoe Bend, Indian Cove, Indian Spring, Shoestring Ridge
Oregon Map Starting Point:	Antelope

East 15 miles from Antelope is the put-in at Clarno on OR 218.

If you're going to see the Lower Canyon unit, you have to see it by river because very limited public access is available by land.

By canoe, raft, kayak, or drift boat this is one of the easiest river trips anywhere (except during the highest runoff). The Clarno Rapids (Class 3) should be scouted (and portaged if you wish), but all the rest is Class 1 and 2. Beware of afternoon upriver winds impeding your progress. Figure on two nights on the river. Detailed information is found in *Oregon River Tours* and *Soggy Sneakers* (see Recommended Reading). Check with the Prineville District BLM office for the latest regulations.

The take-out is at Cottonwood 12 miles southeast of Wasco on OR 206.

51. Eagle Canyon (Spring Basin Unit)

What to Expect:	Clarno formations of colorful clay soils with rugged shapes
Distance:	11.2 miles round trip
Elevation Range:	1,450–2,260 feet
Drinking Water:	Yes
Best Times:	Anytime
USGS 7.5' Maps:	Clarno, Muddy Ranch
Oregon Map Starting Point:	Antelope

From Antelope, proceed 15 miles east on OR 218 to Clarno Road (1.4 miles east of the John Day River crossing). Go south on Clarno Road 2.9 miles to a four-wheel-drive track heading east (you're now going southeast). Park a short distance up this track. This is a two-night backpack.

Walk 1 mile easterly on the four-wheel-drive track to near the top of the ridge. After dead-ending into a north-south four-wheel-drive track, take it southerly (soon moving onto Muddy Ranch quad), looping easterly into Spring Basin Canyon. At 2.2 miles, another four-wheel-drive track takes off easterly 0.8 mile, dead-ending into a four-wheel-drive track in Hay Bottom Canyon. Follow the track southerly down the canyon 0.8 mile to the junction with another four-wheel-drive track, which will take you easterly 0.8 mile into Eagle Canyon. Camp either in Spring Basin Canyon or Hay Bottom Canyon and explore Eagle Canyon the following day.

52. Sutton Mountain Summit (Sutton Mountain Unit)

What to Expect:	Spectacular views of the John Day country, including the Painted Hills from above
Distance:	6.8 miles round trip
Elevation Range:	3,120–4,694 feet
Drinking Water:	No
Best Times:	Spring, summer, fall
USGS 7.5' Maps:	Sutton Mountain, Toney Butte
Oregon Map Starting Point:	Mitchell

1 mile west on US 26 is a turnoff for OR 207. The trailhead is 50 yards north of milepost 15 on OR 207. Park off the highway. Walk down a driveway, through a fence, and bear north to the "Road Closed" sign. A four-wheel-drive track will take you to the summit. You start on the Toney Butte quad and soon move to the Sutton Mountain quad. In about 2.2 miles, you'll come to an 8 x 8 fencepost. Bear south and uphill and don't follow the unmapped track along the fence to the west.

Return as you came.

Because of the paucity of public land in the area, car-camping spots are rare. For primitive car camping, at 100 yards southwest of milepost 20 on OR 207 between Mitchell and Service Creek, take the dirt track through the gate (with the BLM public land sign) northwest into the juniper. Public camping is also available along the John Day River.

OWYHEE UPLANDS ECOREGION

The Owyhee Uplands are a broad undulating plateau cut deep by canyons such as those of the Owyhee and Malheur Rivers. The ecoregion continues into both Idaho and Nevada. The elevation ranges from 2,100 to 6,500 feet, much at an average of about 4,000 feet. Spring is wet, summer scorching, autumn perfect, and winter cold. Most moisture falls in the form of snow.

Though a "Great Basin" desert type, the topography is remarkably different. It is not basin and range, but canyonlands. The welded tuffs yield glorious rock formations reminiscent of Utah's Colorado Plateau.

Notable are the volcanic soils that derive from the underlying deposits of basalt and rhyolite. Of particular interest are the soils that come from welded tuff and volcanic ash, such as at Leslie Gulch, Succor Creek, the Rome Cliffs, and other locales.

The soils, with their unusual and distinctive chemical composition and high clay content, support a rich endemic flora. Take Ertter's senecio (*Senecio ertterae*), which according to the Oregon Biodiversity Project is "found only in parts of two adjacent gulches on less than 500 acres of habitat."[1]

Plant communities in the Owyhee Uplands include big (Wyoming and mountain) sagebrush, low sagebrush, black sage, salt desert scrub, and mountain mahogany woodlands. Riparian forests, including massive cottonwood gallery forests at the confluence of the Snake, Malheur, and Owyhee Rivers, have mostly given way to agriculture and urbanization. Magnificent Great Basin wildrye and needlegrass communities supported by the deep soil along river bottoms have essentially disappeared.

Juniper can also be found, but far less abundantly than in most of the other ecoregions of the Oregon Desert.

The Oregon Biodiversity Project has estimated that 2.1 percent of the ecoregion is adequately protected to conserve and restore biodiversity.

Given the lack of roads (especially paved ones), the Owyhee Uplands of Oregon, Idaho, Nevada, and Utah is the wildest region in the Lower Forty-Eight states.

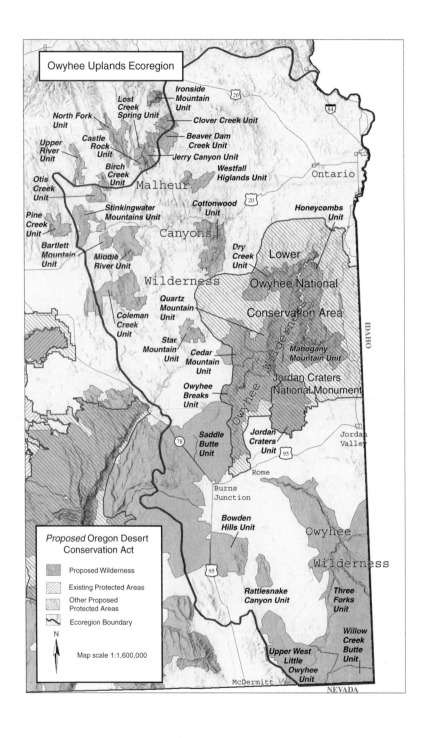

Owyhee Uplands Ecoregion

Ironside Mountain Unit
Lost Creek Spring Unit
North Fork Unit
Clover Creek Unit
Castle Rock Unit
Beaver Dam Creek Unit
Upper River Unit
Jerry Canyon Unit
Birch Creek Unit
Westfall Higlands Unit
Otis Creek Unit
Malheur
Ontario
Pine Creek Unit
Stinkingwater Mountains Unit
Cottonwood Unit
Honeycombs Unit
Bartlett Mountain Unit
Canyons
Dry Creek Unit
Lower
Middle River Unit
Wilderness
Owyhee National
Quartz Mountain Unit
Conservation Area
Coleman Creek Unit
Mahogany Mountain Unit
Star Mountain Unit
Cedar Mountain Unit
Jordan Craters National Monument
Owyhee Breaks Unit
Saddle Butte Unit
Jordan Craters Unit
Jordan Valley
78
95
Rome
Burns Junction
Bowden Hills Unit
Owyhee
95
Wilderness
Rattlesnake Canyon Unit
Three Forks Unit
Willow Creek Butte Unit
Upper West Little Owyhee Unit
McDermitt
NEVADA
IDAHO
26
84
20

Proposed Oregon Desert Conservation Act

Proposed Wilderness
Existing Protected Areas
Other Proposed Protected Areas
Ecoregion Boundary

N

Map scale 1:1,600,000

JORDAN CRATERS NATIONAL MONUMENT (PROPOSED)

A stark expanse of bare lava, some less than a century old.

Location:	Malheur County, 15 miles northwest of Jordan Valley
Size:	132 square miles (84,430 acres)
Terrain:	Mostly lava flows, vegetated and not, and some open water
Elevation Range:	4,180–4,806 feet
Managing Agencies:	Vale District BLM (present); National Park Service (proposed)
Recreation Map:	North Half Jordan Resource Area, Vale District BLM

Craters, spatter cones, lava tubes, caves, cracks, sinks, domes, pits, blisters, and gutters. To the geologic connoisseur, each tells a separate story. Encompassing several lava flows of varying ages, the area shows how nature reclaims the flows using wind and water erosion as well as vegetation.

Over time, and assuming no more volcanic events, some day in the far distant future the flows won't be recognizable to the untrained eye. But now they are unmistakable and unimaginable.

Coffeepot Crater is the most prominent feature in Jordan Craters. It is the main source of a 27-square-mile olivine basalt flow estimated to be four thousand to nine thousand years old.

Volcanically speaking, Jordan Craters may well not be extinct. Scientists have discovered 18 acres of the bare lava that's really bare—no lichens and mosses. That means this part of the flow is less than a hundred years old.

Flows to the south in the Clarks Butte area are much older and more covered with vegetation. They provide excellent and diverse wildlife habitats. The terrain is essentially too rugged for domestic livestock. Hence the vegetation is pristine.

Sometimes the lava flowed around points of higher land, leaving the vegetated kipukas.

Where there is vegetation it is usually the big sagebrush/bluebunch wheatgrass community common to the Oregon Desert. Because of the diversity of habitats, the presence of water, and the lack of livestock, wildlife thrive.

From eight bat species (including the very rare Townsend's big-eared) to the cougar and bobcat, which have restricted range in the desert, Jordan Craters is a haven for wildlife. Sage grouse, mule deer, and pronghorn can often be seen (herds of the latter sometimes swim at night to the island in Lower Cow Lake and can be seen in the moonlight). Because of the open water of the lakes and marshes, one also finds beaver, otter, and muskrat.

The water is concentrated in a few spots like Upper Cow, Lower Cow, Batch, and Crater Lakes, which are the most diverse and are stops for migratory water-

Coffeepot Crater in the proposed Jordan Craters National Monument

fowl. Over three hundred species of wildlife, including white pelican, long-billed curlew, and bald eagle, have been counted in the area.

The proposed national monument is within the Oregon Biodiversity Project's Middle Owyhee River Conservation Opportunity Area.

The BLM's Cow Lakes Campground (take a hint on the name) is a pathetic excuse for a recreational facility and typifies why, as an agency, BLM does a poor job of managing special natural areas and/or people in the absence of specific congressional direction to do so. The campground is set in a crested wheatgrass seeding, and cattle have free range among the picnic tables. If they aren't rubbing up against your tent and/or bellowing all night, evidence enough is still present (watch your step). If only they could be trained to use those fancy outhouses.

WHAT TO DO

There are two major visitor entrances: Cow Lakes and Coffeepot Crater. One can't easily get from one to the other without returning to Jordan Valley.

To reach the do-not-miss Coffeepot Crater, drive approximately 8 miles north of Jordan Valley on US 95. Turn west (left) on a good BLM road (signs say "Jordan Craters"). In about 24 miles (you see Coffeepot Crater well before it), take an unmarked road south 1.4 miles to a parking lot.

A short interpretive walk available is at Coffeepot Crater. Don't try it at high noon in August when surface temperatures can reach 120 degrees Fahrenheit.

To visit Cow Lakes from Jordan Valley, go west approximately 5 miles (southbound in the grander scheme) on US 95, which then turns to the southwest. Continue west on a county road, following signs to Cow Lakes.

After checking out the BLM Cow Lakes cowground for yourself, take the West Peninsula exploration (below).

53. West Peninsula
(Jordan Craters Unit, Owyhee Wilderness)

What to Expect:	Great birding and scenery
Distance:	2.4 miles round trip
Elevation Range:	4,347–4,381 feet
Drinking Water:	In the lake
Best Times:	Spring, summer, fall
USGS 7.5' Map:	Cow Lakes
Oregon Map Starting Point:	Jordan Valley

See above for directions to Cow Lakes Campground.

From the BLM campground, cross at The Narrows below the little dam on Upper Cow Lake. Old pavement across the wide stream channel marks the way. Depending on the time of year, you may have to wade or you may not want to try it at all. Cow Lakes is regulated for irrigation use downstream. During spring high water or summer irrigation releases, the water may be too dangerous. Assuming it's not, hike the unimproved way south and then west along the north shore of Lower Cow Lake. (The USGS 7.5' quad map shows the route as ending, but it continues west along the lakeshore and then turns northwest over a gentle saddle toward the lava flow that abuts Upper Cow Lake.) Shortly you'll come to the interface of the sagebrush grassland, black lava flow, and open water. The way continues a short way west into the Lava Flow. While you are there, bag "peak" 4381 for a panoramic view.

LOWER OWYHEE NATIONAL CONSERVATION AREA (PROPOSED)

A forgotten wild wonderland.

Location:	Malheur County, 20 miles southeast of Adrian
Size:	1,706 square miles (1,091,721 acres)
Terrain:	Rugged river canyons, vast plateaus, and geologic wonders
Elevation Range:	2,320–6,522 feet
Managing Agency:	Vale District BLM
Recreation Map:	South Half Malheur Resource Area, North Half Jordan Resource Area, Vale District BLM

A national conservation area is needed to protect outstanding natural features, restore degraded landscapes, and manage increasing numbers of people. The Lower

Owyhee National Conservation Area would include Birch Creek Ranch, Dry Creek watershed, Honeycombs, Leslie Gulch, Lower Owyhee Canyon, Mahogany Mountain, Middle Owyhee Canyon, Owyhee Reservoir, Owyhee Wilderness, Rome Cliffs, Succor Creek State Recreation Area and vicinity, and Twin Springs.

Much of the area is threatened by cyanide heap leach mining for gold, including at Grassy Mountain, the Honeycombs, and several other sites. Livestock are also a serious ecological irritant and an increasing recreational conflict.

Establishment of a national conservation area would be an important step in defining a new mission for the BLM. Livestock use would be fairly phased out, and a priority of the BLM would be to restore degraded ecosystems.

Birch Creek Ranch

BLM acquired this historic ranch and is now managing it as a river take-out point, campground, nascent resort, and historic site. Besides the impropriety of using too much fossil fuel to pump too much river water to keep too many acres of lawns green in the middle of August, the incessant droning of the pumps defeats the intended relaxing effect.

Dry Creek Watershed

"The Dry Creek watershed is recognized by the American Fisheries Society for its importance both as a reference watershed (highest ecological integrity) and a genetic refuge," says the Oregon Biodiversity Project.[2]

Honeycombs

Visiting the Honeycombs is like a trip to southern Utah. The geologic splendor is not surpassed in Oregon.

Leslie Gulch

Home to several rare plant species, including at least two found here and nowhere else, Leslie Gulch is strikingly scenic. It is also a take-out for river trips and a boat ramp for motorized use of the reservoir. Increasing human use requires special management. The highly inappropriate cabin on a highly inappropriate inholding of private land should be acquired by the BLM and then burned to the ground.

Lower Owyhee Canyon

Including 14 miles of the Owyhee River (below the dam), the area is a popular wildlife-viewing area and includes Snively Hot Spring.

Mahogany Mountain

The highest point in the Owyhee Uplands supports several of the ecoregion's largest blocks of mountain mahogany woodland, while Mahogany Creek to the south is a genetic refuge for numerous aquatic species. Unfortunately, many of these public values are presently in private ownership. Private holdings should be acquired.

Middle Owyhee Canyon

The unit includes about 66 miles of the free-flowing Owyhee River, including the incomparable The Hole in the Ground and unforgettable canyons.

Owyhee Reservoir

This area gets a great deal of recreational use, which could be better managed within a national conservation area under the management of the BLM. The U.S. Bureau of Reclamation currently manages the reservoir shoreline.

Owyhee Wilderness

The national conservation area would add an additional layer of protection to a good portion of the proposed Owyhee Wilderness, including the Mahogany Mountain, Honeycombs, Dry Creek, Quartz Mountain, and Middle Owyhee units.

Rome Cliffs

Fantastic white chalky cliffs rise in the Rome Valley. Highly scenic, only half are in public ownership, and in a 1-mile-square checkerboard ownership at that. BLM plans to divest of these holdings.

Succor Creek State Recreation Area and Vicinity

The Succor Creek Canyon includes canyon walls the color of slate gray with mineralized splotches of greens, yellows, oranges, and reds. Rock spires rise hundreds of feet in the air.

There is not a more forgotten and forlorn state park in Oregon. Far from the beaten path and receiving relatively little use, the 1,900-acre park suffers from a serious lack of maintenance and management. Additionally, the current boundaries do not include much of the geologic features in the Succor Creek watershed. Two decades ago, a similar situation existed for three other Oregon Desert state parks. They are now the John Day Fossil Beds National Monument.

Succor Creek in the proposed Lower Owyhee National Conservation Area

Twin Springs

An oasis in some of the most remote country in Oregon, Twin Springs is the gateway to Dry Creek, which is even more remote.

The ecological values of the proposed national conservation area are well documented. The Oregon Biodiversity Project has recognized two conservation opportunity areas that overlap much of the proposed national conservation area (Middle Owyhee River and Dry Creek).

WHAT TO DO

There are six gateways to the proposed national conservation area.

Succor Creek Canyon

From Adrian, drive south on OR 201 and follow the signs to Succor Creek State Recreation Area.

Leslie Gulch

A high-quality graded road makes this trip almost too easy. Continue southerly through Succor Creek State Recreation Area to the turnoff to Leslie Gulch (21 miles after leaving OR 201). Continue westerly 13 miles to the end of the road.

Several short hikes are available, including Juniper Canyon to the north and Dago Gulch to the south. The latter has a relic stand of four-hundred-year-old ponderosa pines. If you want to see bighorn sheep close up, Leslie Gulch is the place, especially in winter.

Birch Creek Ranch

Returning to the intersection that would take you back through Succor Creek Canyon, instead turn southerly toward US 95. At US 95 drive south 10 miles (to a point approximately 8 miles north of Jordan Valley) and turn west on a good (when dry) county road. This is the same road that takes you to Coffeepot Crater (see Jordan Craters National Monument). Follow the signs to Birch Creek Ranch, which is roughly 30 miles from US 95.

The intersection at which you must choose to go to Birch Creek or Coffeepot Crater is near where about 6 miles of *very* steep road take you to Birch Creek Ranch. Drive very slowly and carefully going down in a low gear to prevent brake overheating. Going up, watch your engine temperature indicator and a keep a nose out for overheating. If you do start to overheat, park and let it cool. Running with the heater at full blast helps keep the engine—though not you—cool. Don't run air-conditioning.

After Birch Creek, continue to Coffeepot Crater (Jordon Craters National Monument).

Coming back to the main road from having done Coffeepot Crater, go not easterly but first continue westerly for 4.1 miles to an intersection. Turn north and proceed 0.4 mile to the canyon rim to take in one of the most incredible views in Oregon. The Hole in the Ground is where the Middle Owyhee Canyon widens to expose an exquisite palette of geologic color. In the right light it is incomparable.

Lower Owyhee Canyon

From Nyssa, go south on OR 201 and follow signs to Owyhee Reservoir and/or Lake [sic] Owyhee State Park. As you drive the scenic river canyon before reaching the dam, stop off for a dip in the Snively Hot Spring and watch some wildlife.

Continuing past the dam, the road ends at a boat ramp. If you do have a motorboat, it is the easiest way to see the Honeycombs.

Rome Cliffs

From downtown Rome, drive northwesterly to view the Rome Cliffs.

Twin Springs Vicinity

The entire proposed national conservation area west of the Owyhee River is much harder to get to. The easiest is the Twin Springs area. It has a very nice primitive campground, both because of the time it takes to reach it and because it has running water in an area where little water ever runs. It qualifies as Oregon's most remote campground.

From downtown Vale, drive westerly about 5 miles to an intersection. Turn south on the county road, which turns into BLM Road 7320. Follow 7320 to Twin Springs Campground in approximately 30 miles (the Vale District's Malheur Resource Area recreation map is almost required to find it). This road is better in summer and fall.

MALHEUR CANYONS WILDERNESS (PROPOSED)

Eighteen wild refugia, each worthy of wilderness designation on its own.

Location:	Grant, Harney, and Malheur Counties, centered 30 miles northeast of Burns (five forest ecotone units, three Castle Rock units, two Upper Bully Creek units); 10 miles southwest of Ironside (Ironside Mountain unit); 15 miles south-southwest of Harper (Cottonwood unit); 10 miles west-south-west of Juntura (Middle River unit); 5 miles west of Westfall (Westfall Highlands unit); 15 miles east of Crane (Coleman Creek unit); 32 miles east-northeast of New Princeton (north of Crowley; Star Mountain unit); 5 miles southwest of Drewsey (two Stinkingwater Mountains units)
Size:	512 square miles (328,186 acres)
Terrain:	Forested headwaters to rugged desert rocky canyons to open rolling hills
Elevation Range:	2,680–7,811 feet
Managing Agencies:	Burns and Vale Districts BLM
Agency Wilderness Status:	76,900-acre BLM wilderness study area; 45,650 acres recommended
Recreation Maps:	North and South Halves, Malheur Resource Area, Vale District BLM; Northeast Quarter, Burns District BLM

An extremely diverse set of units comprise this proposed wilderness. From lovely forested headwaters, through the ecotone transition from forest to sagebrush steppe, to some very stark and beautiful canyons, these units are related ecologically and serve as the anchors of biodiversity of the Malheur River Basin.

The wildlife is as diverse as the landscape. Of greatest concern is the fate of the redband trout, for which several of the proposed wilderness units serve as refugia or repopulation habitats.

Pacific salmon once spawned in the Malheur River Basin, but dams on the Snake River downstream presently prevent it.

The proposed wilderness is comprised of seven BLM wilderness study areas: Malheur River–Bluebucket Creek, Beaver Dam Creek, Castle Rock, Camp Creek, Cottonwood Creek, Gold Creek, and Sperry Creek.

The area is best categorized in ten separate regions: Castle Rock, Coleman Creek, Cottonwood, the Forest Ecotone, Ironside Mountain, Middle River, Stinkingwater Mountains, Star Mountain, Upper Bully Creek, and Westfall Highlands. Several of the units are actually in the Blue Mountains ecoregions (see map).

Castle Rock Region: Castle Rock, Jerry Canyon, and Lost Creek Spring Units

Interspersed among the bluebunch wheatgrass, mountain big sagebrush, and Idaho fescue are significant stands of western juniper, mountain mahogany, Douglas-fir, and ponderosa pine. Mule deer, Rocky Mountain elk, and sage grouse are common.

Castle Rock is the neck of an extinct volcano and reaches 6,780 feet in elevation. It last erupted 15 million years ago. One of the most prominent landmarks in the desert, it can be seen from much of the Malheur and adjoining basins. It served as a vision quest site for the Northern Paiutes.

Coleman Creek Unit

Coleman Creek arises in the south end of the Stinkingwater Mountains. It soon forms into a magnificent canyon lined with quaking aspen, willows, western juniper, and mountain mahogany. Redband trout have a stronghold here, and elk and deer are abundant.

Castle Rock in unit of the same name in the proposed Malheur Canyons Wilderness

Cottonwood Unit

Comprised of four major creek drainages (Camp Creek, Gold Creek, Sperry Creek, and Cottonwood Creek), this is a very steep and rugged area. It is a pure sagebrush steppe ecosystem. Most streams flow into Cottonwood Creek. The average slope ranges from 25 to 90 percent. Impressive basaltic canyons dissect tablelands covered with low sagebrush/bluebunch wheatgrass or big sagebrush/ Idaho fescue communities. The tablelands are rich in wild onion, violet, daisy fleabane, phlox, clover, and buckwheat.

Numerous pockets of riparian vegetation are scattered through the canyon bottoms with willows, golden currant, bittercherry, wild rose, sedges, and rushes. Pockets of Great Basin wildrye may be found on the side slopes.

The unit is also home to Rocky Mountain elk and pronghorn. It has some crucial mule deer winter range and outstanding sage grouse and raptor habitat, including habitat for golden eagles, prairie falcons, turkey vultures, kestrels, red-tailed hawks, and great horned owls.

Several archaeological sites exist.

Forest Ecotone Region: North Fork, Upper River, Pine Creek, Otis Creek, and Birch Creek Units

These units are generally high tablelands cut deeply by streams with canyons averaging 600 to 1,000 feet deep. Adjacent (as well as additional wilderness units) lands on the Malheur National Forest upstream are heavily forested. Cliffs and talus slopes are common to the area. Blue, ruffed, and sage grouse can be found here. The streams are home to significant numbers of redband trout.

Malheur River in Upper River unit of the proposed Malheur Canyons Wilderness

Ironside Mountain Unit

A prominent landmark visible from US 26, Ironside Mountain is the tallest point in the proposed wilderness. It is on the edge of two conservation opportunity areas identified by the Oregon Biodiversity Project: Malheur River Headwaters and Bully Creek.

Middle River Unit

The main feature is the Malheur River, which flows through this unit of rolling hills, high plateaus, and broad, flat expanses. Scattered juniper are found among the big and low sagebrush. The unit includes crucial deer winter range and year-round pronghorn habitat. The flats atop Upton Mountain, because of its defensive topography, have never been grazed by livestock.

Stinkingwater Mountains Region: Stinkingwater Mountains and Bartlett Mountain Units

The Stinkingwater Mountains are characterized by steep uplift and faulted volcanics that form rock outcroppings. Stiff sage, western juniper, and big sagebrush are the dominant vegetation. Sage grouse, pronghorn, and mule deer are the most common wildlife species. Teepee rings have been discovered.

Star Mountain Unit

The Bureau of Land Management first proposed Star Mountain as a wilderness study area and then caved in to local pressure. "The unit is generally free of the imprints of man's work but does not offer outstanding opportunities for solitude and primitive recreation," noted the agency. BLM did allow that the area had "geological and ecological features that are of scientific, educational and scenic value."

But under BLM's rules, unless the primitive recreation or the solitude was "outstanding," the area was dropped from further consideration. Star Mountain was marked down because the recreation was only "moderate," as most slopes were "exposed to a full view from the majority of the unit." It also lost points in the solitude category because only the northwest slope is "sparsely covered with juniper trees," and the "remainder of the unit has little vegetative screening" for the visitor. Only the Crowley Creek drainage provides adequate "topographic screening."

The greatest loss of wilderness-quality land in the Oregon BLM wilderness review process was lands that the agency determined to be generally natural, but not "outstanding" enough in terms of primitive recreation and/or solitude.

BLM hypothesized a Star Mountain being overrun with visitors who couldn't stay out of each other's sight because the country was too open. The heaviest period of recreation use is hunting season, and even then one need not fear being overrun.

Nonetheless, wildlife like Star Mountain. It is important pronghorn habitat and also supports mule deer. High up the mountain, the sparse western juniper (also on the south-facing slope) provides a habitat type sparse in the Owyhee Uplands. Sage grouse also inhabit the area.

Crowley and Little Crowley Creeks have willow and aspen in the draws. Most of the area is covered with sagebrush, bunchgrass, and juniper. The very rare and endangered Barren Valley collomia (*Collomia renacta*), a forb, is found here and in only a few other sites.

Star Mountain is out in the middle of nowhere and is little known and even less visited. The Oregon Official State Map only grants it 5,500 feet of elevation, though it is actually 6,037 feet at the summit. It provides an important ecological link between the larger wildlands of the proposed Malheur and Owyhee Wildernesses.

Upper Bully Creek Region: Beaver Dam Creek and Clover Creek Units

Both units are in the Bully Creek Conservation Opportunity Area, as identified by the Oregon Biodiversity Project. It was recognized for its extensive mosaics of aspen groves, big sagebrush, mountain mahogany, western juniper, and ponderosa pine habitats. It contains a significant example of big sagebrush communities with squaw apple and Thurber's needlegrass.

"The unusually diverse combination of habitats support species ranging from woodland-nesting goshawks to sage grouse, pronghorn, deer and elk," notes the Oregon Biodiversity Project.[3] The juniper/steppe woodland is an ecotone between ponderosa pine forest and the sagebrush steppe and is of limited extent in Oregon.

Westfall Highlands Unit

The western portion of the Westfall Highlands unit is comprised of steep buttes covered with western juniper, quaking aspen, and mountain mahogany that give way eastward to broad expanses of open sagebrush grasslands dissected by Cottonwood Creek. At first glance, one's attention focuses on the long view of the vastness of the landscape. The medium view can be rather monotonous. Take the time to look closely. One can find much, including the delicate mariposa lily.

The area is known for its stiff sage, which grows in the most harsh soil conditions, including near superficial bedrock. In its old age, stiff sage can take on a bonsai-like appearance.

"The unit offers considerable zoological study opportunities, geologic and botanical interest, scenic vistas, and some cultural and historic sites," notes the BLM, which then dropped it from further wilderness consideration.

54. Beaver Dam Creek (Beaver Dam Creek Unit)

What to Expect:	A pleasant mosaic of mountain mahogany, aspen, juniper, and sagebrush
Distance:	7.2-mile loop or 6.4 miles round trip
Elevation Range:	4,200–5,580 feet
Drinking Water:	Yes
Best Times:	Spring, fall
USGS 7.5' Maps:	DeBord Peaks, Hunter Mountain
Oregon Map Starting Point:	Ironside

(High clearance and/or four-wheel drive and an attitude is required to get to the hike site.) At 0.5 mile west of Ironside on US 26, take the Rose Creek Road south and follow this county road with signs toward Juntura. After approximately 15 miles on the main road, you'll come to a "major" (consider where you are) intersection. There is a tiny reservoir east of the intersection. Take the south road (still toward Juntura) 3.3 miles. Proceed east (immediately fording a stream) approximately 6.6 miles to where the road passes through a saddle. Park.

Hike south (DeBord Peaks quad) along the ridge between Godding and Beaver Dam Creeks (Hunter Mountain quad) to Buckskin Spring and then to Pinto Springs. Continue walking down Beaver Dam Creek as far as you'd like. (If you go too far, you'll reach private land and arguably some of the most cow-bombed landscape anywhere.) Return the way you came or hike east and then up Steamboat Creek, or west and then up Godding Creek, to the road and back to your vehicle.

55. Bluebucket Creek (Upper River Unit)

What to Expect:	A strenuous hike down canyons, across talus slopes, through forest, on open hillsides, and with rattlesnakes
Distance:	4.6-mile loop
Elevation Range:	4,020–4,856 feet
Drinking Water:	Yes
Best Times:	Spring, summer, fall
USGS 7.5' Map:	Moffit Table
Oregon Map Starting Point:	Drewsey

Go upriver (northwest) for 13 miles on the Van-Drewsey Road to a major Forest Service road (if you've crossed the river, you've gone too far). Proceed northeasterly approximately 5 miles and park where an unimproved way takes off to northwest.

Hike westerly across Moffit Table toward elevation 4856 on the rim of Malheur River Canyon. It is rugged looking, but one can scout routes down to the river. Cattle and game trails will lead you to the confluence of Bluebucket Creek and then up Bluebucket Creek to the side canyon that takes you south, up, and back to your vehicle. This can either be a day hike or an overnight trip with a campsite near the river. *Lots* of rattlesnakes (guess which subspecies).

56. Castle Rock Circumnavigation (Castle Rock Unit)

What to Expect:	Easy hike around a big old volcanic plug
Distance:	4.5-mile loop
Elevation Range:	5,605–6,400 feet
Drinking Water:	Yes
Best Times:	Spring, summer, fall
USGS 7.5' Map:	Castle Rock
Oregon Map Starting Point:	Juntura

Proceed northerly on a good county road to the northeast side of Beulah Reservoir. After crossing a bridge over Warm Springs Creek, proceed along the north side of the reservoir to a major intersection in 1.4 miles. Turn north on BLM road (follow signs to Ironside). Drive northerly on the main road 8.4 miles to an intersection where another road comes in from the south. You can car camp here (the best spot) or drive south on the other lower-quality road (additional car camps) 1.1 miles to where a four-wheel-drive track leaves the road for Castle Spring.

From wherever you park, the goal is to circumnavigate Castle Rock. It is approachable from all sides. Backpackers can either camp at Castle Spring or south in the Castle Rock Creek headwaters.

57. Coleman Creek Canyon (Coleman Creek Unit)

What to Expect:	A little old-growth Douglas-fir and a beautiful stream canyon with redband trout
Distance:	5.6 miles day hike or 9 miles backpack round trip
Elevation Range:	4,680–5,562 feet
Drinking Water:	Yes
Best Times:	Spring, summer, fall
USGS 7.5' Maps:	Coleman Mountain, Warm Springs Creek
Oregon Map Starting Point:	Burns

Proceed 27 miles east on US 20 to Stinkingwater Pass. Take a major BLM road approximately 12 miles south to a major intersection. Go easterly (left) 6.4 miles

Coleman Creek Canyon in the proposed Malheur Canyons Wilderness

and park at the intersection of an unimproved way (elevation 5,562 feet). At this point you are headed northeast, and the way takes off to the south.

Walk southerly on unimproved ways 2.4 miles to where a way crosses the uppermost headwaters (probably dry) of Coleman Creek. Hike downstream 0.4 mile to a relic stand of old-growth Douglas-fir interspersed with numerous cool meadows, springs, and ponds. If you're day hiking, return the way you came or walk the northerly side canyon back to your vehicle. If you're backpacking, press onward down the creek (it is slower and lovelier than you can imagine).

Walk down Coleman Creek Canyon as far as you like and camp. You can always bail out back to your vehicle to the north. You may want to plan *two* days and hike 2 miles down Coleman Creek with its many springs to where the creek turns south and a tributary canyon comes in from the north. Walk 0.7 mile up and out of this canyon to Chicken Flat. Set a 3.5-mile course northwesterly across Coleman Mountain to your vehicle.

58. Cottonwood Creek (Cottonwood Unit)

What to Expect: Wide-bottomed meandering river canyon
Distance: 13.2 miles round trip
Elevation Range: 3,360–3,680 feet
Drinking Water: Yes
Best Times: Spring, summer, fall
USGS 7.5' Maps: Alder Creek, Tims Peak
Oregon Map Starting Point: Harper Junction (just south of Harper on US 26)

A four-wheel-drive or high-clearance vehicle is nice, but not usually required. Take the county road southerly from Harper Junction (yes, in the Harper Valley; whether they have a PTA is unknown) approximately 10 miles to an intersection with an unimproved road that heads up Cottonwood Creek (often dry here). A huge old cottonwood marks the spot. Drive southwesterly 3 miles to an intersection. Drive southerly about 1 mile and park (Tims Peak quad).

Hike 1.5 miles southwesterly to the end of the unimproved "road." You can continue up Cottonwood Creek Canyon southwesterly 4.8 miles to near the confluence with Alder Creek (Alder Creek quad). This is best done as a 1- or 2-night backpack.

Cottonwood Creek in unit of the same name in the proposed Malheur Canyon Wilderness

59. Ironside Mountain Summit (Ironside Mountain Unit)

What to Expect:	An extremely rugged cross-country assault on the summit, with incredible views
Distance:	8.6 miles round trip
Elevation Range:	5,078–7,811 feet
Drinking Water:	No
Best Times:	Late spring, summer, fall
USGS 7.5' Maps:	Clevenger Butte, DeBord Peaks, Eldorado Pass
Oregon Map Starting Point:	Unity

Drive approximately 10 miles easterly of Unity on US 26. Turn southwesterly on County Road 513, which soon turns into FS Road 16. After 2.9 miles take the southerly fork (FS Road 1684). Continue on FS Road 1684 for approximately 8 miles (FS Road 1684 goes southerly up King Creek, easterly along a ridge, and northerly down Middle Willow Creek.) Park at the intersection of a road to the right (southerly), where a culvert has washed out.

Cross Middle Willow Creek (Eldorado Pass quad) and walk 1.1 miles *up* east to the open ridge (elevation 7,432 feet). Continue 3.2 miles southwesterly along the ridge to the summit (a tiny bit of DeBord Peaks quad onto Clevenger Butte quad). Return the way you came. This is an insane hike. *Only* attempt it if you are in *really* good shape. Start *very* early and plan to return late. Take *plenty* of water and *at least* two lunches. It is worth it.

60. Star Mountain Summit (Star Mountain Unit)

What to Expect:	Great views all around from the summit
Distance:	8.5-mile loop
Elevation Range:	4,503–6,037 feet
Drinking Water:	Available
Best Times:	Late spring, fall
USGS 7.5' Maps:	Crowley, Star Creek Reservoir, Stockade Mountain
Oregon Map Starting Point:	New Princeton

Continue southeast on OR 78 for 32 miles. Turn northeast on the gravel county road toward Crowley and drive 26 miles to where the road takes sharp right turn to the east and a lesser (but adequate) quality road takes off to the west (Crowley quad). Go through the gate (not north into private land). Proceed westerly, then northerly, approximately 7.5 miles (now on Stockade Mountain quad) to an even lesser-quality road to the northeast. You are in a very flat and wide ephemeral stream bottom. Drive 0.3 mile northeast to ensure that you park on public land.

Hike the unimproved way up the south slope of Star Mountain. The summit is an easy bag (just on Star Creek Reservoir quad). Proceed southeasterly along the Star Mountain ridge to Twin Springs and then back to your vehicle. Water can be had at several springs or in the creeks at certain times of the year. This can either be a long day hike or an overnight backpack.

61. Upton Mountain (Middle River Unit)

What to Expect:	A cow-free table of pristine grassland
Distance:	2.8-mile loop/round trip
Elevation Range:	3,785–4,829 feet
Drinking Water:	No
Best Times:	Spring, fall
USGS 7.5' Map:	Upton Mountain
Oregon Map Starting Point:	Drewsey Junction (2 miles south of Drewsey on US 20)

Go east 1 mile and turn south on a good road. Go southerly 9.1 miles and park at an unimproved way heading east. You've just crossed two wide stream drainages, are pointed east, and are just about to turn southeast.

Hike easterly 0.9 mile to the intersection with a four-wheel-drive trail. Take the trail southerly about 1.1 miles until you decide to head east and up 0.3 mile onto the very distinct saddle of Upton Mountain. In the saddle, you have to find your route through the rock rims to either the south or north benches. The north bench is smaller, but a little higher, and overlooks the south table. Return the same way you came, or head cross-country. This is an easy day hike, or you can backpack to the base of the notch to camp.

62. Westfall Butte (Westfall Highlands Unit)

What to Expect:	A nice easy walk to some nice views
Distance:	3.2-mile loop
Elevation Range:	4,500–5,741 feet
Drinking Water:	No
Best Times:	Spring, fall
USGS 7.5' Map:	Westfall Butte
Oregon Map Starting Point:	Westfall

About 1 mile west of Westfall is a bridge. West 0.5 mile from the bridge take BLM's "Lawrence Road" approximately 3 miles to an intersection. Take the right (straight west, not south) fork 1.6 miles to a gate. Go through the gate (west) and continue 8 miles and park directly east of Westfall Butte.

Proceed directly to the summit. Continue southerly on the ridge to Hart Spring and return to your vehicle.

OWYHEE WILDERNESS (PROPOSED)

A magnificent wild river flowing through some of the wildest country in the Lower Forty-Eight.

Location:	Malheur County, 40 miles north of McDermitt (Bowden Hills unit); 44 miles south of Harper (Cedar Mountain unit); 20 miles south-southeast of Harper (Dry Creek unit); 30 miles north-northwest of Jordan Valley (Honeycombs unit); 15 miles northwest of Jordan Valley (Jordan Craters unit); 20 miles north-northwest of Jordan Valley (Mahogany Mountain unit); 6 miles north of Rome (Owyhee Breaks unit); 30 miles northwest of Jordan Valley (Quartz Mountain unit); 30 miles north-northeast of McDermitt (Rattlesnake Canyon unit); 6 miles west of Rome (Saddle Butte unit); 10 miles southeast of Rome (Three Forks unit); 15 miles east-northeast of McDermitt (Upper West Little Owyhee unit); 25 miles east of McDermitt (Willow Creek Butte unit)
Size:	2,130 square miles (1,363,054 acres)
Terrain:	Roaring river canyons, desert mountain peaks, big flats, high tablelands, fantastic geologic formations, wide and flat lava flows, and more
Elevation Range:	2,540–6,522 feet
Managing Agency:	Vale District BLM
Agency Wilderness Status:	796,065-acre BLM wilderness study area; 405,106 acres recommended (additional wilderness in Idaho and Nevada)
Recreation Map:	South Half Malheur Resource Area, North and South Halves, Jordan Resource Area

The Owyhee River drains a huge area—parts of Oregon, Idaho, and Nevada. The mouth of the Owyhee River is at a confluence with the Snake River. (The Oregon-Idaho line heads due south from the mouth, explaining why there is a small part of Oregon *east* of the Snake River.) Moving upstream through some serious agriculture, the river is dammed by the Owyhee Dam. South of the reservoir, the river is a river again, and a wild one at that.

At Three Forks the North Fork and the Middle Fork join the mainstem (mistakenly called by some the South Fork). Upstream from Three Forks the West Little Owyhee River joins the mainstem. Continuing up the mainstem into Idaho, the East Fork and the South Fork converge to create the mainstem. A tributary of the South Fork is the Little Owyhee River (sometimes called the East Little Owyhee River). Confused yet?

Within the proposed wilderness are most of the Upper West Little Owyhee and Owyhee National Wild and Scenic Rivers.

The Owyhee country was even more wild before the Owyhee Dam cut off the magnificent salmon runs. According to the Oregon Biodiversity Project's *Oregon's Living Landscape:*

> *Runs of spring and fall chinook salmon (Oncorhynchus tshawytscha spp.) once traveled up the Owyhee River as far as Nevada. These hardy fish averaged only 10-14 pounds, far smaller than the huge salmon that spawned in the Columbia River system, but they endured a longer and more arduous journey to their spawning grounds.*
>
> *In some years the vagaries of precipitation in the ecoregion's arid environment left insufficient water for both the salmon's upstream passage and their spawning habitat. But in good years, input of thousands of salmon in the upper reaches of these desert rivers resulted in local abundance for many other species of fish and wildlife. Local Paiute tribes also benefited from the successful fish runs.*
>
> *These salmon were central to a complex food web of predators and prey, scavengers, and other fish that all depended on the annual salmon runs. With the eradication of the salmon, many of these other species similarly declined or disappeared altogether.[4]*

The biodiversity values of the region are well recognized. The Oregon Biodiversity Project has identified four conservation opportunity areas: Crooked Creek–Alvord Basin, Dry Creek, Middle Owyhee River, and the Upper Owyhee River.

The proposed Owyhee Wilderness has thirteen units: Bowden Hills, Cedar Mountain, Quartz Mountain, Dry Creek, Honeycombs, Jordan Craters, Mahogany Mountain, Owyhee Breaks, Rattlesnake Canyon, Saddle Butte, Three Forks, Upper West Little Owyhee, and Willow Creek Butte. Adjacent wildlands in Idaho and Nevada are also proposed for wilderness designation.

The proposed wilderness includes seventeen wilderness study areas: Bowden Hills, Blue Canyon, Clarks Butte, Cedar Creek, Dry Creek, Dry Creek Buttes, Owyhee Breaks, Upper Leslie Gulch, Slocum Creek, Honeycombs, Wild Horse Basin, Saddle Butte, Jordan Craters, Lower Owyhee Canyon, Upper West Little Owyhee, Lookout Butte, and Owyhee Canyon.

The most popular way to explore the Owyhee country is by river. The easiest river trip is Rome to Owyhee Reservoir. Take-out is either at Birch Creek Ranch (a very steep road out, which can be impassable in rain) or Leslie Gulch (bring a motor or get towed through the reservoir). The segment from Three Forks to Rome is quite exciting, perhaps too exciting for some. Starting in Idaho on either the South Fork or East Fork, one can float—early in the spring when enough water is present—downstream to Three Forks. Guided trips are available for all sections. (See Recommended Reading.)

Bowden Hills Unit

Sublime, the Bowden Hills are not. The wilderness values of this unit are very important to the native flora and fauna, but humans won't likely appreciate it, unless on a vision quest.

But what solitude! As BLM notes, "There is nothing in the area to attract or concentrate visitors."

The unit is characterized by rolling hills. Some rimrock is exposed, giving a little visual variety. There are no perennial water sources.

The Bowden Hills lies in the Crooked Creek–Alvord Basin Conservation Opportunity Area.

Most of the unit is composed of equal parts of Wyoming big sagebrush/bluebunch wheatgrass, black sagebrush/bluebunch wheatgrass, and shadscale/Indian ricegrass. The remainder is divided between the black sagebrush/bottlebrush squirreltail community and the low sagebrush/Sandberg's needlegrass community. A little Great Basin wildrye can also be found.

Black sage (*Artemisia arbuscula nova*) is a subspecies of dwarf or low sagebrush. The unit is the northernmost extent of the range of black sage. Extensive patches can be found in the northern end of the unit because of unusual associations of poor soils and exposure.

Bowden Hills unit of the proposed Owyhee Wilderness

Pronghorn prefer the low sage both because of nutritional value and because it doesn't get in the way of seeing predators.

About fifty each of mule deer and pronghorn summer in the unit. In the winter, deer numbers rise to about two hundred and pronghorn to between two hundred and four hundred.

The rims provide excellent habitat for raptors, including golden eagle, red-tailed hawk, ferruginous hawk, northern harrier, turkey vulture, great horned owl, and burrowing owl. The rimrock and talus slopes are home to woodrats, bats, and bobcats. Other mammals include black-tailed jackrabbits, mountain cottontails, deer mice, and pocket gophers.

Other birds include the mourning dove, western meadowlark, Say's phoebe, loggerhead shrike, common nighthawk, and raven.

Reptiles include the side-blotched lizard, western fence lizard, sagebrush lizard, desert collared lizard, Great Basin western rattlesnake, gopher snake, and yellow-bellied racer. Likely also are the western whiptail lizard, short-horned lizard, and the desert striped whipsnake.

There is one extensive prehistoric site.

Cedar Mountain and Quartz Mountain Units

The misnamed Cedar Mountain should have been more properly called Juniper Mountain. Juniper is far less abundant in the Owyhee Uplands than any other Oregon Desert ecoregion, but what's the originality in that? A dense juniper stand covers the summit and gives way to Wyoming big sagebrush and understory grasses and forbs as one moves downslope. This juniper stand is isolated from others by at least 10 miles; hence it is an "island ecosystem." Rocky Mountain elk are expanding into the unit.

Compared with its surroundings, the Quartz Mountain unit is less interesting topographically, geologically, aesthetically, and recreationally. It can't all be outstanding. Something has to make the rest look good. Nonetheless, the area is generally wild, quite remote, and integral to the wilderness proposal.

Dry Creek Unit

The year-round water of Dry Creek supports redband trout and has numerous small waterfalls. The unit is also excellent reptile habitat. Pronghorn and mule deer are evident. Much of the vegetation is pristine because of natural topographic defenses against livestock. Mock orange, willow, rushes, and sedges are unusual for their abundance.

Dry Creek Canyon is both remote and beautiful. It has a diverse topography with steep walls, meanders, and angular ridges. The numerous gulches and ravines create a complex pattern of twisting drainages, including badlands, spires, and deeply eroding slopes.

The layered cliffs of basalt and other formations contribute to the great variety of landforms and their vivid color combinations. Because of unusual soils, the clay cliff ash deposits and other areas support either practically no vegetation or very rare species. For botanical types, it is a great place to see shadscales and buckwheats.

Honeycombs Unit

When you first see the Honeycombs, if you didn't know better, you'd think you were in Southern Utah.

Only covering about 12,000 acres, the Honeycombs are extremely scenic steep-walled canyons with sculpted, multicolored rock formations. The thick deposits of volcanic tuff have been cut by numerous and mostly intermittent streams. The result is impressive: a very broken surface of ridges, hills, and drainages, often adorned with outcrops and pinnacles.

The vegetation is mostly classic sagebrush steppe, but salt desert scrub along the reservoir includes greasewood, spiny hopsage, and shadscale. A few junipers can be found.

Bighorn sheep are the most noticeable wildlife species.

Jordan Craters Unit

The Jordan Craters unit of the proposed Owyhee Wilderness includes the undeveloped portions of the proposed national monument by the same name. See Jordan Craters National Monument for more details.

Mahogany Mountain Unit

At 6,522 feet, Mahogany Mountain is the highest point in the Owyhee Uplands. Unfortunately, most of it is private land. The mountain is an extinct volcanic caldera. Volcanic tuff deposits 2,000 feet thick have been cut with intermittent streams, leaving outcrops and spires.

The unit is very steep: 85 percent of the slopes exceed 25 percent, says BLM.

The mountain has two dense groves of curlleaf mountain mahogany and in fact is the largest contiguous stand of mountain mahogany in western North America (mostly privately owned).

The predominantly sagebrush steppe ecosystem has pockets of juniper and also a small relic stand of four-hundred-year-old ponderosa pine. Located in the Dago Gulch drainage, the species is little known elsewhere in the Owyhee Uplands.

California bighorn sheep are common in the area, as increasingly are Rocky Mountain elk. Uncommon are five plant species of very special interest. Two are found only in Leslie Gulch.

Owyhee Breaks Unit

The topographic and geologic diversity reaches out and grabs you: cliffs, outcrops, steep bluffs, dramatic erosional features, twisting gulches, deep river canyons, razorback ridges, breaks, badlands, dissected ridges, colorful sedimentary rock spires, buttes, tablelands, plateaus, wind- and water-sculpted formations, palisades, talus slopes, and barren soils. One does not tire of the expansive panoramas overlooking the river and off into the distance.

Owyhee River above Birch Creek in the proposed Owyhee Wilderness

Salt desert scrub communities can be found alongside the more typical sage-brush with bluebunch wheatgrass, bottlebrush squirreltail, Sandberg's bluegrass, Thurber's needlegrass, and Indian ricegrass understory species. Shadscale and greasewood are also known here. Western juniper can be found in certain draws like Birch Creek. The common riparian species along the streams include alder, currant, mock orange, clematis, willow, hackberry (an unusual species for the desert and sometimes occurring here in groves), chokecherry, sedges, and grasses.

Because of the river and diverse habitats, wildlife abounds. Twenty to thirty bald eagles use the river regularly. Rocky Mountain elk are moving into the area. There is a high density of raptors. The river supports Canada geese and several duck species. It is too warm for rainbow trout, but channel catfish, black bull-head, yellow perch, whitefish, and small-mouth bass have been caught.

Numerous archaeological sites have been inventoried in the unit.

Last, but not least, some of the oldest packrat middens (nests) yet discovered in the Intermountain sagebrush province are found here, offering a scientific record of use going back thirty thousand years.

Rattlesnake Canyon Unit

This outlier unit of the proposed wilderness serves as an important wild island connector between the greater Owyhee and greater Steens-Alvord wildlands. The canyon itself is quite dramatic, scenic, and geologically interesting. Above the canyon are broad rolling flats of sagebrush and grass.

Owyhee River near Idaho border in the proposed Owyhee Wilderness

Saddle Butte Unit

The Saddle Butte Lava Field is south of Saddle Butte, a prominent landmark visible from OR 78. It is a very large and flat flow that forms rough-surfaced ridges, numerous hillocks, and depressions. An extensive system of lava tube caves is also present.

Vegetation is primarily big sagebrush and bunchgrass.

Permanent water is almost nonexistent. Only Tub Spring on the ephemeral Ryegrass Creek can be counted on.

Seven hundred pronghorn make this one of the most important game ranges in southeast Oregon. Coyotes, mule deer, and mourning doves are also common. The breaks, caves, and collapsed lava tubes provide habitat for desert woodrats, yellow-bellied marmots, and bobcats. The area is also the northernmost range of the northern kit fox.

At least four species of bats have been observed, including the threatened Townsend's big-eared bat *(Plecotus townsendii)*. Of Oregon bats, this medium-sized (more than 1 inch long) gray to brown bat is most associated with caves. It will quickly vacate a roost if disturbed.

An extensive system of lava tubes winds through the Saddle Butte Lava Field. Twenty-two uncollapsed segments have been discovered.

BLM has designated a 7,040-acre area of critical environmental concern that includes 8 to 10 miles of lava tubes.

Geologically, lava tubes are formed quickly. As molten lava flows from a vent across the ground, a faster-moving current develops inside the flow, not unlike a swifter channel of current in a wide river. The outer portion flows slower because it is much cooler (though still molten). As the flow begins to solidify, the hotter lava inside continues to flow. A lava tube is created when the still molten lava drains out of the emerging lining of the soon-to-be lava tube. The lining can be a few inches to several feet thick. Where erosion, especially freezing and thawing, creates a small hole in the ceiling, a skylight is formed. Often the collapsed area is large enough to expose two cave openings.

The caves are of great educational and scientific interest as they provide a habitat of constant humidity and temperature, which promotes the growth of mosses and ferns uncommon to the dry climate.

Three Forks Unit

Most of the Three Forks unit is unending plateau and gently rolling hills. Several lake playas break up the vegetation and scenery. It is the vastness of the expanse that one cannot forget.

The plateau is unending except for numerous deeply carved and massive river canyons, be they trickling streams or rushing rivers. The reddish brown cliffs of the mainstem Owyhee Canyon rise hundreds of feet above the water. Brilliant green, yellow, and orange microflora covering the walls add to this palette of nature. Deep green communities of vegetation can be seen at seeps and springs. Diversely eroded spires add to the geologic mix.

Charismatic fauna include cougar, bobcat, river otter, and bighorn sheep.

Upper West Little Owyhee Unit

"Some of the state's most extensive wildlands," says the Oregon Biodiversity Project. "Portions of the Upper West Little Owyhee have never been grazed and support virtually pristine native vegetation."[5]

The unit is dissected by a national wild and scenic river, with vertical cliffs, prominent rimrock, and very steep slopes that rise to several hundred feet above the canyon bottom. Reds, browns, greens, and tans color the canyon landscape.

In places, the canyon narrows so the stream is forced through very constricted gaps.

The unit has the largest concentrations of sage grouse and white-tailed jack-rabbits in Malheur County. Raptors found here include kestrel, red-tailed hawks, prairie falcons, and golden eagles.

The river is quite seasonal as it has no snowpack or major springs at its source. It runs high in the spring, and barely at all in the fall. Water is left in deep, clear, cool pools as the flow recedes in the late summer.

Scattered groves of aspen, mahogany, and willow are found in the canyons, with sagebrush on the plateaus, including the Owyhee sagebrush (*Artemesia papposa*), rare in Oregon, but more common elsewhere.

Willow Creek Butte Unit

Recreationally speaking, compared to the Owyhee River and tributaries in the vicinity, the Willow Creek unit is a yawner. It has gently rolling hills and flats of sagebrush steppe. Nonetheless, it is good for wildlife. If you want solitude, even in your car, this is the place. Very few come this way.

63. Anderson Crossing (Upper West Little Owyhee and Three Forks Units)

What to Expect:	Incredibly deep and textured canyon full of color
Distance:	2 to 120 miles (your call) loop or round trip
Elevation Range:	5,200–5,800 feet
Drinking Water:	Yes
Best Times:	Summer, fall
USGS 7.5' Maps:	Guadeloupe Meadows, Oregon Butte
Oregon Map Starting Point:	McDermitt

Approximately 14 miles north on US 95, turn east onto a good BLM road. Proceed northeasterly for 1.2 miles and go right (northeast, not north) at the intersection. Continue easterly and then northerly on the main road for approximately 14 miles. At a major intersection (you're now pointed northeast) turn southeast (right). Staying to the main road, go approximately 19 miles to Anderson Crossing (Guadeloupe Canyon quad). You can park before the ford or on the other side.

Test the water depth before you cross in your vehicle. Some suspicious rock dams—first thought to be made by the grazing permittee to provide water for livestock—have been found here. Closer inspection revealed an engineering marvel far beyond the reach of most humans, especially ranchers usually given to damming streams with bulldozers and plastic sheeting. These dams were very even in height and had a very smooth arc. The rocks were well interlaced and evenly sized. It is thought to be the handiwork of beavers.

From Anderson Crossing, one can walk either upstream into the Upper West Little Owyhee unit (Oregon Butte quad) or downstream into the Owyhee Canyonlands unit (Guadeloupe Meadows quad). Since the river drains a much smaller area and has no snowpack or large springs at its source, by late summer it is a series of pools. The wet-shoes option is the only option for walking in the canyons.

For day hikes, walk either upstream or down. If there is too much water, go to plan B and walk the rims above the river. How far you want to go is up to you. The canyon meanders extensively, so your time returning on the plateau is a fraction of the time spent in the canyon. If you choose to go a *long* way in the canyon, you will need the adjacent quad maps.

Some have carried an inner tube and floated their pack and themselves through the deep pools. The summer air soon dries one's clothes. One option is to walk the canyon until you want to get out, then find a way up to the rim. They will be strenuous, but there are relatively short escapes to the surrounding plateau. Return to your start.

64. Batch Lake (Jordan Craters Unit)

What to Expect:	A stark landscape of recent lava with an oasis lake
Distance:	2 miles (very slow walking) round trip
Elevation Range:	4,321–4,340 feet
Drinking Water:	Yes
Best Times:	Spring, fall
USGS 7.5' Map:	Cow Lakes
Oregon Map Starting Point:	Jordan Valley

Go west approximately 5 miles (southbound in the grander scheme) on US 95, which then turns to the southwest. Continue west on a county road, following the signs to Cow Lakes. After approximately 8 miles the road turns from northwesterly to due north and gets very straight for 1.4 miles After the *end* of the straight stretch, where it curves first to the northwest (left), go 1.2 miles to the intersection with a dirt road. The good road bends sharply to northeast (right) and crosses a dry streambed. Continue straight (north-northeasterly) for 0.2 mile. At the intersection turn left (southwesterly). Continue westerly for 1.9 miles. Park at Parks Dam.

Batch Lake is 1 mile due west, but—because of the broken terrain, and depending on the season and wetness of the year—you'll have to climb "high" (it is relative) points to scout your course. Depending on how good/lucky you are, this journey may take anywhere from 1 to 5 hours (no kidding). You'll be walking over recent (within the last few thousand years) black lava flows, so make sure you are properly shod. This is a day hike, but you could backpack if you want. Camp back at least 200 feet from the water. Setting up a tent isn't a problem.

Jordan Craters unit of the proposed Owyhee Wilderness

65. Bowden Hills Summit (Bowden Hills Unit)

What to Expect:	Total solitude
Distance:	11.2 miles round trip
Elevation Range:	4,244–5,467 feet
Drinking Water:	No
Best Times:	Spring, fall
USGS 7.5' Map:	Flat Tom Mtn. SE
Oregon Map Starting Point:	Burns Junction (where OR 78 joins US 95)

Go approximately 13 miles south on US 95. Turn east (left) onto the county road (marked only by stop sign). Go 3.9 miles and park at the intersection with a north-south way.

Walking southward on this way will take you to within a mile of the highest point in the area, a USGS benchmark named Medina. This can either be done as a day hike, or you may dry-camp at the head of the dry stream in a protected little canyon (with exposed rock on the east side) just north of Medina benchmark.

You can't get lost, just keep bearing south on the way. After a sharp turn to the east followed immediately by a turn again to the south, you'll cross a dry stream channel and rise slightly and then cross another dry stream channel. At this point the way turns south-southeast and is marked by two old stock-watering tanks. You're now in one of the four named natural features in the entire area, and original it is: "The Basin." (There is actually a fifth: Mendi Gori Posue, along the southern boundary. The translation from Basque suggests that either a babbling Basque named it or the USGS misplaced the name, as there is no pond or well at a red mountain.)

Walk south-southeast on this way about 0.8 mile before making your assault of the summit. Return as you came or head due north across The Basin and up the north-south ridge that parallels your way in. Stay high until you see the broad valley and your vehicle.

66. Chalk Basin (Owyhee Breaks Unit)

What to Expect:	Unique ecological sites with a bit of badlands, barren soils, and sparse vegetative communities, all quite scenic
Distance:	4.6 miles round trip
Elevation Range:	3,400–3,740 feet
Drinking Water:	Yes
Best Times:	Spring, fall
USGS 7.5' Map:	Lambert Rocks
Oregon Map Starting Point:	Rome

In downtown Rome head northwest (US 95 runs east-northeast and west-southwest) for 1.8 miles. The road turns to the north-northeast for 0.2 mile to an intersection. Continue westerly (enjoy the Rome Cliffs as you drive by) for 4 miles. You now come to an intimidating-looking gate, probably with a "No Trespassing" sign that would turn back lesser souls. In fact, this is a public right-of-way, according to the BLM staffer in Rome. Proceed northerly through the gate 0.6 mile. Where the good road turns west, take the worse road that forks to the right, which passes the butte to the west, across Crooked Creek and then turns north. After 0.6 mile from leaving the good road, take the left (northwesterly) road for 3.7 miles to another intersection. Stay on the main road, which turns northeasterly and then northerly for 1.4 miles to another intersection. Continue northerly 3.4 miles and park at the intersection.

Hike the unimproved way to the east steeply down off the flat and into the Chalk Basin. In 2 miles, after having crossed the second (likely) dry stream channel, walk this channel downstream to several springs. Even in late summer the creek has a little water. You might have to dig in the mud and let it collect and then filter. Continue downstream for a view of the Owyhee River. Continuing downstream to the river is highly problematic because of rough terrain.

This can either be a day hike or you can camp in the basin.

67. Honeycombs (Honeycombs Unit)

What to Expect:	With the right light, vibrant oranges, reds, yellows, golds, tans, and browns
Distance:	21 miles round trip
Elevation Range:	2,655–4,388 feet
Drinking Water:	At reservoir
Best Times:	Spring, fall
USGS 7.5' Maps:	Pelican Point, Three Fingers Rock
Oregon Map Starting Point:	Adrian

Go southerly on OR 201 8.0 miles. As OR 201 turns east, continue south on the county road to Succor Creek State Recreation Area. After approximately 26 miles turn westerly to Leslie Gulch. After approximately 3.0 miles turn westerly (you're pointed southwesterly) onto a lower-standard road. The road soon turns northwesterly and then northerly. After approximately 12.3 miles park where a jeep trail takes off westerly.

This is a two-night backpack. Hike (Three Fingers Rock quad) this four-wheel-drive track 1.2 miles to the end (Pelican Point quad). Pick up the cattle/game/human trail down-canyon. It comes and goes, so keep an eye out. Walk 2.7 miles to Carlton Canyon and then 2.6 miles down-canyon to the reservoir for water. Camp in lower Carlton Canyon. The next day, hike to the summit of Saddle Butte for great views and then to Bensley Flat. Walk up the unnamed stream bottom into the heart of the Honeycombs (4 miles one way from camp). Return as you came.

68. Lambert Rocks (Owyhee Breaks Unit)

What to Expect:	A fantastic lava flow on a bench above the Owyhee River
Distance:	8.8 miles round trip
Elevation Range:	3,020–3,700 feet
Drinking Water:	Yes
Best Times:	Spring, fall
USGS 7.5' Map:	Lambert Rocks
Oregon Map Starting Point:	Rome

At the Rome store head northwest (US 95 runs east-northeast/west-southwest) for 1.8 miles. The road turns to the north-northeast for 0.8 mile until crossing the Owyhee River. Continue on the main road, and always northerly if you have a choice, for approximately 13.6 miles. You are now at a road intersection and in the middle of an airstrip (in fact, you've been on it for the last 0.3 mile). Take the road to the north (get off the runway, which runs north-northeast), which turns northwesterly. Park at about 3 miles.

Hike out the unimproved way along the peninsular point and then steeply down to Bogus Creek. Hike the four-wheel-drive track to the river (4.4 miles total).

This can be done as a long day hike but is best enjoyed as a backpack to a riverside camp. There is much to explore coming and going.

The most geologically interesting views across the river are not actually of Chalk Basin, but of the unnamed drainages to the south, though most postcards and calendars identify this scene as Chalk Basin.

69. Saddle Butte Lava Field (Saddle Butte Unit)

What to Expect:	Several collapsed segments of lava tubes allowing cave exploration
Distance:	14.1-mile loop
Elevation Range:	3,900–4,254 feet
Drinking Water:	No
Best Times:	Spring, summer, fall
USGS 7.5' Maps:	Iron Mountain, Palomino Lake, Saddle Mountain, Wrangle Butte
Oregon Map Starting Point:	Burns

On OR 78, 0.3 mile east of milepost 83 (measured from Burns), turn northerly onto a dirt road. Proceed 4.9 miles to an intersection. Continue northwesterly 1.8 miles and park at the intersection of an unimproved way to north. On your left coming in was Coyote Trap Cave, worthy of a side trip.

Hike (Palomino Lake quad) the way northerly 1.8 miles to Tire Tube Cave. Continue northeasterly 1.4 miles to Fortymile Cave. If you are feeling adventurous, can navigate by maps, and have a good sense of direction, continue easterly 0.3 mile to a key intersection of ways. Continue easterly 2.6 miles on the way, and beyond cross-country (Iron Mountain quad), to the Owyhee River Cave at the east

Tire Tube Cave in the Saddle Butte unit of the proposed Owyhee wilderness

end of about a mile of numerous tube collapses. Follow the tube northeasterly 0.4 mile to Burns Cave (Wrangle Butte quad). Another 0.6 mile northeasterly is Rattle-snake Cave. Set a course west-southwesterly 2.5 miles to the end of an unimproved way (Saddle Butte quad). Follow this way back 1 mile to the key intersection (Palomino Lake quad). Return to your vehicle the way you came.

The entire exploration is definitely a carry-your-own-water backpack. The cross-country can be very slow going. Though open and flat—and Saddle Butte to the north always serves as a landmark—you should know how to read topographic maps and the land. A Global Positioning System receiver could be a lifesaver because it all starts to look the same. Day hikers should return after Fortymile Cave.

70. Slocum Creek–Schoolhouse Gulch (Mahogany Mountain Unit)

What to Expect:	Fantastic, colorful, and towering rock formations
Distance:	11.8-mile loop
Elevation Range:	2,700–5,289 feet
Drinking Water:	No
Best Times:	Spring (best for flowers), fall
USGS 7.5' Map:	Rooster Comb
Oregon Map Starting Point:	Adrian

Go southerly on OR 201 8 miles. As OR 201 turns east, continue south on the county road to Succor Creek State Recreation Area. After 26 miles turn westerly for Leslie Gulch. At approximately 13 miles is the boat ramp/campground at the mouth of Slocum Creek.

Hike up Slocum Creek far enough to cross over to return down Schoolhouse Gulch and Spring Creek and then the reservoir edge back to your vehicle.

This is a *rugged* and *long* day hike. Get an early start. If you find the going too slow for the time available, just turn around (assuming you've gone less than half way).

71. Three Forks (Middle Owyhee River Unit)

What to Expect:	Magnificent cliffs, scenic overlooks, pristine grasslands, historic military road, and a warm bath
Distance:	7-mile loop
Elevation Range:	3,900–4,800 feet
Drinking Water:	Yes
Best Times:	Summer, fall
USGS 7.5' Map:	Three Forks
Oregon Map Starting Point:	Jordan Valley

Drive 16 miles west on US 95 (southbound in the greater scheme). Turn south at milepost 36 and drive 41 miles to Three Forks. Park and camp at Three Forks.

Owyhee River above Three Forks in the proposed Owyhee Wilderness

Wade across the river (usually anytime after June) and hike the Military Grade (the steep and zigzagging old roadbed you noticed driving in) due west of Three Forks to the top of the river's west rim. Hike westerly across the flat to the head of Warm Springs Canyon. (Identify as many grasses as you can.) Catch the four-wheel-drive trail on the south side down and east to the two lovely pools at the mouth of Warm Springs Creek. Shade is available. Explore upstream to the source of Warm Springs Creek.

Don't get too intimate with the poison ivy and/or poison sumac that can be found at the water's edge.

After you've had your 95-degree-Fahrenheit bath, ford the Owyhee again and catch the old road grade northerly and uphill. This soon crosses a low divide into the Middle Fork Owyhee drainage. Continue northerly and wade the Middle Fork. You soon reach a bridge across the North Fork and are soon back to your vehicle. If the mainstem Owyhee is too high to ford, you can reverse this hike and explore the hot springs on the opposite bank from Warm Springs Canyon. Several small rock-lined pools exist, as do some showers.

REFERENCES

NATURAL HISTORY

1. George Wuerthner. *Oregon Mountain Ranges.* Helena, Mont.: American Geographic Publishing, 1987, 54.
2. A. Joy Belsky. "Viewpoint: Western Juniper Expansion: Is It a Threat to Arid Northwestern Ecosystems?" *Journal of Range Management* 49 (1996): 53–59.
3. C. Maser, J. W. Thomas, and R. G. Anderson. *Wildlife Habitats in Managed Rangelands—The Great Basin of Southeastern Oregon: The Relationship of Terrestrial Vertebrates to Plant Communities, Part 2, Appendices.* USDA Forest Service and USDI Bureau of Land Management, General Technical Report PNW-172, 1984, 1–6.
4. *Oregon Bighorn Sheep Management Plan 1992–1997.* Portland, Ore.: Oregon Department of Fish and Wildlife, n.d., 3.
5. Oregon Biodiversity Project. *Oregon's Living Landscape.* Portland, Ore.: Oregon Biodiversity Project, 1998, 157.
6. B. J. Verts and Leslie N. Carraway. *Land Mammals of Oregon.* Berkeley and Los Angeles: University of California Press, 1998, 258–259.
7. Mayo W. Call and Chris Maser. *Wildlife Habitats in Management Rangelands—The Great Basin of Southeastern Oregon: Sage Grouse.* USDA Forest Service and USDI Bureau of Land Management, General Technical Report PNW-187, 1985, 19.

UNNATURAL HISTORY

1. Cited in Robert R. Kindschy, Charles Sundstrom, and James D. Yoakum. *Wildlife Habitats in Managed Rangelands—The Great Basin of Southeastern Oregon: Pronghorns.* USDA Forest Service and USDI Bureau of Land Management, General Technical Report PNW-145, 1982, 6.
2. D. S. Wilcove, D. Rothstein, J. Dubow, A. Phillips, and E. Losos. "Quantifying Threats to Imperiled Species in the United States: Assessing the Relative Importance of Habitat Destruction, Alien Species, Pollution, Overexploitation, and Disease," *BioScience* 48, no. 8 (August 1, 1998): 607–615.
3. Studies cited in J. Belsky, A. Matzke, and S. Uselman. "Survey of Livestock Influences on Stream and Riparian Ecosystems in the Western United States," *Journal of Soil and Water Conservation* 54, no. 1 (1999): 419–431.
4. Ibid.
5. E. A. Weiss, M.D. *Wilderness 911.* Seattle: The Mountaineers Books, 1998, 194.
6. H. D. Radtke and S. W. Davis, *Economic Study of Implementing the Proposed Oregon Desert Protection Act.* Bend, Ore.: Oregon Natural Desert Association, 1998.

POLITICAL FUTURE

1. The Keystone Center. "Final Consensus Report of the Keystone Policy Dialogue on Biological Diversity on Federal Lands." Keystone, Colo.: The Keystone Center, 1991, quoted in R. F. Noss and A. Cooperrider, *Saving Nature's Legacy: Protecting and Restoring Biodiversity,* Washington, D.C.: Defenders of Wildlife and Island Press, 1994, 5.

2. R. F. Noss. "The Wildlands Project: Land Conservation Strategy." *Wild Earth* (Special Issue, 1992): 11.
3. Ibid., 12.
4. M. Soulé and R. F. Noss. "Rewilding and Biodiversity: Complementary Goals for Continental Conservation." *Wild Earth* 8, no.3 (1998): 25.
5. Ibid., 26.
6. Adapted from Andy Kerr. "The Voluntary Retirement Option for Federal Public Land Grazing Permittees." Published simultaneously in *Rangelands* 20, no. 5 (October 1998) and *Wild Earth* 8, no. 3 (fall 1998).

BASIN AND RANGE ECOREGION
1. Wilderness Study Report. Portland, Ore.: USDI Bureau of Land Management, 1991, 52.
2. R. Cooley. "Wilderness Therapy Can Help Troubled Adolescents." *International Journal of Wilderness* 4, no.3 (December 1998).
3. Oregon Biodiversity Project. *Oregon's Living Landscape.* Portland, Ore.: Defenders of Wildlife, 1998, 131.
4. Ibid., 130.
5. Ibid.
6. Ibid., 132.
7. Ibid., 132.
8. Ibid., 146.
9. Ibid.
10. Ibid., 132.
11. Ibid., 131.
12. Ibid.

BLUE MOUNTAINS ECOREGION
1. Wilderness Study Report. Portland, Ore.: USDI Bureau of Land Management, 1991, 360.

COLUMBIA BASIN ECOREGION
1. Oregon Biodiversity Project. *Oregon's Living Landscape.* Portland, Ore.: Defenders of Wildlife, 1998, 188.

KLAMATH MOUNTAINS ECOREGION
1. Oregon Biodiversity Project. *Oregon's Living Landscape.* Portland, Ore.: Defenders of Wildlife, 1998, 85.

LAVA PLAINS ECOREGION
1. Oregon Biodiversity Project. *Oregon's Living Landscape.* Portland, Ore.: Defenders of Wildlife, 1998, 176.

OWYHEE UPLANDS ECOREGION
1. Oregon Biodiversity Project. *Oregon's Living Landscape.* Portland, Ore.: Defenders of Wildlife, 1998, 139.
2. Ibid., 146.
3. Ibid., 145.
4. Ibid., 139.
5. Ibid., 143.

RECOMMENDED READING

Many books were lovingly read or consulted for the preparation of this volume. The author is thankful for the numerous authors who came before.

A primary source worth special mention is the numerous government documents, especially those prepared by the Bureau of Land Management in conjunction with their wilderness review. This book would have not been possible had not a legion of public servants gone before.

Book titles and authors are noted below, but the publisher, publication year, and price are not. For books, both in and out of print, your first stop is either the library or a bookstore. If they don't have it, they can often obtain it. A vibrant market in used books is growing, both expanding knowledge and extending the lives of books.

(Though some of the books recommended below are published by The Mountaineers Books, publisher of this book, this was not a factor in the author's selection.)

OUTDOOR SKILLS AND SAFETY

Where's a doctor when you need one? Probably a long way from you when a medical emergency strikes. *Wilderness Medicine: Beyond First Aid,* by William W. Forgey, M.D., and *Wilderness Medical Society Practice Guidelines for Wilderness Emergency Care,* edited by Forgey, are both very readable. The former is longer and more directed toward the layperson. The latter includes succinct treatments of subjects. *Wilderness 911: A Step-by-Step Guide for Medical Emergencies and Improvised Care in the Backcountry,* by Eric Weiss, M.D., is strong on both prevention and improvisation in emergency situations.

For learning the art of land navigation, try *The Essential Wilderness Navigator,* by David Seidman. A classic in the field is *Be an Expert with Map and Compass,* by Björn Hjellstrom.

A pocket Global Positioning System (GPS) receiver (our tax dollars at work) saved the author at least some lost time and miserable nights, if not his life. It is possible to get turned around even in treeless terrain. *GPS Made Easy,* by Lawrence Letham, is quite good. GPS is no substitute for maintaining your sense of direction and paying attention to the landscape as you traverse it, however.

When you do get in trouble (it is best to assume you will and be prepared for it), *The Basic Essentials of Desert Survival,* by Arizona survival expert Dave Ganci, and *Desert Survival Handbook,* by Charles Lehman, are no-nonsense books that make for interesting and important learning. During the summer, even a "cold" desert like the Oregon Desert can kill the ignorant and unprepared.

Backpacking One Step at a Time, by Harvey Manning, is a fine general guide to the art of backpacking. For the art, science, and Zen of backpacking, one must turn to the classic *The Complete Walker III,* by Colin Fletcher. John Hart's *Walking Softly in the Wilderness* is the bible on low-impact techniques.

If you have experience backpacking, doing so in the desert should not be a problem. Water availability is the primary factor. *Desert Hiking,* also by Dave Ganci, and *Desert Hiking Tips,* by Bruce Grubbs, have suggestions specific to tree-free regions.

Everyone does it, so why not do it expertly? *How to Shit in the Woods: An Environmentally Sound Approach to a Lost Art,* by Kathleen Meyer, is a small volume that exhaustively covers the subject.

It can be fun to learn about weather, but it can also save your life. The *National Audubon Society Field Guide to North American Weather,* by David Ludlum, is helpful.

DESERT WALKING AND RIVER RUNNING

All guidebook authors are deeply indebted to their predecessors.

Although *Hiking the Great Basin: The High Desert Country of California, Nevada, Oregon and Utah,* by John Hart, covers only one Oregon area (Steens), it gives a fine overview of some of the greatest hiking in the Great Basin.

Similarly, while it is about forests, *A Walking Guide to Oregon's Ancient Forests,* by Wendell Wood, is an inspiration for this book.

William Sullivan pioneered the concept of presenting both the protected and unprotected wild areas in his *Exploring Oregon's Wild Areas.* He does include eleven Oregon Desert areas in his collection of primarily forest and alpine areas.

It is long out of print and was never well distributed, but *Unobscured Horizons, Untravelled Trails: Hiking the Oregon High Desert,* by Bruce Hayse and published by the late Oregon High Desert Study Group, deserves a mention if for no other reason than it was the first.

For those wanting to continue desert explorations eastward, there is *Exploring Idaho's High Desert,* by Sheldon Bluestein (now online at www.hikeidaho.com).

There is not a lot of cross-country skiing in the Oregon Desert, but Steens Mountain and some of the other high mountains can be skied. The last chapter of *Cross-Country Ski Routes: Oregon,* by Klindt Vielbig, is about Steens Mountain.

Hiking Hot Springs in the Pacific Northwest, by Evie Litton, includes four springs in the Owyhee country.

If you have the equipment and expertise to run a river (the only real way to see the Lower Canyon unit of the John Day Wilderness and one of the best ways to see the Owyhee Wilderness), *Oregon River Tours,* by John Garren, and *Soggy Sneakers,* by the Willamette Kayak and Canoe Club, are the standards. A new standard may be *Paddling Oregon,* by Robb Keller. *John Day River Drift and Historical Guide,* by Arthur Campbell, is exhaustively specific.

TRAVEL AND EXPLORATION

Since you won't want to do the long drive without taking some time to explore what else can be found along the way, you'll need some other guidebooks.

Oregon's Outback: An Auto Tour Guide to Southeast Oregon, by Donna Lynn Ikenberry, is the newest of the genre and should be packed for desert travel. *Oregon's Great Basin Country,* by Denzel and Nancy Ferguson, centers on Harney County and environs. Since you'll undoubtedly want to break up the long drive, the *Birder's Guide to Oregon,* by Joe Evanich Jr., reveals key birding areas in and on the way to the Oregon Desert. *Oregon Wildlife Viewing Guide,* by James A. Yuskavitch, is a guide to all those binocular icon signs along Oregon's roadways. Finally, it is so old it is quaint, but the classic *Oregon for the Curious,* by Ralph Friedman, is a fine road guide. Friedman doesn't short the forgotten quarter of Oregon as do so many other tour books.

Eastern Oregon: Portrait of Its Land and People, by Allan D. St. John, has lots of beautiful pictures and narrative to give you a nice natural and cultural overview of the Oregon Desert. *America's Secret Recreation Areas,* by Michael Hodgson, covers official BLM recreation opportunities nationwide, with an extensive Oregon chapter.

FLORA AND FAUNA

Good field guides to birds and other species are a must. Two books dominate the field: *Field Guide to the Birds of North America*, edited by Shirley L. Scott (National Geographic Society), and *A Field Guide to Western Birds,* by Roger Tory Peterson. The latter is more limited in geographic range and therefore includes fewer birds that are unlikely to be seen. Especially good for beginners is *Birds of North America,* by Chandler Robbins, Bertel Bruun, and Arthur Singer.

A fine little natural history of desert birds to supplement your bird identification guide is *Birds of the Malheur National Wildlife Refuge, Oregon,* by Carrol D. Littlefield.

Though not a birder, the author enjoyed *Birds of the Great Basin: A Natural History,* by Fred A. Ryser Jr.

Atlas of Oregon Wildlife: Distribution, Habitat and Natural History, by Blair Csuti et al., is an excellent encyclopedic guide.

To help identify those wildflowers, try *Sagebrush Country: A Wildflower Sanctuary,* by Ronald J. Taylor.

Desert reptiles can be looked up in *Reptiles of Washington and Oregon,* Robert M. Storm and William P. Leonard, coordinating editors.

For desert amphibians, the choice is *Amphibians of Oregon, Washington and British Columbia,* by Charlotte Corkran and Chris Thoms.

For those really into grasses (and forbs and sedges), no decent field guide exists. *Range Plants: Their Identification, Usefulness and Management,* by Ben Roché (Washington State University Department of Natural Resource Sciences Forestry Publications, Pullman), is somewhat helpful.

A desert can have trees. *Trees to Know in Oregon,* by Edward C. Jensen (published by Oregon State University Extension Service), is an excellent identification guide for the layperson. *Trees of the Great Basin,* by Ronald M. Lanner, is more of a natural history.

Between the grasses and the trees are many plants documented in *Shrubs of the Great Basin: A Natural History,* by Hugh N. Mozingo.

Land Mammals of Oregon, by B. J. Verts and Leslie N. Carraway, is the definitive word on the subject.

Rattler!: A Natural History of Snakes, by Chris Mattison, is an excellent treatise on rattlesnakes. Knowledge can conquer fear. Great pictures.

Fish freaks will love *Fishes of the Great Basin: A Natural History,* by William F. Sigler and John W. Sigler.

Ovis: North American Wild Sheep, by Guy Tillett, includes bighorn sheep but merges the California subspecies into the Rocky Mountain subspecies, a convention not of taxonomy, but of trophy hunting.

Pronghorn aficionados will relish *Pronghorn: Portrait of the American Antelope,* by Gary Turbak.

Track of the Coyote, by Todd Wilkinson, details the natural history of the trickster.

Fans of cougar, mountain lion, puma, catamount, or whatever you prefer, might like *The Cougar Almanac,* by Robert Busch, or *Mountain Lion,* text by Rebecca Grambo and photographs by Daniel Cox. For an excellent literary examination of this species, see *Shadow Cat,* edited by Susan Ewing and Elizabeth Grossman.

For a fascinating discussion of the natural history of and the history of wiping out the beaver, see *Water: A Natural History,* by Nancy Outwater. To go deeper on beavers, see *Beavers: Where Waters Run,* by Paul Strong.

ECOLOGY AND CONSERVATION BIOLOGY

To start with the big-picture overview of American deserts and grasslands, see the National Audubon Society nature guide *Deserts,* by James A. MacMahon, and *Grasslands,* by Lauren Brown. Then get more specific with *The Sagebrush Ocean: A Natural History of the Great Basin,* by Stephen Trumble. The latter serves as an excellent introduction to the Oregon Desert, though somewhat Nevada-centric.

Natural Vegetation of Oregon and Washington, by Jerry F. Franklin and C. T. Dyrness, is loaded with pictures and descriptions so an interested layperson can understand the major landforms and vegetative communities of the Oregon Desert (actually it is not real desert, but steppe and shrub-steppe).

To grasp the basics of the increasingly important science of conservation biology, see *Saving Nature's Legacy: Protecting and Restoring Biodiversity,* by Reed F. Noss and Allen Cooperrider.

Continental Conservation, edited by Michael Soulé and John Terborgh, contains the wisdom of over two dozen prominent biologists who argue that to have fully functioning ecosystems, across both the landscape and time, nothing less than the rewilding of North America will do.

Oregon Mountain Ranges, by George Wuerthner, devotes a fine chapter to the natural history of the Basin and Range mountains, reminding us that mountains in Oregon are not always covered by trees.

You'll never find it in a bookstore, but a fourteen-volume collection (the volumes are small) under the title of *Wildlife Habitats in Managed Rangelands—The Great Basin of Southeastern Oregon* is well worth finding. (Don't be bothered by "managed"—it was a funding thing. The series is a fine example of how your tax dollars can be spent wisely.) The technical editors were Dr. Jack Ward Thomas, who later rose on the back of the spotted owl to be chief of the Forest Service, and Chris Maser, then with the Bureau of Land Management, but later forced out for his ecological views.

The fourteen volumes were first published separately, in conjunction with

BLM, as General Technical Reports (GTRs) of the U.S. Forest Service's Pacific Northwest Research Station (then known as the Forest and Range Experiment Station). All the following titles begin with *"Wildlife Habitats in Managed Rangelands—The Great Basin of Oregon"*:

1. *Introduction*, by Chris Maser and Jack Ward Thomas (GTR PNW-160, 1983).
2. *Plant Communities and Their Importance to Wildlife*, by J. Edward Dealy, Donavin A. Leckenby, and Diane M. Concannon (GTR-PNW-120, 1981).
3. *The Relationship of Terrestrial Vertebrates to Plant Communities, Part 1, Text,* by Chris Maser, Jack Ward Thomas, and Ralph G. Anderson (GTR PNW-172, 1984).
4. *The Relationship of Terrestrial Vertebrates to Plant Communities, Part 2, Appendices*, by Chris Maser, Jack Ward Thomas, and Ralph G. Anderson (GTR PNW-172, 1984).
5. *Native Trout*, by Wayne Bowers, Bill Hosford, Art Oakley, and Carl Bond (GTR PNW-84, 1979).
6. *Sage Grouse*, by Mayo W. Call and Chris Maser (GTR PNW-187, 1985).
7. *Pronghorns*, by Robert R. Kindschy, Charles Sundstrom, and James D. Yoakum (GTR PNW-145, 1982).
8. *Mule Deer*, by Donavin A. Leckenby, Dennis P. Sheehy, Carl H. Nellis, Richard J. Scherzinger, Ira D. Luman, Wayne Elmore, James C. Lemos, Larry Doughty, and Charles E. Trainer (GTR PNW-139, 1982).
9. *Bighorn Sheep*, by Walter A Van Dyke, Alan Sand, Jim Yoakum, Allan Polenz, and James Blaisdell (GTR PNW-159, 1983).
10. *Riparian Zones*, by Jack Ward Thomas, Chris Maser, and Jon E. Rodiek (GTR PNW-80, 1979).
11. *Edges*, by Jack Ward Thomas, Chris Maser, and Jon E. Rodiek (GTR PNW-85, 1979).
12. *Geomorphic and Edaphic Habitats*, by Chris Maser, J. Michael Geist, Diane M. Concannon, Ralph Anderson, and Burrell Lovell (GTR PNW-99, 1979).
13. *Manmade Habitats*, by Chris Maser, Jack Ward Thomas, Ira David Luman, and Ralph Anderson (GTR PNW-86, 1979).
14. *Management Practices and Options*, by Frederick C. Hall (GTR PNW-189, 1985).

Of course they're dated (and just forget No. 14), but they still have great value.

The Interior Columbia Basin Ecosystem Management Project (a joint Forest Service and Bureau of Land Management project) has managed to spend a lot of tax money without any improvement in the management of ecosystems to date. However, the draft environmental impact statement and especially *An Assessment of Ecosystem Components of the Interior Columbia River Basin and Portions of the Klamath and Great Basins* (GTR PNW-GTR-405), although flawed, are fairly impressive for ecological information, though they are depressive on management issues.

LAND AND WATER

To learn more about the diverse and spectacular natural history of the region, start from the ground up. An advantage of the desert is that the geology isn't obscured by trees. *Geology of Oregon,* by Ewart Baldwin, is the classic in the literature and gives an overview of Oregon Desert geology. *Geology of the Great Basin,* by Bill Fiero, focuses primarily on Nevada, but nonetheless is helpful in understanding the forces that shaped the Oregon Desert. Windshield geologists will enjoy *Roadside Geology of Oregon,* by David D. Alt and Donald W. Hyndman. Also consider *Hiking Oregon's Geology,* by Ellen Morris Bishop and John Elliot Allen, which includes twelve routes in the desert. *The Desert's Past: A Natural Prehistory of the Great Basin,* by Donald Grayson, is a classic.

Oregon Rivers, with photographs by Larry Olson and essays by John Daniel, gives a fair shake to the state's formally designated wild and scenic desert rivers.

WILDERNESS AND LAND MANAGEMENT

BLM's body of publications for their wilderness review (all published by the Oregon State Office) includes a foot-high stack of environmental impact statements and inventories. The last and the best is *Wilderness Study Report (Oregon),* which includes two volumes plus a statewide overview. You'll likely be exasperated by the agency's rationalizations to not designate most areas as wilderness. Fortunately Congress, not BLM, makes the final decision.

BLM's draft *Southeast Oregon Resource Management Plan Environmental Impact Statement* offers more information than protection.

LITERATURE

The best literary product of the Oregon Desert is William Kittredge, who grew up on the MC Ranch in the Warner Valley. His *Owning It All, Hole in the Sky,* and *Who Owns the West* are stories of the desert and human attitudes toward it.

Though set in the American Southwest, *Desert Solitaire,* by Edward Abbey, is a paean to all deserts and a rage against any who would desecrate them.

Desert Notes, by Barry Lopez, has some inspiration from the Oregon Desert.

C. E. S. Wood, an absolutely amazing turn-of-the-(last)-century author, lawyer, civic leader, radical, writer, nature freak, free-lover, and much more, wrote *Poet in the Desert,* which was inspired by his experiences in the Donner und Blitzen country. He's best known for having translated Chief Joseph's surrender speech. *Wood Works: The Life and Writings of Charles Erskine Scott Wood,* edited by Edwin Bingham and Tim Barnes, gives a good taste of the man, as does *Two Rooms: The Life of Charles Erskine Scott Wood* by Robert Hamburger.

A rapid ecological, economic, and social transition is happening throughout the American West. *Lasso the Wind: Away to the New West,* by Timothy Egan, tells stories from across the West, several of which could just as well have been set in the Oregon Desert. (For the record, the author is featured.)

CONSERVATION POLICY

The harm to America's deserts is not all caused by livestock. Inappropriate cultivation, aquifer and stream depletion, and relatively new stresses such as mining and exotic plants (livestock related to a large degree) are laid out in stark and compelling terms in *Desertification of the United States,* by David Sheridan, published in 1981 by the U.S. Council on Environmental Quality. It is so powerful that the government soon took it out of circulation, though the demand was high and the information important.

Oregon's Living Landscape, by the Oregon Biodiversity Project, is an excellent source of biodiversity information by ecoregion. It suggests numerous conservation opportunity areas that are remarkably compatible with many of the protection proposals in this book.

Ernest Callenbach, best known for *Ecotopia,* has written *The Buffalo Commons.* Though this book is focused on the Great Plains and not the Great Basin, Callenbach paints a grand and better future for a similarly abused landscape. We can emulate.

The environmental literature on the horrible destruction that livestock do to arid lands is not well developed. Not just the masses but many conservationists and writers have also been duped by the cowboy myth. I'm sure it will change as the literati begin to pay more attention to the ecosystem rather than just continuing to glamorize and mythologize the cowboy.

Two people who haven't been deceived, and who deserve much credit for educating generations of environmental activists dedicated to removing livestock from the public lands, are Denzel and Nancy Ferguson. Their classic, *Sacred Cows at the Public Trough,* is now a hallowed ancient text. If you don't already comprehend the great wrong in allowing these aliens run of the arid West, do read this book, but read the first chapter last. Even to the committed conservationist it can seem unduly harsh. After reading the rest of the book, however, this chapter will seem too kind.

Also of note is the exhaustively documented and detailed *Waste of the West,* by Lynn Jacobs, who has done as much in the Pacific Southwest to educate the public about the livestock scourge on the public lands as have the Fergusons in the Pacific Northwest. This book can be hard to find, but it is online at *www.sw-center.org/swcbd/grazing/waste.html.*

Sharman Apt Russell's *Kill the Cowboy: A Battle of Mythology in the New West* is an interesting and entertaining treatment of the livestock debate, but her conclusion is that better grazing is the solution—not because humans need the meat or the ecosystem needs the livestock—but because she needs her cowboy myth. It also profiles the antigrazing work of Denzel and Nancy Ferguson.

For a general discussion about the environmental, social, and health impacts of bovine meat, consider *Beyond Beef: The Rise and Fall of Cattle Culture,* by Jeremy Rifkin. If you want to swear off beef for sure and likely all other meats as well, consider *Mad Cowboy: Plain Truth from the Cattle Rancher Who Won't Eat Meat,* by Howard Lyman.

There is a crying need for a modern book that examines the government's animal damage control efforts. To learn of both the ecological and fiscal idiocy of this subsidy to livestock operators, see *Waste, Fraud & Abuse in the U.S. Animal Damage Control Program* (available from Wildlife Damage Review—see Appendix C) or *Audit of the USDA Animal Damage Control Program*, by Randal O'Toole of the Thoreau Institute (online at www.ti.org/adcreport.html).

HISTORY AND ARCHAEOLOGY

To learn about native peoples of the Oregon Desert, start with *The First Oregonians: An Illustrated Collection of Essays on Traditional Lifeways, Federal-Indian Relations, and the State's Native People Today*, edited by Carolyn M. Buan and Richard Lewis. For an archaeological overview, start with *Archaeology of Oregon*, by C. Melvin Aikens.

To understand how the Paiutes endured in such a seemingly harsh environment, see *Survival Arts of the Primitive Paiutes*, by Margaret M. Wheat. A classic is *Life Among the Piutes: Their Wrongs and Claims*, by Sara Winnemucca Hopkins. (Both Paiute and Piute are correct spellings.)

Donald Grayson's *The Desert's Past: A Natural Prehistory of the Great Basin* is a synthesis of the environmental and human history of the Great Basin.

To learn about the European invasion and the pioneers, settlers, cowboys, sheepboys, and the rest, you might enjoy *The Oregon Desert*, by E. R. Jackman and R. A. Long, *Owyhee Trails*, by Mike Hanley with Ellis Lucia, and *High Desert*, by Raymond R. Hatton. The former two especially were written by cowboys and cowboy wannabes and are of an era since passed.

The definitive source on place names is *Oregon Geographic Names*, by Lewis A. MacArthur and Lewis L. MacArthur. It also contains natural history tidbits.

NIGHT SKIES

There is no better place to scan the heavens than the Oregon Desert on a moonless night in the dry winter air. You'll enjoy it more with all the warm clothes you own and a good book on stars like the *National Audubon Society Field Guide to the Night Sky*, by Mark Charttrand.

OTHER METHODS OF LEARNING

The High Desert Museum on US 97 on the south end of Bend offers several well-done natural history displays, though you would never know from them that livestock are the major ecological irritant to the Oregon Desert. The Desert Museum in Tucson shows that natural history and the human impacts—including livestock—can be properly interpreted and still draw large crowds and contributions.

APPENDIX A:
GOVERNMENT AGENCY CONTACTS

Bureau of Land Management

Oregon State Office
1515 Southwest Fifth Avenue
P.O. Box 2965
Portland, OR 97208
503-952-6001
www.or.blm.gov

Burns District BLM Office
HC 74 - 12533 Highway 20 West
Hines, OR 97738
541-573-4400
www.or.blm.gov/burns

Lakeview District BLM Office
1000 South Ninth Street
HC 10 Box 337
Lakeview, OR 97630
541-947-2177
www.or.blm.gov/lakeview

Medford District BLM Office
3040 Biddle Road
Medford, OR 97504
541-770-2200
www.or.blm.gov/medford

Prineville District BLM Office
3050 Northeast Third Street
P.O. Box 550
Prineville, OR 97754
541-416-6700
www.or.blm.gov/prineville

Vale District BLM Office
100 Oregon Street
Vale, OR 97918
541-473-3144 (Mountain Time Zone)
www.or.blm.gov/vale

Baker Resource Area (Vale District)
    Office
3165 Tenth Street
Baker City, OR 97814
541-523-1256
www.or.blm.gov/vale

U.S. Forest Service

Pacific Northwest Regional Office
333 Southwest First Avenue
P.O. Box 3623
Portland, OR 97208
503-808-2644
www.fs.fed.us/r6

Crooked River National Grassland
(Ochoco National Forest)
813 Southwest Highway 97
Madras, OR 97741
541-475-9272
www.fs.fed.us/r6/ochoco

Fremont National Forest
1300 South Street
HC 10 Box 337
Lakeview, OR 97630
541-947-2151
www.fs.fed.us/r6/fremont

Malheur National Forest
431 Patterson Bridge Road
P.O. Box 909
John Day, OR 97845
541-575-1731
www.fs.fed.us/r6/malheur

Ochoco National Forest
3160 Northeast Third
P.O. Box 490
Prineville, OR 97554
541-416-6500
www.fs.fed.us/r6/ochoco

Wallowa-Whitman National Forest
P.O. Box 907
Baker, OR 97814
541-523-6391
www.fs.fed.us/r6/w-w

U.S. Fish and Wildlife Service

Western Regional Office
911 Northeast Eleventh Street
Portland, OR 97232
503-231-6121
www.r1.fws.gov

Malheur National Wildlife Refuge
HC 72 Box 245
Princeton, OR 97721
541-493-2612
www.r1.fsw.gov/malheur

Sheldon/Hart Mountain Refuges
    Complex
P.O. Box 111
Lakeview, OR 97630
541-947-3315

National Park Service

Columbia Cascades Systems
    Support Office
909 First Avenue
Seattle, WA 98104
206-220-4010
www.nps.gov

John Day Fossil Beds National
    Monument
HC 82 Box 126
Kimberly, OR 97848
541-987-2333
www.nps.gov/joda

APPENDIX B:
WHAT YOU CAN DO TO HELP

Congress will only enact the Oregon Desert Conservation Act if it senses a groundswell of massive and sustained public support. Below are easy things you can do to help.

Tell your congressional delegation that you support the Oregon Desert Conservation Act and urge them to co-sponsor the legislation.

Oregon has two United States senators and five members of the House of Representatives. As of publication their names and addresses are:

Senator Ron Wyden (D)
Senate Office Building
Washington, DC 20510
503-326-7525
503-326-7528 fax
senator@wyden.senate.gov

Senator Gordon Smith (R)
Senate Office Building
Washington, DC 20510
503-326-3386
503-326-2900 fax
oregon@gsmith.senate.gov

Rep. David Wu (1st District D)
House Office Building
Washington, DC 20515
503-326-2901
202-326-5066 fax
david.wu@mail.house.gov

Rep. Greg Walden (2nd District R)
House Office Building
Washington, DC 20515
541-776-4646
541-779-0204 fax
greg.walden@mail.house.gov

Rep. Earl Blumenauer (3rd District D)
House Office Building
Washington, DC 20515
503-231-2300
503-230-5413 fax
earl@mail.house.gov

Rep. Peter DeFazio (4th District D)
House Office Building
Washington, DC 20515
541-465-6732
541-465-6458 fax
pdefazio@mail.house.gov

Rep. Darlene Hooley (5th District D)
House Office Building
Washington, DC 20515
503-588-9100
503-588-5517 fax
darlene@mail.house.gov

If you aren't sure who your member of Congress is, call your local library. If you are from out of state, write your own senators and representative.

APPENDIX C:
CONSERVATION ORGANIZATIONS

The most important step you can take to protect the Oregon Desert is to join an organization that is working to protect it. Besides lending your support, you'll get a newsletter and special alerts so you can stay involved in the legislative process. Regular memberships are reasonably priced.

No one organization can save the Oregon Desert alone. Below are some of the major organizations fulfilling key roles in the conservation and restoration of the Oregon Desert:

American Lands
726 Seventh Street Southeast
Washington, DC 20003
202-547-9105
202-547-9213 fax
wafcdc@americanlands.org
www.americanlands.org
          or
5825 North Greeley
Portland, Oregon 97217
503-978-1054
503-978-1757 fax

Audubon Society of Portland
5151 Northwest Cornell Road
Portland, OR 97210
503-292-9471
503-292-1021 fax
general@audubonportland.org
www.audubonportland.org

Defenders of Wildlife
West Coast Office
1637 Laurel Street
Lake Oswego, OR 97035
503-697-3222
503-697-3268 fax
kstirling@defenders.org (book orders)

ajohnson@defenders.org (conservation issues)
www.defenders.org

Native Plant Society of Oregon
P.O. Box 902
Eugene, OR 97440
www.teleport.com/nonprofit/npso

Oregon Natural Desert Association
16 Northwest Kansas Street
Bend, OR 97701
541-330-2638
541-385-3370 fax
onda@onda.org
www.onda.org
          or
732 Southwest Third Avenue
Suite 407
Portland, OR 97204
503-525-1093
503-228-9720 fax

Oregon Natural Resources Council
5825 North Greeley Avenue
Portland, OR 97217
503-283-6343
503-283-0756 fax
info@onrc.org
www.onrc.org

Oregon Trout
117 Southwest Front Avenue
Portland, OR 97204
503-222-9091
503-222-9187 fax
info@oregontrout.org
www.oregontrout.org

Sierra Club (Oregon Chapter)
2950 Southeast Stark Street
Suite 110
Portland, OR 97214
503-238-0442
503-238-6281 fax
orsierra@spiritone.com
www.oregon.sierraclub.org

The Wilderness Society
Northwest Office
1424 Fourth Avenue
Suite 816
Seattle, WA 98101
206-624-6430
206-264-7101 fax
Info@twsnw.org
www.wilderness.org

Trout Unlimited
213 Southwest Ash Street
Suite 211
Portland, OR
503-827-5700
503-827-5652 fax
jcurtis@tu.org
www/tu.org

Two organizations working to protect their parts of the Oregon Desert include:

Hells Canyon Preservation Council
P.O. Box 2768
La Grande, OR 97850
541-963-3950
541-963-0584 fax
hcpc@hellscanyon.org
www.hellscanyon.org

Soda Mountain Wilderness Council
P.O. Box 512
Ashland, OR 97520
541-482-0526
541-488-1682 fax
sodamtn@mind.net

If predator control offends you, two fine organizations are leading the charge to end this ecologically undesirable and socially unacceptable practice:

Predator Conservation Alliance
P.O. Box 6733
Bozeman, MT 59771
406-587-3389
406-587-3178 fax
pca@predatorconservation.org
www.predatorconservation.org

Wildlife Damage Review
P.O. Box 85218
Tucson, AZ 85754
520-884-0883
520-884-0902 fax
wdr@azstarnet.com
www.azstarnet.com/~wdr

Fortunately, wilderness does not stop at the Oregon border. For more information on wilderness issues on adjacent deserts, you may contact:

Friends of Nevada Wilderness
200 Bartlett Street
Reno, NV 89512
702-348-1759
702-348-1986 fax
fnw@nevadawilderness.org
www.nevadawilderness.org

Committee for Idaho's High Desert
P.O. Box 2863
Boise, ID 83701
208-429-1679
ktfite@earthlink.org
www.cihd.org

You should also join an organization advocating population and consumption control. An organization founded by the author is:

Alternatives to Growth Oregon
205 Southeast Grand Avenue, #203
Portland, OR 97214
503-222-0282
503-222-0180 fax
info@AGOregon.org
www.AGOregon.org

APPENDIX D: THE DESERT TRAIL

In 1974, a beloved high school biology teacher had a vision of a hiking trail from Canada to Mexico. Yes, it has been done along the Pacific Crest and is being done along the Continental Divide, but not through the deserts and grasslands of the Interior West. Russ Pengelly founded the Desert Trail Association to make his vision a reality.

Living in Burns, he naturally started with segments on and near Steens Mountain. Russ has passed on to that 0 percent grade in the sky, but his fine work is being carried on by the Desert Trail Association.

> Much of the trail is not actually a trail, but a corridor marked by cairns (don't knock over these rockpiles).

The Desert Trail Association has published eight detailed "trail" guides (see table) and continues its methodical plotting and plodding northward and southward, staying to public lands where possible. Someday the Desert Trail will reach the nation's borders. In the meantime, several sections of the trail have been recognized as national recreational trails under the National Trails System Act. Such an administrative designation isn't as good as a congressionally designated national scenic trail, a status that this route richly deserves.

You can obtain each trail guide for $7 postpaid. While you're at it, also fork over enough to become a member ($12/year or $20/2 years individual; $18/year or $28/2 years family) and to receive a newsletter. While it is an all-volunteer outfit, the Desert Trail Association still has overhead costs worthy of your support. Of course, they would greatly welcome your direct participation as well.

If you're planning to do long stretches, walk north. The weather is better earlier in the year in the south and the sun isn't in your eyes. You also need to time your traversing of Steens Mountain during the snow-free season of late July through September.

The Desert Trail presently traverses the proposed Pueblo Mountains, Steens Mountain, and Alvord Wildernesses, the proposed Steens Mountain National Conservation Area, and the proposed Diamond Craters National Monument.

Desert Trail Guides

Section	Southern Terminus	Northern Terminus	Published
High Rock Canyon, NV	High Rock Lake	Cottonwood Canyon	1990
Sheldon NWR, NV	Cottonwood Canyon	Denio	1991
Pueblo Mountains, OR	Denio	Fields	1981
Alvord Desert, OR	Fields	Frog Spring (Alvord Desert)	1984
Steens Mountain, OR	Frog Spring (Alvord Desert)	Near Steens Mountain summit	1983
John Scharff Section, OR	Near Steens Mountain summit	Page Springs	1985
Malheur National Wildlife Refuge, OR	Page Springs	Diamond Craters	1987
Riddle Mountain, OR	Diamond Craters	Oregon Highway 78	1989

For more information:

Desert Trail Association
Box 34
Madras, OR 97741
dta@madras.net
www.madras.net/dta.htm

APPENDIX E: HOME ON THE RANGE

While this popular folk song is associated with cowboys, it does not contain a single reference to domestic livestock. Instead, it extols the natural richness of the western range, mentioning a number of species now in decline. Perhaps conservationists will reclaim this folk song, sing it in camp, and teach it to their children.

Oh, give me a home where the buffalo roam,
Where the deer and the antelope play;
Where seldom is heard a discouraging word,
And the skies are not cloudy all day.

CHORUS:

Home, home on the range,
Where the deer and the antelope play.
Where seldom is heard a discouraging word,
And the skies are not cloudy all day.

Where the air is so pure, the zephyrs so free;
The breezes so balmy and light;
That I would not exchange my home on the range,
For all of the cities so bright.

How often at night when the heavens are bright,
With the light from the glittering stars;
Have I stood here amazed and asked as I gazed,
If their glory exceeds that of ours.

Oh, I love these wild flowers in this dear land of ours,
The curlew I love to hear scream.
And I love the white rocks and the antelope flocks,
That graze on the mountain tops green.

Oh give me a land where the bright diamond sand,
Flows leisurely down the stream,
Where the graceful white swan goes gliding along,
Like a maid in a heavenly dream.

Yes, give me the gleam of the swift mountain stream,
And the place where no hurricane blows,
Oh give me the park where the prairie dogs bark,
And the mountains all covered with snow.

Then I would not exchange my home on the range,
Where the deer and the antelope play;
Where seldom is heard a discouraging word,
And the skies are not cloudy all day.

In the honored folk tradition, the author penned a new last verse, which is hereby granted to the public domain:

Oh it will not be long 'til the livestock are gone,
And the bighorn range without fear,
When the native biotic will retake the exotic,
And the streams again will run clear.

INDEX

ABOUT THE AUTHOR

Andy Kerr first fell in love with the wild as a kid. After dropping out of Oregon State University, he spent two decades with the Oregon Natural Resources Council, the organization best known for having brought you the spotted owl. He has been hung in effigy (at least twice) and received death threats (lost count).

He consults, writes, and speaks on environmental issues through The Larch Company (the western larch has a contrary nature as a deciduous conifer). Kerr is on the board of the North American Industrial Hemp Council and is founder of Alternatives to Growth Oregon.

Andy Kerr

A fifth-generation Oregonian, he was born and raised in Creswell, a recovered timber town in the upper Willamette Valley. Until recently, he lived near Joseph, a recovering timber town in the upper Wallowa Valley. He now resides in the recovered timber town of Ashland.

He is happily married, child-free, and lives with two dogs and one cat. He likes to canoe, raft, hike, read, listen to shortwave radio, and move his home toward energy self-sufficiency.

He knows all the words to "Home on the Range" (see Appendix E).

ABOUT THE PHOTOGRAPHER

Family backpacking adventures in the High Sierra inspired an early respect for nature and seeded Sandy Lonsdale's love for wilderness.

After a decade of public lands activism, Sandy now brings remote places to people, utilizing visuals, narrative, and description to inspire others and to compel action to protect and restore our natural world.

He contributes a wealth of imagery to the conservation community, and his work is widely published in educational and adventure publications.

Wandering the backroads of Oregon, Sandy discovered what a few have long known: rarely seen treasures of great complexity and wonder dot the landscape.

Sandy Lonsdale

His hope is that others who see the visual record presented here will visit these places to discover their sublime beauty and rich diversity, then work collectively to preserve, rebuild, and celebrate our public inheritance.

All royalties from the sale of this book are being donated to Oregon Desert conservation.

THE MOUNTAINEERS, founded in 1906, is a nonprofit outdoor activity and conservation club, whose mission is "to explore, study, preserve, and enjoy the natural beauty of the outdoors . . . . " Based in Seattle, Washington, the club is now the third-largest such organization in the United States, with 15,000 members and five branches throughout Washington State.

The Mountaineers sponsors both classes and year-round outdoor activities in the Pacific Northwest, which include hiking, mountain climbing, ski-touring, snowshoeing, bicycling, camping, kayaking and canoeing, nature study, sailing, and adventure travel. The club's conservation division supports environmental causes through educational activities, sponsoring legislation, and presenting informational programs. All club activities are led by skilled, experienced volunteers, who are dedicated to promoting safe and responsible enjoyment and preservation of the outdoors.

If you would like to participate in these organized outdoor activities or the club's programs, consider a membership in The Mountaineers. For information and an application, write or call The Mountaineers, Club Headquarters, 300 Third Avenue West, Seattle, WA 98119; 206-284-6310.

The Mountaineers Books, an active, nonprofit publishing program of the club, produces guidebooks, instructional texts, historical works, natural history guides, and works on environmental conservation. All books produced by The Mountaineers are aimed at fulfilling the club's mission.

Send or call for our catalog of more than 450 outdoor titles:

The Mountaineers Books
1001 SW Klickitat Way, Suite 201
Seattle, WA 98134
800-553-4453
mbooks@mountaineers.org
www.mountaineersbooks.org